New Forms of Revolt

A volume in the SUNY series in Gender Theory

Tina Chanter, editor

New Forms of Revolt

Essays on Kristeva's Intimate Politics

Edited by

Sarah K. Hansen

and

Rebecca Tuvel

SUNY PRESS

Published by State University of New York Press, Albany

Printed in the United States of America

For information, contact State University of New York Press, Albany, NY
www.sunypress.edu

Production, Diane Ganeles
Marketing, Kate R. Seburyamo

Library of Congress Cataloging-in-Publication Data

Names: Hansen, Sarah K., editor.
Title: New forms of revolt : essays on Kristeva's intimate politics / edited by Sarah K. Hansen and Rebecca Tuvel.
Description: Albany, NY : State University of New York, 2017. | Series: SUNY series in gender theory | Includes bibliographical references and index.
Identifiers: LCCN 2016031496 (print) | LCCN 2016048539 (ebook) | ISBN 9781438465210 (hardcover: alk. paper) | ISBN 9781438465203 (pbk. : alk. paper) | ISBN 9781438465227 (ebook)
Subjects: LCSH: Kristeva, Julia, 1941–
Classification: LCC B2430.K7544 N49 2017 (print) | LCC B2430.K7544 (ebook) | DDC 194—dc23
LC record available at https://lccn.loc.gov/2016031496

10 9 8 7 6 5 4 3 2 1

Contents

Part III
Language and Narrative in Kristeva

Acknowledgments

Editing a book is a challenging and rewarding task. We are grateful to the many colleagues who have supported this project since its inception at the 2014 meeting of the Kristeva Circle. Andrew Kenyon of SUNY Press has been a thoughtful and patient guide through the process of publication. Special thanks are also due to Kelly Oliver for her mentorship and friendship.

Kara Walker, Greg Bright and Eugenio Dittborn have generously given permission to reproduce images that appear in Chapters 3, 4, and 5. A different version of Alice Jardine's essay "At the Risk of Thinking: On Writing an Intellectual Biography of Julia Kristeva" will appear in *Being Contemporary: (Un)Timely Essays in French Culture*, eds. Lia Brozgal and Sara Kippur, forthcoming from Liverpool University Press.

Introduction

Twenty Years of Revolt

Sarah K. Hansen and Rebecca Tuvel

> "Intimacy is not the new prison.
> The need for connection might one day initiate another politics."
>
> —Julia Kristeva, "New Forms of Revolt"

The notion of intimate revolt has been a continuing theme in Julia Kristeva's writing for almost twenty years. Since its initial formulation in *The Sense and Nonsense of Revolt* (1996), Kristeva has theorized it in numerous texts, from her studies of religious belief and artistic production to her series on feminine genius and her series on the "powers and limits of psychoanalysis." Across this ever-growing body of work, she describes revolt as a basic condition of social life imperiled by global crises. It is an event that regenerates symbolic bonds and empowers individuals to make meaning. Yet today, she warns, it is not clear *who can revolt* or *against whom*. From economic collapse to climate change, from terrorism to social inequality, our psyches are deprived of supportive social relations and deep inner experiences. In this context, against whom or what should our fragile psyches revolt? It is hard to locate contemporary power because it is disseminated in numerous institutions, parties, and normalizing forces. And if power cannot be located, how can it be opposed or overthrown?

This volume engages with the theory of revolt, focusing especially on its maturation. Kristeva's shift away from the revolutionary stance of *Revolution in Poetic Language* (1974) has been addressed in countless publications. However, few texts engage with the development of intimate revolt itself.

How is psychic revolt a mode of political action? What is the meaning of politics, for Kristeva? Which social and political conditions encourage and support this event? Conversely, which conditions challenge or imperil it? How accurate is Kristeva's account of contemporary power? Is it elitist or Eurocentric? By posing these questions, the chapters in this volume consider the contemporary political relevance of revolt. They examine xenophobia and psychic estrangement; Kara Walker's antiracist art; media spectacles and global capitalism; Hannah Arendt and Ferdinand Saussure's politics of language; colonization and linguistic identities in Latin America; radical caregiving and doctor-patient relationships. Kristeva's own eponymous contribution, "New Forms of Revolt," is a wide-ranging commentary on today's "popular uprisings, indignant youth, toppled-down dictators" (2014, 1). In her view, revolt is not only relevant but also urgent; without the psychic resources provided by revolt, there can be no social bonds, let alone social change.

From Poetic Revolution to Intimate Revolt

Many Anglophone readers first became familiar with Kristeva's politics through her 1974 text *Revolution in Poetic Language*, translated into English in 1985. There, Kristeva famously posits the notion of a *semiotic chora*, understood as the drives, rhythms, and charges that compose early psychic space. Unlike patriarchal narratives that associate the Symbolic with disembodied masculinity and embodiment with nonlinguistic femininity, Kristeva draws on the semiotic *chora* to affirm the body's relation to language. As a *chora*, semiotic drives are both motile and regulated. They are not opposed to language but rather exhibit its logic, supporting the child's later transition into the Symbolic. For instance, in the early mother-child relationship, the two fused semiotic bodies physically communicate and signal to one another in ways that ultimately encourage language development (Oliver, 34). Given its association with the maternal body, it is not surprising that the notion of the semiotic earned Kristeva a wide, and sometimes wary, readership among Anglophone feminists. Some celebrated the semiotic as an important intervention in psychoanalytic theory and phallocentric philosophies of language; others worried that the *chora* essentializes maternity or makes it compulsory for women (Oliver, 48).

In the 1970s, Kristeva herself embraced a revolutionary vision, broadly construed, and resisted feminism, which she narrowly associates with a politics of parity. In her view, language itself can be revolutionary because it is heterogeneous. Just as the semiotic is already and not yet symbolic, the Symbolic is still but no longer semiotic; amid its logical and grammatical structures, there is the insistent presence of drives. The Symbolic order may attempt to repress or obscure them, but semiotic drives are an essential, and sometimes disruptive and revolutionary, aspect of meaning making. In *Revolution in Poetic Language*, Kristeva highlights poetry and avant-garde writing as examples of how "the signifying process joins social revolution." Poetry and avant-garde writing neither destroy the Symbolic nor allow semiotic drives to devolve into chaos. Instead, they transform the Symbolic order by provoking reflection on its heterogeneous elements. Poetry exposes the materiality of language through its music, tones, and rhythms; avant-garde writing transgresses and loosens grammatical rules, opening language to bodily conditions.

In a trilogy of texts published in the 1980s—*Powers of Horror* (1985), *Tales of Love* (1985), and *Black Sun* (1987)—Kristeva begins to revise the positive revolutionary claims of *Revolution in Poetic Language*. To be sure, the 1974 text never imagined revolution in the sense of a full-scale destruction of or emancipation from the Symbolic. However, the 1980s trilogy tempers even promises of subversion and disruption. In this period, Kristeva begins to rethink the semiotic-Symbolic relation and reassess the shape of contemporary power and values. Where *Revolution in Poetic Language* emphasizes how some texts might mobilize semiotic elements in the Symbolic to promote revolution and *jouissance*, the trilogy more deeply explores symbolic elements in the semiotic and the "conditions in which resources are lacking for the semiotic to take on symbolic form" (Beardsworth, 45). The three volumes are effectively case studies of *abjection*, *idealization*, and *primal melancholia*, three psychic processes that are necessary for the child's separation from the semiotic *chora*. If they fail or go awry, children struggle to develop social bonds and make meaning in basic ways, let alone to write poetic texts or to be moved by them. Instead of pointing to literatures that agitate the semiotic-Symbolic relation in transformative ways, Kristeva highlights how this entanglement can leave subjects silent and suffering or violent and alone. When she talks about artistic forms, such as the literature of abjection or stories of loving connection, it is to encourage healing practices rather than to mobilize "social revolution."

In many ways, the pessimism and seriousness of the 1980s trilogy deepens in Kristeva's 1990s writings on revolt as she develops a more sustained critique of the "empty" Symbolic order that imperils revolutionary texts and speaking subjects. To be subversive, poetry or avant-garde writing must transgress or oppose substantive laws, authorities, and values. Twenty years after the publication of *Revolution in Poetic Language*, Kristeva begins to wonder if such laws, authorities, and values can even be found. In *The Sense and Nonsense of Revolt* (1996) and *Intimate Revolt* (1997), she argues that the form-giving aspects of social life ("symbolic laws") are eroding. In their place, "disciplinary and administrative punishments multiply, repressing or rather normalizing everyone" (1996, 5). Kristeva uses the term "power vacuum" to describe this expansion of disciplinary power and the loosening of contemporary authority. In the power vacuum, "there are no longer laws [as much as] measures [. . .] susceptible to appeals and delays, to interpretations and falsifications" (1996, 5). Legal interpretation amounts to the pursuit of loopholes, to "finding omissions in the law that allow otherwise unlawful acts to be carried out within the terms of the law" (Oliver 2009, 67). The media also exacerbate the power vacuum. Across their spectacle of images, the absence of authority is confirmed on every stage, from the celebrity judges to the incessant and ever-revising judgment of celebrities themselves. In this context, Kristeva offers a difficult picture of resistance. She asks: How can individuals revolt against authority if they cannot find it? How can individuals challenge authority if they are too rapt by the spectacle to even search for it? "Who can revolt and against what? Can a patrimony of organs revolt against a normalizing order? How? Through remote-controlled images?" (Kristeva 1996, 8)

Intimate Revolt in Dark Times

Kristeva's questions reflect a critique of the social order, but they are not meant to retreat from it, as some have charged. On her view, intimate revolt is a political and cultural necessity because it "keeps our inner lives alive" (1996, 8). But how, exactly? "Through remote-controlled images?" The French etymology points to some of its operation—sullying, reversal, detour, cycle, stalling, upheaval, recovery, and reassessment, among other meanings and mutations. Where "revolution" has intellectual associations via *revolvere* (to consult, to reread, to tell), revolt is more surprising. It "twists and turns—indeed, veers off—depending on history" (1996, 1–3). The Freudian history of revolt is also suggestive, for Kristeva. In his well-known fable of the origin of civilization, Freud describes how primitive men live in hordes where the father prohibits his son's access to women. One day, in an act of rebellion, the sons murder the father, replace him with the totem symbol, feast, and, in their guilt, develop a social bond. This "Oedipal revolt" is not a transgression of law but a surprising confrontation with and displacement of power that authorizes the individual. Drawing on Freud's twists and turns, Kristeva celebrates a broad practice of revolt that confronts, displaces, and assimilates authority in the psyche. For the developing child, the rebellious incorporation is a condition for entering the Symbolic order. In adult life, revolt is a regenerative return to the past that questions and renews symbolic ties. In each case, it is a necessity. Only through revolt can one find and make meaning. Its "fruits" lie in the social belonging and the capacity to represent; its failure marks the onset of nihilism and what Kristeva calls the "new maladies of the soul."

Today the power vacuum makes these failures more likely. For instance, when authority cannot be located, subjects struggle to abject the maternal semiotic body, an important process undertaken in primary narcissism. The inability to abject can lead to depression at the individual and cultural levels (2002a, 83). Disempowered, excluded, and lacking social bonds, a depressed culture experiences (and economizes) the symptoms a depressed individual feels in isolation—despair, symbolic collapse, a severance of social ties. Alongside depression, the power vacuum also bears another destructive trajectory—the eruption of abjection in social life. When identification with power no longer works, individuals feel excluded in a depressive mode, or, in an attempt to overcome that feeling, they lash out, renewing exclusions at the lower echelons of the social edifice (1996, 14). Subjects in search of a nonlocatable authority or a purified social order can reinvoke violent processes of identity differentiation against the lower echelons of society. In the absence of resources to give meaning to the archaic processes of loss and abjection, "life becomes a life of death, a life of physical and moral violence, barbarity" (1996, 7).

Kristeva's accounts of cultural depression and abject violence have perhaps earned her "an image as someone who willfully depicts and even enjoys exaggerating the seriousness of the present state of affairs" (2014, 4). Nevertheless, she does offer a way to navigate and perhaps avert the "barbaric" threats of the power vacuum—loving social supports. Her model of loving support is the "imaginary father," or what Freud referred to as "the father of individual prehistory." In the process of separating from the maternal body within primary narcissism, the child identifies with and idealizes the site of the mother's love, an "accepting or loving third" or "imaginary father." Kristeva describes this site as "not a 'pure signifier' but as the very space of metaphorical shifting: a condensation of semantic features as well as non-representable drive heterogeneity that subtends them, goes beyond them and slips away" (1983, 38). In effect, the loving third is a figure of the semiotic element of language, "not just the semiotic rhythms of the maternal body, but those rhythms as they show up in the speech of the other" (Oliver 2005, 83). Identifying with the third, the child transfers drives and affects to the site of meaning and begins the entrance into the Symbolic order. In this way, the figure of the semiotic in language is an important aid to revolt and symbolic authorization. By mobilizing loving support in the power vacuum, Kristeva hopes that we might encourage the upheavals of revolt. Without supportive sites of transference for drives, with only empty laws and regulatory mechanisms, individuals in the power vacuum lose their sense of belonging to the social order, their openness to finding and making meaning. Today, loving relations are urgently needed. "It is not the time of great works, or perhaps, for us, contemporaries, they remain invisible. Nevertheless, by keeping our intimacy in revolt we can preserve the possibility of their appearance" (1997, 13).

The loving third makes clear that intimate revolt is not a "retreat" to the psychic realm. For Kristeva, the boundary between psyche and social, personal and political, is porous, ambiguous, and exposed. Troubled psyches can pose real social and political dangers; loving connections can provide real psychic support. This aspect of revolt culture is often misunderstood. Lacanians, feminists, and Marxists have all criticized Kristeva for "individualizing the political and ignoring the need for new forms of solidarity" (Sjöholm 2004, 80). For instance, Nancy Fraser has suggested that Kristeva's speaking subject is split between two politically useless halves that cannot be united (Fraser 1990, 98). In her view, Kristeva's semiotic subject cannot be a political agent because she is "beneath, rather than within, culture and society," forever caught in an apolitical realm (1990, 98). However, far from positing a divide between realms—apolitical and political, psychic and social, semiotic and Symbolic—Kristeva laments any severance between the two. As Sara Beardsworth puts it, such a "categorical distinction can appear only in conditions where modern institutions and discourses have *failed* to provide everyday social and symbolic sites or practices for the adequate connection of the semiotic and symbolic" (2004, 14, authors' emphasis). By calling for loving relations, Kristeva attempts to redress the failures of the power vacuum and repair the severed bond between drives and meaning. Instead of turning away from the political, she argues for the need to rehabilitate the political potential of the psychic space—a space that still harbors the possibility for interrogation, thought, and resistance to the normalizing, technocratic forces of modern society.

New Forms of Revolt

Given her call for an intimate politics, it is not surprising that Kristeva's most recent writings wade into the psychic stakes of current events, from disability rights to terrorism, immigration to social inequality. Across various texts, Kristeva argues that the retrospective returns of revolt can shape these debates by provoking reflection on broader political ideals. For instance, in *Hatred and Forgiveness* (2005), Kristeva makes a case for vulnerability. On her view, vulnerability lies in the "crossroad" of "biology/language" and is "integral to the identity of the human species and the singularity of the speaking subject" (2010, 42). Failure to acknowledge the vulnerable junction of bodies and words encourages "rejections caused by race, social origin or religious differences" (2010, 43). Subjects either disavow vulnerability, in a manner that promotes violence against others, or they are swallowed up by vulnerability, in the sadomasochism of depression and other flimsy defenses. In *Hatred and Forgiveness*, these threats are real, but there is an alternative. Through revolt, one can return to the early crossroads of biology/language and recover the love and pleasure that also characterize vulnerability. The indefinite questioning of revolt allows subjects to work through rather than act out psychic wounds. Quite dramatically, Kristeva promotes vulnerability as the absent fourth term of the French Enlightenment; it "inflects" liberty, equality, and fraternity "towards a concern for sharing" (2010, 42).

In addition to vulnerability, Kristeva's recent writings also celebrate humanism as part of her intimate politics. In "New Forms of Revolt" and elsewhere, she argues that this humanism might be mobilized against the power vacuum, in particular its threat of "soft totalitarianism." When the ambition of power is to normalize and manage life, it bears the totalitarian threat of destroying life after having devalued the question of its meaning (2001, 13). Deprived of supportive social relations and deep inner experiences, human beings are reduced to "patrimonial individuals" or "conglomerates of organs" (2002, 4). Patrimonial individuals are normalized, unquestioning, and dogmatic. They are not subjects who can transgress authority; they are not subjects of revolt. In "New Forms of Revolt," Kristeva attempts to reinvigorate the question of life's meaning by setting forth a humanism that "puts 'a big question mark on matters of weighty seriousness' " (2014, 3). As she sees it,

> we are undergoing not only an economic, political, and social crisis, but also an existential one in which we are confronted with a major unknown: *What is a man? What is a woman? What is humanity?* The interminable response to this question associates, I believe, today's crisis with the crisis of *Homo Sapiens.* Concretely speaking, it is a question of human identity in general, and subsequently of the crisis of our multiple identities: sexual, ethnic, racial, national, religious, familial, and so on. (2014, 3)

Averting the threat of "soft totalitarianism" requires restoring our capacity for revolt and reinvigorating humanism and humanistic questioning. For Kristeva, it is a process that spurs the "knowing subject's questioning of himself and his truth" (2002, 8).

While her recent writings on vulnerability and humanism can hardly be accused of being apolitical, their political content itself has been widely criticized. Many commentators charge that Kristeva's interest in vulnerability and humanism reflects her failure to attend to the role of racism and colonialism in the "power vacuum" (see Ahmed 2005; Gratton 2007; Miller 2014). These critics worry not only that her work effaces colonialism and racism, but also that, as a result, she misunderstands how the power vacuum operates and its psychic effects. For instance, Peter Gratton raises this concern with respect to Kristeva's analysis of France's national depression. Gratton argues that Kristeva consistently betrays a "resistance to thinking the colonial apparatus, notably absent in works that again and again consider nations and nationality, particularly the French nation-state" (2007, 9). Similarly, Elaine P. Miller criticizes Kristeva's contention that religious fundamentalism and the psychic "need to believe" caused the 2005 French suburban uprisings. According to Miller, Kristeva does not address the history of French colonialism in Africa and thereby distorts France's "suburban troubles" as problems of religion (43). For the predominantly North African immigrant population of the French suburbs, however, "it is not religious concerns that cause most unrest . . . but rather unemployment and discrimination and a *de facto* second class citizen status" arising from a history of colonialism (Miller, 41).

Kristeva's calls to embrace vulnerability and to question humanity may evidence a universalizing tendency, but Miller and Gratton's criticisms highlight a reductionist tendency as well. If Kristeva fails to explore the role of racism and colonialism in the power vacuum, her account of intimate revolt applies to a very narrow subject position unaware of its own racialization. Indeed, during the 2014 meeting of the Kristeva Circle at Vanderbilt University, Elaine P. Miller questioned Julia Kristeva about the role of structural racism in the 2005 uprisings. Kristeva's answer was telling.

> EM: In particular, I wanted to ask you about the role of racism in France, the U.S., and in other parts of Europe and all over the world in the development of a kind of adolescent pseudo-rebellion. You talked about the failure of the French model of secularism. What kinds of ways have you thought about [. . .] addressing the issue of racism, not only at the personal level, but also at a structural level?
>
> JK: Thank you very much for the question, especially because it reaches a very conflictual situation. I've been asked this question quite often in stronger terms than you—you did it with a lot of the delicacy. Because I don't ignore the political lacks, the feminine lacks, and the lack of education that is criticized and developed by politicians, sociologists, and social workers, and philosophers also. I took a tiny portion of this big problem—which is the relation of this age of the human behavior [adolescence] with the need to have ideals. So my interest is focused on this very slim portion, but I do not ignore the other aspects.

Kristeva's response to Miller's query is striking in its description of the psychic space as "slim" or "tiny," language that seems to treat the intimacy as if it could be portioned from bigger problems like economic and structural inequities. Kristeva claims that she "does not ignore other aspects." However, when she continues on to reconnect the intimate and the political, she refers only to reductive abstractions like public space, modern democracy, and the French revolution.

> When we say *liberté*, *fraternité*, *egalité*, and other examples that teachers and politicians have in order to make rules for behavior in the city, we don't have the narrative, the personal experience, the sexual experience, the hallucinatory experience, the place for the need, of the belief, the desire, of the reflection upon death.

> All these aspects are kept from the public space and [placed] into the fetish of art or are forgotten. We see this in the political space in modern democracy. We have the parliament that deals with social works and to discuss if it is necessary or not to make social security. On other hand, we have religious people who can deal with the solidarity, with the critique, and so on. What the French revolution tries to do and what the republic tries to do through secularism is to develop humanism and to develop more proximity and more closeness with individuals. This is the program, but it is not yet the reality. This is why we fail in the suburbs. But, it continues to be discussed and we continue to try to work with the mothers, with the families, and with adolescents and try to make more specific our attitude towards them.

Instead of separating the "slim" or "tiny" psyche from the social, Kristeva now speaks of the politicized dimensions of intimacy like "proximity," "closeness," personal, sexual, and hallucinatory experiences. Nevertheless, she fails to frame the political in concrete terms that are relevant to an analysis of the 2005 uprisings, for instance, histories of racism, colonialism, immigration, and segregation. The effect of her abstractions is most evident when she describes the analysis as trying "to make more specific *our* attitude towards *them*." In this moment, the subject of revolt is not abstract; she is a white, Francophone, European, non-Muslim woman. In this exchange, Kristeva's reductions not only compromise the political potential of revolt, but they also ensure that it will be complicit in the histories she ignores.

It could be otherwise. With deeper analyses of racism, colonialism, and segregation, intimate revolt might play an important role in antiracist political practice. In the United States, the peculiar psychic manifestations of racism have been on horrifying display in the recent killings of Terence Crutcher, Korryn Gaines, Philando Castile, Alton Sterling, Samuel DuBose, and Jessica Hernandez. Public discussion and media coverage of these cases suggest that the most dangerous and insidious form of racism lies in individuals who refuse to question themselves and unravel their own implicit racist attitudes. Intimate revolt—a relentless refusal to give up self-interrogation—might help to combat this pernicious form of racism, but only if it attends to the concrete psychosocial realities of white supremacy and other relevant dimensions of racist Symbolic orders. For white writers like Kristeva, this attention may be more difficult to achieve. In racist societies that prohibit the acknowledgment of white domination, whites are taught to "see the world wrongly, but with the assurance that their mistaken ways of making sense of events count as accurate explanations" (Bailey 2007, 80). Like the adolescent, whites move out of questioning into a stubborn assurance of the accuracy of their worldview. Their need to believe is deeply rooted because it is a form of "not knowing"—a constant disavowal of the "erasing, dismissing, distorting, and forgetting about the lives, cultures, and histories of peoples whites have colonized" (Bailey 2007, 85).

Because Kristeva's comments about the 2005 uprisings betray her participation in this "not knowing," imagining an antiracist intimate revolt may involve *revolting* against her texts. For instance, readers might displace and question her authority in order to identify some of her theory's white adolescence. By disrupting her unmarked, unraced persona, readers could also expose the heterogeneous subject behind comments about "us" and "them." This mode of reading promises to unsettle and surprise, but isn't this the spirit of revolt? As Kristeva says, "it is our responsibility to be interpreters, givers of meaning" (1996, 8). Indeed, many of the essays in this volume can be described as revolts against and through Kristeva's texts. There is an emphasis on revolt in non-European and nonwhite contexts, an attempt to shift Kristeva's center and reimagine and reassess concepts accordingly. There is also a continuing interest in heightening the subversions of Kristeva's intellectual inheritances, from Ferdinand Saussure to Hannah Arendt. The essays take up many specific political foci—from Latin American linguistic identities to the aesthetic representation of slavery and trauma—but they are united in their reckoning with Kristeva's theorization of intimate politics over the last twenty years.

Essays on Intimate Politics

The volume begins with a section titled *Kristeva: Revolt and Political Action* and Julia Kristeva's own contribution, "New Forms of Revolt." Given as a keynote address at "The Kristeva Circle" conference at Vanderbilt University in 2014, this essay is a representation of Kristeva's mature theory of revolt. She stresses the totalitarian risks that accompany the power vacuum and argues forcefully for revolt's promise and political relevance. Surti Singh's and Sara Beardsworth's essays discuss figures that might refine and sharpen Kristeva's grip on these totalitarian risks. In "Spectacle and Revolt: On the Intersection of Psychoanalysis and Social Theory in Julia Kristeva's Work,"

Singh interrogates Kristeva's inheritance of the figure of the spectacle and asks whether Guy Debord's masculinist perspective makes its way into the analysis. In "The Chiasmus of Action and Revolt: Julia Kristeva, Hannah Arendt, and Gillian Rose," Beardsworth introduces the figure of *chiasmus* to characterize the surprising experience of being "strangers to ourselves." For Beardsworth, the *chiasmus* provides a lens through which to observe Kristeva's and Rose's different approaches to the impasses of modernity and the motility of the modern subject.

In the section "Imagining New Intimacies: Antiracist, Aesthetic, and Clinical Revolts," Elena Ruiz and Amy Ray Stewart consider revolt vis-à-vis non-European and/or nonwhite traditions and contexts. In "Revolt and the Lettered Self," Ruiz problematizes several Eurocentric tendencies at work in Kristeva's notion of subject formation. She aims also to rehabilitate a Kristevan insurrectional subject for *non*-European indigenous resistance and Amerindian dissent. Similar themes emerge in Amy Ray Stewart's "Extimate Trauma, Intimate Ethics: Kristevan Revolt in the Artwork of Kara Walker." Stewart argues that Kara Walker's "cutting" style attempts to work through legacies of racial abjection and cultural trauma. Finally, Melinda C. Hall's essay, "Patient Interpretation: Kristeva's Model for the Caregiver," applies Kristeva's practice of "patient interpretation" to doctor-patient relationships. Emphasizing the stakes for vulnerable populations, Hall attempts to break from doctor-patient models that are stuck in the twin stranglehold of authoritative diagnostic criteria and purely somatic understandings of disease.

The book's final section, "Language and Narrative in Kristeva," reframes language as the long-standing and varied terrain of Kristevan revolt—myths, mystery novels, biographies, artworks, and more. Beata Stawarska's chapter, "Language as *Poeisis*. Linguistic Productivity and Forms of Resistance in Kristeva and Saussure," shows how recently discovered writings reveal subversive, and underappreciated, dimensions of Saussure's semiotics. She wonders whether Kristeva might inherit or mobilize these subversions. In "Peregrine Genius and Thought-Things: Julia Kristeva and Hannah Arendt on Salutary Estrangement," Elaine P. Miller traces the theme of estrangement in Kristeva's writings, from "The Ruin of a Poetics" to the recent trilogy on feminine genius, illustrating how estrangement is figured in extralinguistic, protolinguistic, and aesthetic modes. Sarah Kathryn Marshall's "Eurydicean Revolt and Metam-Orphic Writing in Arendt and Kristeva" compares Arendt and Kristeva's discussions of the myth of *Orpheus*, a myth that represents the abstract thinking of the philosophical tradition and the "burning need" for truth. For Kristeva, Arendt's use of the Orpheus myth is a kind of revolt against, and subtle transformation of, the Western philosophical tradition. The volume concludes with Alice Jardine's autobiographical reflections on Kristeva's life and friendship, "At the Risk of Thinking: On Writing an Intellectual Biography of Julia Kristeva." Jardine argues that autobiographies can help develop new models of the intellectual in the twenty-first century, but only if they are "strong," highly personal, and intensely honest. For Jardine, the experience of reading and writing such an autobiography is risky, but it offers the possibility of revolt and rebirth.

Works Cited

Bailey, A. 2007. "Strategic Ignorance," in *Race and Epistemologies of Ignorance*, edited by Shannon Sullivan and Nancy Tuana, 77–94. New York: State University of New York Press.

Beardsworth, Sarah. 2004. *Julia Kristeva: Psychoanalysis and Modernity*. New York: State University of New York Press.

———. 2005. "From Revolution to Revolt Culture." In *Revolt, Affect, Collectivity: The Unstable Boundaries of Kristeva's Polis*, edited by Tina Chanter and Ewa Plonowska Ziarek. Albany: State University of New York Press.

Clément, Catherine, and Julia Kristeva. 2001. *The Feminine and the Sacred*. New York: Columbia University Press.

Fraser, N. 1990. "The Uses and Abuses of French Discourse Theories for Feminist Politics." *boundary 2* 17 (2): 82–101.

Gratton, Peter. 2007. "What Are Psychoanalysts for in a Destitute Time? Kristeva and the Community in Revolt." *Journal for Cultural Research* 11 (1): 1–13.

Kristeva, Julia. 1974. *Revolution in Poetic Language*. New York: Columbia University Press.

———. 1983. *Tales of Love*. New York: Columbia University Press.

———. 2000. *The Sense and Non-Sense of Revolt*. New York: Columbia University Press.

———. 2002. *Intimate Revolt*. New York: Columbia University Press.

———. 2002a. *Revolt, She Said*. New York: Semiotext(e).

———. 2010. *Hatred and Forgiveness*. New York: Columbia University Press.

———. 2014. "New Forms of Revolt." *Journal of French and Francophone Philosophy* XX (2): 1–19.

Miller, E. 2014. "Investing in a Third: Colonization, Religious Fundamentalism, and Adolescence." *Journal of French and Francophone Philosophy* XXI (2): 36–45.

Oliver, Kelly. 1993. *Reading Kristeva: Unraveling the Double Bind*. Bloomington: Indiana University Press.

———. 2005. "Revolt and Forgiveness." In *Revolt, Affect, Collectivity: The Unstable Boundaries of Kristeva's Polis*, edited by Tina Chanter and Ewa Plonowshka Ziarek. Albany: State University of New York Press.

———. 2009. "Bodies against the Law: Abu Ghraib and the War on Terror." *Continental Philosophy Review* 42: 63–64.

———. 2009a. *Animal Lessons: How They Teach Us to Be Human*. New York: Columbia University Press.

Sjöholm, C. 2004. "The Temporality of Intimacy: Kristeva's Return to the Political." *The Southern Journal of Philosophy* XLII: 73–87.

Part I

Kristeva

Revolt and Political Action

1

New Forms of Revolt

Julia Kristeva

I would like to summarize the lecture of *New Forms of Revolt* without repeating it, by briefly touching on my understanding of humanism.

I am referring to an event that happened in Europe (and nowhere else) and that cut ties with religious tradition, leading to Nietzsche's "God is dead"—an unprecedented event whose way was paved by the Greco-Judeo-Christian tradition. But "God is dead" also means that some use religion as a political tool if not a political weapon, as in the case of religious fundamentalism. Hannah Arendt already established that those who use God for political aims are also nihilistic, if not more so than the self-declared nihilists. We cannot respond to the crisis of the global world without continuously refounding this other ethical space, which detached itself from the religious continent and which is precisely *secularization* or *humanism*. Humanism was built in Europe—it began in the Renaissance and was developed during the eighteenth century by Erasmus, Diderot, Voltaire, Rousseau, Goethe, and many other rebels, continuing on until Freud and his successors, who have inspired my thought.

I understand humanism in the Nietzschean sense of a "transvaluation of values" (*Umwertung aller werte*) that puts "a big question mark on matters of weighty seriousness." Such work is endless, exorbitant, and long term. We are undergoing not only an economic, political, and social crisis, but also an existential one in which we are confronted with a major unknown: *What is a man? What is a woman? What is humanity?*

The interminable response to this question associates, I believe, today's crisis with the crisis of *Homo sapiens*. Concretely speaking, it is a question of human identity in general, and subsequently of the crisis of our multiple identities: sexual, ethnic, racial, national, religious, familial, and so on. This crisis calls on the human sciences, which developed following the disintegration of the theological continent more than two centuries ago, but the response depends equally on our ability (or inability) to create new languages: new literature, new painting, new dance, new music.

In the thirteenth and fourteenth centuries, Dante Alighieri (1265–1321) in his *Divine Comedy* (cantica I, 69) looked for a language capable of "exceeding the human": "trasumanare" was the term he used, a neologism representative of what is called his "new style." Today my conviction is that the human sciences could be a radical means to this *trasumanare* that humanity needs—that is, if we refuse to wallow in this endemic, inevitable crisis that the growth of technology and virtual finance has imposed on men and women; and if, on the contrary, we want to sense the seeds germinating while awaiting the much desired renaissance to come.

On the invitation of Pope Benedict XVI to a recent interreligious meeting for peace in Assisi in October 2011, as a humanist at the head of a delegation of non-believers (and this for the first time in the long history of religions), I developed ten principles of humanism, which I will not develop here, but which you can consult on my Web site.

Allow me, though, to mention just the first principle of humanism according to my understanding, because it echoes with the theme of Revolt.

The humanism of the twenty-first century is not a theomorphism. Neither "value" nor ulterior "goal," Man with a capital M does not exist. After the Holocaust and the Gulags, humanism has a duty to remind men and women that we are not the sole legislators, but it is uniquely through the continuing questioning of our personal, historical, and social situation that we can make decisions for society and history.

Revolt is this permanent questioning: revolt, as return/turning back/displacement/change, constitutes the internal logic of a certain culture whose acuity seems rather threatened these days, and which I would like to revive in my paper. But let us return to the meaning of this revolt, which seems to me to indicate what is most alive and promising about our culture.

Generally, when the media use the word "revolt," what we understand is the nihilistic suspension of questioning in favor of so-called new values, which, precisely as they *are* values, have neglected to operate a return onto themselves and have thereby essentially betrayed the meaning of the revolt that I am trying to make you appreciate here. The nihilist is not a man in revolt. The pseudo-rebellious nihilist is, in fact, a man reconciled with the stability of new values. This stability, which is illusory, is in fact deadly and totalitarian. I cannot stress enough the fact that totalitarianism and its modern version, the automatization of species, are the result of a certain fixation of revolt in what is precisely its betrayal—namely, the suspension of retrospective return, which amounts to a suspension of thought.

I am therefore seeking experiences in which this work of revolt, which opens psychical life to infinite re-creation, continues and reoccurs, even at the price of errors and dead ends. Indeed, we should not delude ourselves: it is not enough to revive the permanence of revolt, which technology may have inhibited, in order to secure happiness or some sort of serene stability of being. Revolt exposes the speaking being to an unbearable conflictuality, and our century has assumed the daunting privilege of manifesting the necessary enjoyment (*jouissance*) and morbid dead ends associated with this conflictuality. But this functions in an altogether different way from the nihilist, who is focused on the celebration of his unmitigated rejection of the "old" or on the unflinching positivity inspired by the "new" path of *trasumanare.*

I briefly touch on how new political actors are incarnating and realizing this refoundation of humanism that the globalized world direly needs. I take as examples two of these experiences that cruelly lack a means of expression in today's codes of humanism: adolescents in want of ideals and maternal passion at the crossroads of biology and meaning.

Adolescence: A Syndrome of Ideality

As opposed to the child, who, according to Freud, is a polymorphic pervert—the child who wants to know where babies come from and whom Freud compares to a "laboratory researcher"—the adolescent is a *believer.* The adolescent is not a "researcher" *in a laboratory*; *he is a believer.* The adolescent is a mystic of the object of love. Adam & Eve, Dante & Beatrice, Romeo & Juliet: we are all adolescents. We are all adolescents when we are in love.

But the belief that there exists an ideal object (be it a partner, a profession, or a creation) is accompanied by the absolute belief that the parental couple must be surpassed and even abolished so that the adolescent subject can escape into an idealized, paradisiacal variant of absolute satisfaction.

When this fantasy fails to direct the adolescent toward a process of sublimation (school, profession, vocation), the failure of the paradise syndrome inevitably leads to depressivity, which takes the banal form of common boredom—"If I don't have Everything, I get bored"—and opens the way to delinquent conduct. But this conduct is merely the flip side of the malady of ideality, because the need for ideality persists beneath this delinquency and supports aggressive behavior; it in no way signals the abolition or ongoing destruction of ideality.

Civilizations commonly referred to as primitive have long used *initiation rites* to assert symbolic authority (divine for the invisible world, political for this world here) and to justify the acting out of what we would qualify today as perverse by condoning initiatory sexual practices. In our Western culture, notably in medieval Christianity, *mortification rituals and excessive fasting* channeled the anorectic and sadomasochistic behaviors of adolescents and, in so doing, alternatively downplayed or glorified them.

In yet another way—this time secular—what seems to me to be an imaginary elaboration of the adolescent's crisis is the *birth of the European novel* during the Renaissance, shaped around the adolescent character.

Those are some solutions from the past, but today the question for psychoanalysis and education is: are we able to innovate when confronted with adolescent crises?

Only the analyst's and the teacher's capacities to recognize and name the idealizing course of adolescent drives will allow them to provide a credible and effective transference and thus enable a metabolization of the need to believe through the pleasure that comes with thinking, questioning, and analyzing rather than through nihilist acting out. This way, analysts and teachers will be able to accompany the adolescent's rebellions, doubts, and malaises while conserving this universal component, this need to believe, which structures the adolescent.

Motherhood Today

Secular civilization is the only civilization lacking a discourse on motherhood. We believe we understand what a Jewish or a Christian mother is—but what about a modern mother? What is she in this space between the lover, the working woman, and the activist for women's liberation and artificial reproduction, or, on the contrary, returning to the protective values of traditional family?

Contemporary psychoanalysis offers to shed some light on maternal passion. I recently proposed the existence of a maternal eroticism I call *reli-*

ance at an international conference on psychoanalysis (JAPA—*Journal of the American Psychoanalytic Association*). This word, in French, carries echoes of the word "*lien*," to link or to connect, and *confiance*, trust or confidence, as well as an alternative to religion (religion-reliance). Between biology and sense, attachment and expulsion, love and hate, and violent influence and generous transmission, maternal *reliance* is a surprising and necessary version of ethics we might call a *herethic*.

Maternal passion can be understood as a *cleft* between the mother's *hold on her child* and *sublimation*. This division makes the risk of madness ever present, and yet this very risk offers a perpetual opportunity for culture. Religious myths spun their webs around this divide. In the Bible, the woman is a "*hole*" (such is the meaning of the word "woman," *nekayva* in Hebrew) and a *queen*; the Virgin is similarly a "hole" in the Christian trinity of father/son/holy ghost *and* a Queen of the Church. Religions address this maternal division through these imaginary constructions—by recognizing the division, they perpetuated it, but they also found a way of balancing it. A kind of working-through of maternal madness came of this, one that made possible the existence of a humanity endowed with a complex psychic functioning, capable of having an inner life and of being creative in the outer world.

Let me conclude. The adolescent and the mother are two eternal actors in human existence that reveal themselves to be decisive actors in this *trasumanare*, in this passing through the human that concerns us at the beginning of this third millennium; and by incarnating their dramatic experiences, our interdisciplinary research could perhaps accompany modern existential crises with the necessary delicacy lacking in contemporary ethics and politics. The refoundation of humanism necessitates the contribution of our multifaceted field, the humanities. Thank you for having given me the occasion to remind you of this.

2

Spectacle and Revolt

On the Intersection of Psychoanalysis and Social Theory in Julia Kristeva's Work

Surti Singh

Since the publication of Kristeva's *The Sense and Non-Sense of Revolt* and *Intimate Revolt*, renewed forms of revolt have spread across the globe. The rebellious atmosphere of the twenty-first century occasions a reconsideration of Kristeva's thesis that the loss of revolt is a central problem for contemporary politics. Given recent events, how should we understand Kristeva's claim that the spectacular nature of contemporary society damages the culture of revolt (2002, 5)? This claim reflects a profound shift in Kristeva's thinking from her earlier works on revolt and revolution (Beardsworth 2005; Brandt 2005; Margaroni 2007). Kristeva's *Revolution in Poetic Language*, for example, was inspired by the distinctly political meaning of revolt originating with the French Revolution, which implied a transgression against the law and prohibitive political structures, "a protest against already established norms, values and powers" (2002, 3). In contrast, Kristeva's later work questions this meaning of revolt given the changed social and political climate of the late twentieth century. For Kristeva, one of the most striking features of contemporary society is the absence of any definitive power against which we might revolt, and the effects that this absence has on the individual. In this context, Sara Beardsworth notes that Kristeva's return to the concept of revolt in her later works, while renewing the themes that she developed in the 1970s, is profoundly influenced by her psychoanalytic excursions into the problems of subject formation undertaken in works such as *Powers of Horror, Tales of Love,* and *Black Sun* written during the 1980s (2004, 37). Kristeva asks not only how we might think about revolt today when power is much more diffuse and difficult to identify, but, more importantly, how we might think about the *loss* of the desire for revolt forty years after the rebellious atmosphere of the 1960s that inspired the student-worker revolution of May 1968.

While Kristeva ultimately addresses the loss of the desire for revolt within a psychoanalytic register, it is notable that she turns to social theory to explain the conditions for this loss. Explicitly referencing the 1967 text of Guy Debord, *The Society of the Spectacle,* Kristeva argues that the image-saturated environment of the spectacle invades the psychic space of the individual resulting in a lack of imagination and fantasy. The subject's passivity in face of these commercial, standardized images creates an incapacity for revolt. Kristeva's invocation of the society of the spectacle moves her work beyond traditional psychoanalytic concerns by linking them with social and political issues. Kristeva's debt to *The Society of the Spectacle* is noted in the literature, but the wider implications of Kristeva's reliance on Debord's social theory, specifically as a framework for her own psychoanalytic theory of revolt, is little discussed. Part of this neglect is a result of Kristeva's own references to Debord, which, while numerous, are never linked to an explicit engagement with *The Society of the Spectacle* itself. Maria Margaroni's review article (2007), for example, positively explores the viability of a psychoanalytic social theory that emerges in recent work on and by Kristeva. Yet in another essay Margaroni notes, "Kristeva's obsessive and (perhaps, uncritical) use of Debord's term has done little to improve her reputation . . ." (2009, 110). Indeed, Kristeva's shorthand references to Debord potentially pose problems for the legitimacy of her claims, but they also create the possibility of developing this connection further, particularly in light of the prominent role that the spectacle continues to play in the political realm. Fifteen years after writing *Intimate Revolt* and *The Sense and Non-Sense of Revolt,* and in light of current events, Kristeva asks in her lecture "New Forms of Revolt," "Could 'revolt,' called 'riot' on the web, be—at this digital age—in the process of shaking up humankind of its dream of hyperconnectedness? Or could it be just a trick played on us by the culture of the spectacle to last longer?" (2014). Kristeva's turn to Debord is both provocative and timely, for it points to the spectacle's ambivalent character—it creates both the obstacles to revolt but also the resources by which revolt may occur. We can see this double-edged quality of the spectacle in the prominent role that social media, for example, have played in contemporary uprisings. The spectacle contains the means to facilitate revolt and at the same time, by way of these means, perpetuates its own existence and produces new obstacles to revolt.

Because Kristeva accepts Debord's thesis wholesale and often references his theory of the spectacle as an explanatory principle for the nature of society without explicitly engaging with it, her analysis of subject formation does not include a questioning of psychoanalysis itself as a discourse produced within and by the society of the spectacle. According to Debord, the logic of the spectacle structures every aspect of our reality; discourse cannot magically stand outside the spectacle. How, then, can we accept both Kristeva's reliance on traditional psychoanalytic categories to explain contemporary subjectivity and her belief that we live in a society of the spectacle, in Debord's sense of the term? While there may appear to be a disjuncture between psychoanalysis and social theory in Kristeva's work, I contend that Debord's theory of the spectacle offers a framework through which we can broaden Kristeva's psychoanalytic approach to account for the social obstacles to revolt. Hence, we can consider the way in which psychoanalytic categories are already part of the spectacle and perpetuate the spectacle through the discourse of sexuality. At the same time, Kristeva's criticism of the spectacle raises the question of whether Debord's analysis neglects the specifically masculine perspective on which the spectacle turns, and further raises the question of whether contesting the spectacle is a feminist project.

The Logic of the Imaginary

In both *The Sense and Non-Sense of Revolt* and *Intimate Revolt*, Kristeva links the psychic inability to revolt to the advent of the society of the spectacle, in which the creative capacity of our fantasies becomes stunted: "We are inundated with images, some of which resonate with our fantasies and appease us but which, for lack of interpretative words, do not liberate us. Moreover, the stereotype of these images deprives us of the possibility of creating our own imagery, our own imaginary scenarios" (2002, 67). Kristeva's main concern is that the society of images threatens to destroy this "phantasmatic faculty"—the ability to produce and analyze fantasies. In this context, revolt itself no longer can be understood as a transgression against law but instead as "an anamnesis, a movement of 're-volt' that returns to the past, that repeats, interrogates, re-elaborates the most archaic, intimate phases of psychic development" (2000, 64–65). For Kristeva, this return to the past exposes an irreconcilable conflict at the heart of the subject. That is, it exposes a negativity that constantly threatens the wholeness of being. The culture of revolt explores "the permanence of contradiction, the temporariness of reconciliation, the bringing to the fore of everything that puts the very possibility of unitary meaning to the test (such as the drive, the unnamable feminine, destructivity, psychosis, etc.)" (2002, 10). It is only through this investigation of subjectivity that the possibility of transformation arises. As Kristeva notes, revolt is not enacted in the world of action but in psychic life and its social manifestations, such as art, thought, and writing. In this way, Kristeva distinguishes the person in revolt from both "the Christian man, reconciled with God ('coram Deo'), and the nihilist, his enraged but symmetrical opposite" (2002, 7). Unlike the Christian or the nihilist, the person in revolt seeks the contradictions, fractures, ruptures, rejections, and negations that are inherent to subjectivity. Kristeva theorizes that this return, which involves an encounter with a fractured subjectivity, is blocked within the society of the spectacle. The spectacle destroys our capacity for imagination and fantasy, the two components essential to the psychic makeup of individuals who are creative rather than passive, engaged rather than detached, autonomous rather than suppressed. Kristeva also locates this problem within psychoanalysis itself, which after Jacques Lacan becomes invested in a concept of the imaginary that is negligent of the role of fantasy in the individual's psychic life. There is an important convergence between the reifying logic of the image in the spectacle and the masculinist logic of the imaginary in traditional psychoanalysis.

Rather than discarding the concept of the imaginary altogether, Kristeva reinvents it according to the positive potential she finds in fantasy. Her work is aligned with feminist theorists of film who discuss fantasy as a way of dislodging the primacy of the imaginary in psychoanalytic theory. Constance Penley, for example, turns to fantasy as a "counter to the 'maleness' of the cinematic apparatus and its theories" (1989, 79). Kristeva contests the hegemony of the imaginary by pointing to what occurs before the image, which she views to be a more dynamic and fluid process neglected by the Lacanian conception of the imaginary. Melanie Klein's psychoanalytic theory offers Kristeva a way to think about this excess. In her book on Klein, Kristeva highlights the difference between Klein's approach to fantasy and that of Lacan, specifically in their attitudes toward the Greek etymology of fantasy that "evokes appearance-presence-vision" (2001, 141). According to Kristeva, Lacan adopts a Greek approach because he shifts psychic representation "toward the appearance and toward the visibility of the *eidos*" (2001, 141). Conversely, Klein and her followers distance themselves from the Greek etymological and metaphysical origins of the term. They saturate psychic representation "with the reality of drives and with such primary 'contained' contents as greed and envy" (2001, 141), and they recognize the inseparability of drives from thought. Rescuing the concept of negativity from a certain patrilineage, Kristeva reads it according to a specifically feminine logic. While a masculine logic totalizes and creates a unified psychic experience, a feminine logic remains and dwells with the cracks, gaps, and absences. Kristeva mobilizes sensory intimacy as feminine resistance to the reifying images of the spectacle, which operate according to the masculinist logic of the imaginary. In this vein, we can turn to Kristeva's analysis of cinema as a prominent medium that both perpetuates and contests the society of the spectacle.

Cinema and Fantasy

In *Intimate Revolt*, Kristeva discusses cinema as an image of the spectacle that both assumes "the universe of fantasy as a right" and contains the power to destroy fantasy (2002, 69). To develop the connection between cinema and fantasy, Kristeva further clarifies the meaning of fantasy. Turning once again to its etymology, Kristeva conceptualizes fantasy according to "the Greek root—*fae, faos, fos*"—that "expresses the notion of light and thus the fact of coming to light, shining, appearing, presenting, presenting oneself, representing oneself" (2002, 63). From this initial conceptualization of fantasy, Kristeva suggests that we ought not equate fantasy with the faculty of imagining in the philosophical sense, but instead, following Freud, we should consider it the place of imaginary formations. Fantasy designates "an imaginary scenario in which the subject depicts in a more or less distorted way the fulfillment of a desire, ultimately sexual" (2002, 64). Kristeva distinguishes between different types of fantasies: diurnal, subliminal, and unconscious, with unconscious fantasies also including primal fantasies. To briefly reiterate, diurnal fantasies are daydreams, or alternate realties we create—the novels without an audience, as Kristeva refers to them. Through these fantasies we recount our desires—whether fairy tales or nightmares—in counterpoint to our real lives. Subliminal fantasies are unconscious daydreams and have strong sexual connotations, "reflexively conscious or not, which are the precursors of hysterical symptoms" (2002, 64). Finally, unconscious fantasies are the expression of unconscious desires and "are situated at the foundation of the progredient trajectory that ends in dream" (2002, 64). The impossibility of gaining access to unconscious fantasies and their repression are the cause of symptoms in the classical Freudian sense. Kristeva recalls Freud's patient Dora, whose mysterious cough Freud linked to unconscious fantasies arising from an imaginary scenario she conceived of as a young girl. Believing her father to be impotent, she imagined witnessing her father's mistress performing fellatio on him. An intolerable scenario for Dora, this event remained unconscious, and she developed an eroticization of the mouth, tongue, and throat; this eroticization, also inadmissible to Dora, developed into "neurotic spasms manifested by uncontrollable coughing" (2002, 64). Kristeva notes that Freud makes this connection—makes what is unconscious conscious—by starting with language, that is, by analyzing Dora's speech.

When we examine fantasy seriously, and particularly the phenomenon of unconscious fantasies, two points emerge. First, although unconscious fantasies emerge in childhood, they signify a reality that is different from perceptual reality; they signify the reality of desire, which has its own alternative logic. "The subject imagines something; he is having an illusion. But this illusion is nevertheless strong, steady, persistent, and subject to its own rigorous logic: it is the reality of his desire" (2002 65). Fantasy prompts us to take this reality—psychic reality—seriously. Second, the illusions we create are complex formations, they are "transitional organisms, hybrid constructions between two psychical structures—between the conscious and the unconscious—that play with both repression and the return of the repressed" (2002, 65). The hybrid nature of unconscious fantasies is evident in their rootedness in biology, as the expression of sexual drives, and their simultaneous manifestation as "narration, with syntax, grammar, logical construction, and a whole narrative setup" (2002, 65). Kristeva emphasizes that in Freud's work, fantasies were not simply equated with either instinctual drives or symbolic formation. Rather, fantasies indicated the polyvalence of psychic life, an interdependence and translatability among all its levels. Similarly, Freud pointed to the close relation between the different regimes of fantasy in the subject—"the speaking, sexual subject is a subject of fantasies and subject to fantasies" (2002, 66). Finally, Kristeva discusses a subset of our unconscious fantasies—primal fantasies—the oldest and archaic fantasies that are not particular to an individual, but are hereditary structures, scenarios concerning our origins. "The child invents these scenarios, which he represses, but the invention is only an eternal return of hereditary schemas that have actually taken place in preceding generations and are mysteriously encrypted in the psyche" (2002, 66). Given Kristeva's emphasis on the central role of fantasy in defining the subject, she explores the aspects of culture that promote the formation of fantasies, that provide the place where they can be realized, and, in some cases, provide a substitute for action.

Kristeva refers to great works of modernist art—those by Sade, Proust, Goya—as the place for the formation of fantasy. She is skeptical that media images can take on the same role. In fact, contemporary media create the opposite effect. Rather than stimulating the production of fantasies, the society of the spectacle destroys fantasy. The images we consume might very well appease us, but, according to Kristeva, they do not liberate us. Further, the stereotypical nature of these fantasies hinders our capacity to create our own imaginary scenarios. The representation and production of fantasy become blocked, and this impoverishment of fantasy threatens to dissolve our inner depth. In contrast, art and literature perform a similar role to psychoanalysis; "they open the verbal path to the construction of fantasies and prepare the terrain for psychoanalytical interpretation" (2002, 68). It is not surprising then, that Kristeva has an ambivalent view of cinema, which partakes in both realms; it is the central place of the contemporary imaginary and therefore shares the characteristics of traditional art and literature, but it can easily slide into the vacuous realm of mass media images and become one more vehicle that destroys fantasy.

Kristeva discusses different types of cinema with respect to fantasy. In its most basic, realist form, cinema projects fantasies: "Since the visible is the port of registry of drives, their synthesis beneath language, cinema as the apotheosis of the visible offers itself to the plethoric development of fantasies" (2002, 69). Kristeva points to classic early films from the 1920s to 1960s that seduce or scare us—*Arsenic and Old Lace*, *A Man and a Woman*, *Nosferatu*, and *Doctor No*. Not only do these films tap into the fantasies of a particular era, but they also, presumably because of their foundational status, define the era of cinema itself. From its early inception, Kristeva suggests, cinema exhibited a certain capacity to portray fantasies because of its powerful ability to re-create reality—a capacity that drove the other arts, such as literature and painting, to "take refuge in maximal condensation" and explore other regions of the imaginary through "poetry, meditation, distortion, abstraction." Kristeva's analysis echoes André Bazin's discussion of photography as replacing painting's ability to render reality—a development that in turn liberated "Western painting, once and for all from its obsession with realism and allowed it to recover its aesthetic autonomy" (1960, 9). As with subsequent developments in photography, which transcend its early function to reproduce reality, cinema also expands into other forms of representation, veering away from only realist projections of fantasy. Kristeva has greater interest in this second type of image; it is closely related to what she considers great works of literature and painting. Kristeva terms this cinematic image the thought specular, and she attributes it to great art, films produced by directors such as Eisenstein and Godard, which portray fantasies in a way that differs from journalistic or dramatized stereotypes.

Cinema and the Thought Specular

It is through this second type of image—the thought specular—that Kristeva primarily explores the role of fantasy. She asks, "Why does the visible lend itself to a primary and fragile synthesis of drives, to a more supple, less controlled, riskier representability of instinctual dramas, the game of Eros and Thanatos?" (2002, 69). The power of cinema arises from its capacity to literally show fantasies, paralleling the capacity of psychoanalysis to allow the analyst to see the patient's fantasies. When a patient cannot communicate his or her "forms of psychic and somatic ill-being" through words, the therapist suggests a psychodrama through which the patient can

> put his drives into play, to show them to us: gesture and image. The act of psychodrama is in large part a specular act: "one" shows itself, "one" relies on the analyst's speaking action before eventually becoming an "I" capable of deferring this action and this demonstration and acceding to the statement of a subject. (2002, 69–70)

This is an alternative means of signification via the image. Kristeva points to the fundamental role of the specular, or vision, in the classic familial drama—the Oedipus complex—that forms the unspoken foundation of Western subjectivity.

Introducing her own case studies, Kristeva recounts her patient Antoine's recurring nightmare. Antoine is four years old and while on the "potty" experiences an overflow of excrement that turns into an animal, "something like a frog and a crocodile but with transparent skin, as if the membrane of an eye" (2002, 70). At this point in the nightmare, Antoine's father enters and upon seeing the animal threatens to punish the boy. Kristeva interprets this nightmare according to the boy's real, imagined, unconscious, and conscious drives and desires for the mother and the father and in relation to narratives of birth. But importantly, Kristeva also emphasizes the central role that the father's gaze plays in this drama—"the eye of the other, the eye of the third, the menacing and seductive paternal eye" (2002, 71). The presence of the paternal eye is the first instance of separation from the maternal dyad and autoeroticism; it is the intrusion of the other, of the third party; it initiates "the autonomy of the subject and access to thought and language. But nothing guarantees that this separation will ever be clear and definitive in any of us" (2002, 71). The paternal eye takes over the function of the ideal mother with a call to order. As Kristeva explains it, Antoine is an example of an incestuous son who needs the intrusion of a strong paternal figure to detach himself from his mother. "This terrifying father, who is nevertheless a seductive father, refers the very young narcissistic identity to its passive position of being a seduced, feminine, uncertain subject The seductive and terrifying specular endlessly celebrates our identity uncertainties" (2002, 72). Kelly Oliver further develops Kristeva's analysis of the imaginary father by emphasizing its role in providing the primary social support necessary for the individual's psychic development, creativity, and love (Oliver 2002). That is, Oliver emphasizes the connection to the social that the loving third/imaginary father implies.

Fear and seduction embodied in the specular, exemplified by the father's gaze, returns in cinema. Films by Eisenstein, Hitchcock, and Pasolini explore the specular; they reproduce its "untenable logic." Kristeva connects the analysis of Antoine's dream with cinema's reproduction of the specular—"the most direct cinema, which projects more or less modified fantasies, seizes us in this place in our psychical lives where the imagination lets itself be controlled by fantasy, which I call the specular" (2002, 73). The thought specular in cinema refers to "the visible signs that designate fantasy and denounce it as such" (2002, 74). Kristeva turns to Jean-Luc Godard, whose films she reads as "signals captured, cut up, and arranged in such a way that the phantasmatic thought of the writer-director can be made out and invites you first to locate your fantasies and then to hollow them out" (2002, 74). Expanding on Kristeva's reference to Godard, we can think of a classic film of the *French New Wave* such as *Breathless*.

Godard conceived of *Breathless* as a remake of Howard Hawk's *Scarface*, and it ambivalently reproduces both identification and misidentification with American Hollywood cinema, the traditional trope of the gangster film, and its conventional gender roles through several cinematic techniques—the jump cut; the emphasis on artifice, particularly in scenes of violence; the miscommunication between Patricia and Michel; and so on. As Dennis Turner notes, the film's "subject matter, dialogue and characterizations seem always to be sliding from a worshipful endorsement of the narrative conventions and archetypes of American movies to an acknowledgment of the impossibility of the unmediated functioning of those conventions and types in the context of a Continental cinema" (1983, 54). *Breathless* artfully plays with genre conventions and, through the interaction of the young lovers that makes up the heart of the film, reveals the instability of desire, fantasy, and identification. While this film can play the role that Kristeva bestows on the thought specular, Kristeva is suspicious of other films that lull us into a flat complacency, that make us passive receivers of ready-made fantasies instead of their active producers. This ambivalence is expressed by Kristeva's probing question "[D]oes cinema wish to be an exhibition of the sadomasochistic repressed in the spectacle, an authorized perversion, a banalization of evil? Or, on the contrary, its demystification?" (2002, 80). Kristeva's emphasis on the ambivalent character of the specular finds a theoretical counterpart in Debord's theory of the spectacle.

Society of the Spectacle

In *Society of the Spectacle*, Debord locates the specular nature of reality within the tradition of Western philosophy; it exhibits the same logic. "The spectacle is heir to all the weakness of the project of Western philosophy, which was an attempt to understand activity by means of the categories of vision" (1994, 17). This continuation of the philosophical emphasis on vision deploys the technical rationality inherent to the Western project. The spectacle philosophizes reality insofar as it turns material life into a universe of speculation. Martin Jay has masterfully traced the role of vision in the Western philosophical project (1994), and, as he explains, Debord links this emphasis on vision to its social and material basis in capitalist commodification. In such a society, reality is not lived directly, but experienced only through a series of representations. Debord recalls Marx's analysis of commodity fetishism that depicted a mode of production in which the social relations between people are masked by the social relations between commodities. The real social relations necessary for the production of commodities are obscured. Debord's analysis of specularization rests on an analysis of the image and its function in capitalist society. The specularization of consciousness occurs through a process in which the social relations between people become mediated by a social relation between images.

> The spectacle is the self-portrait of power in the age of power's totalitarian rule over the conditions of existence. The fetishistic appearance of pure objectivity in spectacular relationships conceals their true character as relationship between human beings and between classes; a second Nature thus seems to impose inescapable laws upon our environment. (1994, 19)

As Debord notes, the spectacle is not simply a ready-made, standardized collection of images. Rather, the spectacle is the process by which our human interactions and social relations become mediated by images. As a result, the concrete socioeconomic reality, and the inherent inequality within the spectacle, is obfuscated. Individuals experience a separation from reality as it is and become lost in the illusions created by the spectacle. Kristeva theorized how individuals are unable to bring into view their initial separation from the mother. For Debord, subjectivity is falsely constructed through the separation of individuals from the real conditions of capitalism, and from others living within the same system.

For Marx, commodities are fetishized because they obscure the labor that produces them and thus appear to have magical, mystical qualities. For Debord, in the society of the spectacle, the commodities themselves are fetishized. That is, the competition, clash, and competing interests of the commodities on the market create a commoditization of the world, a fetishization of not only labor, but also of desire and thought. Furthermore, the unity that the spectacle creates through consumption hides class division, which is the real unity on which the capitalist mode of production is based. News, propaganda, advertising, and the actual consumption of entertainments are the place of illusion and false consciousness. Debord writes,

> The spectator's alienation from and submission to the contemplated object (which is the outcome of his unthinking activity) works like this: the more he contemplates, the less he lives, the more readily he recognizes his own needs in the images of need

> proposed by the dominant system, the less he understands his own existence and his own desires. . . . The spectator feels at home nowhere, for the spectator is everywhere. (1994, 23)

This absolute invasion of images into the psychic space of the individual produces a loss of boundaries. Drawing upon Joseph Gabel's *Ideology and Schizophrenia*, Debord believes the spectacle erases the boundary between self and the world. While Kristeva's work develops this loss of boundaries through the notion of abjection, thus linking the loss of boundaries to the formation of new personality disorders, Debord's analysis holds a distinctly social dimension. That is, for Debord, the creation of this loss of boundary is symptomatic of a society that is structured through the spectacle, and thus there no longer exists a deeper psyche into which we may delve to examine the site of the fissure that may somehow be healed. For Debord, this would be one more enactment of the operation of the spectacle, for individuality is itself produced by the spectacle. Revolt can no longer occur at the level of the individual, for the individual's fantasies, thoughts, desires, and dreams cannot exist outside of the spectacle. Even in acknowledging that one lives in a society of the spectacle, any activity of resistance at the level of the individual would be co-opted back into the spectacle. There is a false separation constructed between our seemingly private desires and the structure of the spectacle. For Debord, neither the alienated individual nor the separated masses can enact revolution, but rather a subjectivity to come.

Debord's theory of the spectacle has implications for Kristeva's theory of revolt. On Kristeva's view, intimate revolt is a healing of the narcissistic wound. This becomes problematic from the perspective of Debord, for whom revolt would entail a shattering of the conditions by which that wound is created. Debord's theory of the spectacle can assist in introducing this critical element to Kristeva's theory and offer the beginning of a solution to the gap that pertains to her reflections on the individual and its ramifications for wider social and political questions. For example, how can we think about the spectacle as not just an external barrier to the development of subjectivity, but also as implicated within the subject's development itself? Is there a way in which narcissism, abjection, love, and all the other myriad concepts that form Kristeva's theory of subject formation are themselves specularized? Kristeva views the subject to be in a permanent state of revolt, which creates the distance necessary for the subject to rebel against the society of the spectacle, yet what I want to suggest here is that intimate revolt is always already a social revolt, if indeed the subject's psychic life is formed by the society of the spectacle. If one's fantasies are always already determined by the social structure, then intimate revolt is against the construction of this subjectivity itself. In this respect, I see rich possibilities in Kristeva's work for understanding the relationship between the psychoanalytic and the social, the intimate and the external, the inside and the outside, that her work does not fully broach. In other words, Kristeva introduces a psychoanalytic dimension to the sociopolitical readings of fetishism (of commodities, of images) that convincingly asks us to take seriously the obstacles that face the mobilization of the masses. One arena that could help to bridge this gap and allow us to investigate the question of sexual difference with respect to the spectacle is aesthetic experience, something that both Kristeva and Debord privilege. Kristeva thinks that "great art"—certain forms of literature, painting, and cinema—can create the necessary space for reflection because they allow for the production of fantasy. Debord's emphasis on art has a distinctly social dimension.

Aesthetic Experience

Both Kristeva and Debord view the aesthetic sphere as containing the possibility of resisting the logic of the spectacle. Kristeva locates the possibility of this resistance in avant-garde works of modern art. In contrast, Debord writes from the perspective of the end of modern art, marked by what he views as the failure of dadaism and surrealism to fulfill their countercultural or antiestablishment aims. For Debord, the trajectory of dadaism and surrealism in art parallels the proletarian movement in politics. Just as the proletarian movement ultimately failed to bring about social change after its last great offensive, so too did dadaism and surrealism fail in their revolutionary stances within the sphere of art. As a result, dadaism and surrealism are halted in the very aesthetic sphere that they wished to transcend; they both remain one-sided in their critique. "Dadaism *sought to abolish art without realizing it,* and surrealism sought to *realize art without abolishing it* (1994, 191). Against the historical failure of these movements, Debord, writing in the 1960s, proclaims situationism to be the critical position that recognizes the realization and abolition of art as inseparable moments in the transcendence of art. The situationist view of art positions the various tendencies that develop in postmodern or post–avant-garde art as absorbed by the spectacle, with culture itself becoming the society of the spectacle's star commodity. Debord's stance, then, resists either a recuperation of modernism's tendencies in the present or a view of the present as expressing a fundamentally new tendency—the two positions exemplified a short time later by the seminal works of Jürgen Habermas (1997) and Jean-François Lyotard (1979). Given the totalizing function of the spectacle in contemporary capitalist society, Debord envisions the role of aesthetic resistance as emerging in interventionist tactics—*détournement* being the most well-known strategy of the Situationists. Debord's notion of *détournement* reconceives the aesthetic as something that is broader than the artwork—it is something that can emerge in everyday practices but, importantly, can only operate through negation as a disruption of the logic of the spectacle. Debord describes *détournement* as

> the fluid language of anti-ideology. It occurs within a type of communication aware of its inability to enshrine any inherent and definitive certainty. This language is inaccessible in the highest degree to confirmation by any earlier or supra-critical reference point. On the contrary, its internal coherence and its adequacy in respect of the practically possible are what validate the ancient kernel of truth that it restores. *Détournement* founds its cause on nothing but its own truth as critique at work in the present. (1994, 146)

For Debord, *détournement* plays with the paradox inherent to the sphere of culture and the nature of avant-garde art—a paradox that Theodor W. Adorno in *Aesthetic Theory* expressed as the tension between the new and duration. With the advent of modernity, the sphere of culture achieves an autonomy previously denied to it in myth-based societies, yet this liberation also proves to be the basis for culture's annihilation. Debord notes that "culture is the locus of the search for lost unity. In the course of this search, culture as a separate sphere is obliged to negate itself" (1994, 130). The separation of value spheres, which Max Weber theorized as signifying the advent of modernity, leaves each sphere falsely isolated, and thus, while achieving autonomy, culture also becomes excluded or irrelevant within the broader workings of society. Culture becomes caught, ultimately, in the desire to retain its autonomy, on the one hand, and to recover its lost unity, on the other. The development of avant-garde art is at once critical of this historical development and yet, according to Debord, cannot help but become caught within the same paradox.

> Art in the period of its dissolution, as a movement of negation in pursuit of its own transcendence in a historical society where history is not yet directly lived, is at once an art of change and a pure expression of the impossibility of change. The more grandiose its demands, the further from its grasp is true self-realization. This is an art that is necessarily *avant-garde*; and it is an art that *is not.* Its vanguard is its own disappearance. (1994, 135)

From this vantage point, a culture that has become wedded to the spectacle, that has literally become spectacular consumption, preserves the old culture, including its revolutionary or negating impulses, in a deadened or congealed form. This preservation of culture, which has as its aim the promotion of reconciliation or assimilation with the status quo, results in the production of art that continues the historical gestures of the *avant-garde* but emptied of any real import.

Working from this perspective, the strategy of *détournement* is resolutely historical, communicating in the language of contradiction, "dialectical in form as well as in content: the language of the critique of totality, of the critique of history" (1994, 143–44). Debord ties *détournement* to a history of dialectical thinking via Hegel, Feuerbach, and the young Marx, a style of thinking that preserves the negativity that is otherwise eradicated from the affirmative spectacle. *Détournement*, instead of being its own, new development, "restores all of their subversive qualities to past critical judgments that have congealed into respectable truths—or, in other words, have been transformed into lies" (1994, 145). Citing Kierkegaard as an example, the point of *détournement* is to represent some word or phrase from the past to provoke a disturbing recollection. *Détournement* is defined as the opposite of quotation, as the opposite of respecting tradition and attributing authority to a source; it is more akin to plagiarism, which stays close to an author's ideas but exploits them, erases them, replaces them with others. For Debord, the normative project of *détournement* is to replace the old, false ideas with ideas that are correct. Jay further elaborates the meaning of *détournement* as "diversion, deflection, or hijacking, often for illicit purposes. Anticipated by Lautréamont's creative plagiarism, Dada photomontages, Duchamp's readymades, and Brecht's principle of *Umfunktionerung*, it means confronting the Spectacle with its own effluvia and reversing their normal ideological function" (1994, 424). Assessing the legacy of *détournement*, Jay has rightly noted that it seems to be more critical than constructive,

> Twenty years later, the Situationists, who so fervently sought to unite art and life and thus make the Revolution, were in danger of being turned into yet another canonized entry in the dreary succession of modernist movements seeking to outdo their predecessors in radicality. Radical "situations" in the streets were replaced by "artworks" in museums. (1994, 417)

Jacques Rancière further explores the loss of critical power of the situationist project in the *Emancipated Spectator*, where he notes that this practice, while losing its political efficacy, still features in art production, for example in the "parodies of promotional films; reprocessed disco sounds; advertising icons or media stars modeled in wax; Disney animals turned into polymorphous perverts; montages of 'vernacular' photographs showing us standardized petty-bourgeois living rooms, overloaded supermarket trolleys, standardized entertainment or the refuse of consumerist civilization, and so on and so forth" (2009, 76). Capitalism benefits from the paradoxes or undecidability of the critical project itself. What, then, is left of the critical project that Debord and the Situationist International advanced with respect to the spectacle?

Conclusion

Recent revolts, uprisings, and revolutions around the globe have given birth to hope and disappointment, often failing to fulfill their promises. Given this climate of defeat, a perspective that returns to the past to interrogate both this hope and failure is poignant. Debord and Kristeva offer a way to rethink the past in light of the present, and their frameworks can serve to mutually critique the exhaustion of art and the limitations of the psychoanalytic framework. The sensory intimacy of Kristeva's analysis disrupts the masculinist logic of the spectacle; at the same time, the spectacle reveals the reification of subjectivity and the illusory nature of subjective depth.

Tina Chanter, in her essay "The Exoticization and Universalization of the Fetish, and the Naturalization of the Phallus: Abject Objections," provides a clue as to how these discourses can be brought together. Chanter returns to the unquestioned ground of many of our contemporary political discourses and reveals a disturbing logic of fetishization that she convincingly argues perpetuates itself even in the most critical and radical attempts to affirm those who are excluded, such as women or racial minorities. Chanter argues that although feminist thinkers, postcolonial thinkers, and film theorists have criticized Freudian psychoanalysis and its legacy of the sociosymbolic law enshrined by the phallus and built on the construction of woman as other, they have not gone far enough. While feminist critiques illuminate how the Freudian subject is modeled on male experience and how this privileging is conflated with the universality of language, Chanter interrogates the psychological foundations that resurrect fetishization and continue to reenact this privilege at the level of logic rather than the content of theory.

Chanter mobilizes Kristeva's notion of abjection, which offers a way to rework the dominant psychoanalytic model, and extends it to the sociopolitical sphere. She demonstrates how abjection is at work in the differential relations that construct meaning within the sociosymbolic system. Rather than a purely deconstructive procedure, however, Chanter's treatment of abjection allows for the formation of new symbolics. Extending Chanter's observations, abject art is one example of feminine resistance that can offer a meeting point between Debord and Kristeva. Through its excess of representation, abjection contests the flatness of post–avant-garde art by momentarily reaching into the psyche of the subject. At the same time, the abject presents this subjectivity as illusory. The abject potentially has the power to halt the leveling equalization of the commodity sphere and the masculine logic on which it turns through its inassimilable content.

Works Cited

Adorno, Theodor W. 1997. *Aesthetic Theory.* Translated by Robert Hullot-Kentor. Minneapolis: University of Minneapolis Press.

Bazin, André. 1960. "The Ontology of the Photographic Image." *Film Quarterly* 13 (4) (Summer): 4–9.

Beardworth, Sara. 2005. "From Revolution to Revolt Culture." In *Revolt, Affect, Collectivity*, edited by Tina Chanter and Ewa Ziarek. Albany: State University of New York Press.

Brandt, Joan. 2005. "Julia Kristeva and the Revolutionary Politics of *Tel Quel.*" In *Revolt, Affect, Collectivity*, edited by Tina Chanter and Ewa Ziarek. Albany: State University of New York Press.

Chanter, Tina. 2005. "The Exoticization and Universalization of the Fetish, and the Naturalization of the Phallus: Abject Objections." In *Revolt, Affect, Collectivity*, edited by Tina Chanter and Ewa Ziarek. Albany: State University of New York Press.

Debord, Guy. 1994. *The Society of the Spectacle.* Translated by Donald Nicholson-Smith. New York: Zone Books.

Habermas, Jürgen. 1997. "Modernity: An Unfinished Project." In *Habermas and the Unfinished Project of Modernity*, edited by M. P. d'Entréves and S. Benhabib. Cambridge: MIT Press.

Jay, Martin. 1994. *Downcast Eyes: The Denigration of Vision in Twentieth-Century French Thought.* Berkeley: University of California Press.

Kristeva, Julia. 2000. *The Sense and Non-Sense of Revolt: The Powers and Limits of Psychoanalysis.* Vol. 1. Translated by Jeanine Herman. New York: Columbia University Press.

———. 2001. *Melanie Klein.* Translated by Ross Guberman. New York: Columbia University Press.

———. 2002. *Intimate Revolt: The Powers and Limits of Psychoanalysis.* Vol. 2. Translated by Jeanine Herman. New York: Columbia University Press.

———. 2014. "New Forms of Revolt." Paper presented at the Kristeva Circle, Nashville, Tennessee.

Lechte, John. 2004. "The Imaginary and the Spectacle: Kristeva's View." In *Julia Kristeva: Live Theory*, edited by John Lechte and Maria Margaroni. London: Continuum.

———. 2009. "Julia Kristeva and the Trajectory of the Image." In *Psychoanalysis, Aesthetics, and Politics in the Work of Julia Kristeva*, edited by Kelly Oliver and S. K. Keltner. Albany: State University of New York Press.

Lukács, Georg. 1997. *History and Class Consciousness: Studies in Marxist Dialectics.* Translated by Rodney Livingstone. Cambridge: MIT Press.

Lyotard, Jean-François. 1979. "Answering the Question—What Is Postmodernism?" In *The Postmodern Condition: A Report on Knowledge*, translated by Geoff Bennington and Brian Massumi. Minneapolis: University of Minnesota Press.

Margaroni, Maria. 2009. "Julia Kristeva's Chiasmatic Journeys: From Byzantium to the Phantom of Europe and the End of the World." In *Psychoanalysis, Aesthetics, and Politics in the Work of* Julia *Kristeva*, edited by Kelly Oliver and S. K. Keltner. Albany: State University of New York Press.

———. 2007. "Recent Work on and by Julia Kristeva: Toward a Psychoanalytic Social Theory." *Signs*: *Journal of Women and Culture* 32 (3) (Spring): 793–808.

McAfee, Noëlle. 2004. *Julia Kristeva.* New York: Routledge.

Oliver, Kelly. 2002. "Psychic Space and Social Melancholy." In *Between the Psyche and the Social: Psychoanalytic Social Theory*, edited by Kelly Oliver and Steve Edwin. Lanham, MD: Rowman and Littlefield Publishers.

———. 2004. *The Colonization of Psychic Space: A Psychoanalytic Social Theory of Oppression.* Minneapolis: University of Minnesota Press.

Penley, Constance. 1989. *The Future of an Illusion: Film, Feminism, and Psychoanalysis.* Minneapolis: University of Minnesota Press.

Rancière, Jacques. 2009. *The Emancipated Spectator.* Translated by Gregory Elliot. London: Verso.

Turner, Dennis. 1983. "Breathless: Mirror Stage of the Nouvelle Vague." *SubStance* 12 (4): 50–63.

3

The Chiasmus of Action and Revolt

Julia Kristeva, Hannah Arendt, and Gillian Rose

Sara Beardsworth

This essay questions the relation between Kristeva's conception of *revolt* and the modern problem of political action, taking as its starting point the contrast in Kristeva between the worlds of action and revolt. Kristeva phrases this distinction in different ways in her books and essays on revolt, writing that revolt is realized "not in the world of action" or "not so much in the world of action . . . but rather in that of psychical life and its social manifestations (writing, thought, art)."[1] There is an equivocation here. After all, is it *not* or *not so much* that is meant? The equivocation registers the simultaneous need and uncertainty of the distinction between the world of action and that of revolt. I develop the equivocation into what I call a *chiasmus*. The chiasmus of revolt and action in modernity is revealed by comparing Kristeva's thought with that of Gillian Rose.

What Rose and Kristeva broadly share is a critical approach to the problems of modernity that is indebted to Hegel, a critique of modern political idealism understood as the problem of political thinking that does not know the situation it is in, and a discovery of this problem in Arendt. Although Rose and Kristeva share an appreciation of Arendt on the life of the mind, they reject the unmoving distinction in her thought between the social and the political spheres, a distinction upheld by an opposition between the "public" and the "private" realms. Arendt's concept of action is rooted in these oppositions. To Rose and Kristeva, this means that Arendt's conception of the spontaneity of individual action in the political sphere fails to discern the ways in which the political emerges out of the social in modernity. Nevertheless, neither thinker then falls into the symmetrical problem of mistaking the emergence of the political out of the social for the possibility of positing a *historical subject* of the modern versions of revolution or revolt. Rather, each takes the complexities of modernity right into the self-identity of the subject. The parting of the ways comes with their different approaches to the nonidentity of the modern subject, who is *divided* in Kristeva and *aporetic* in Rose. Rose situates the nonidentical subject of modernity within its social and historical conditions, while Kristeva advances the notion of the split subject of psychoanalysis. This essay seeks to recover this parting of the ways and articulate it as the chiasmus of action and revolt in modernity.

We may acknowledge, first, that revolt today aspires to recovery of motility—real and personal—in the face of a problem of modernity that is nowhere more acute than when it fails to be recognized. But this leaves us with a dilemma before we even begin. How can one be sure of the basis of one's own revolt—that it is not experienced as a part of the problem of modernity rather than being part of a response to it? The challenge is that of finding a voice that is equal to this question. There is another voice that spoke out before Kristeva and Rose could speak their parts. Arendt, too, felt the need for revolt, which she saw as a distinctly political concept. To her, human fulfillment lies in the political experience known to the "men of the revolution"—the French Revolution and the American Revolution—as public happiness or public freedom.[2] "Acting in concert" generates the power to keep the public realm in existence (Arendt 1958, 244–45). Here revolt is identified with action. However, to Kristeva, in opposing the political to the social realm, Arendt has raised the public realm to one of "political purity." To Rose, the unmoving distinction between the private and the public turns Arendt's political thought into an "ideal-typical" politics (Rose 1992, 227). The implication for both is that Arendt's response to the problem of modernity merely carries in its voice the condition of *lack* of motility for the subject of modernity and does not actually work to overcome it. It is precisely this work that is carried out in discrete but, as I will argue, strangely complementary ways by Kristeva and Rose.

Kristeva herself does not follow through Arendt's writings on revolution and dissent. Theoretical and existential difficulties stand in the way. What she finds missing in Arendt's approach is that which for her is essential to the whole question: a radical inner experience. What for Arendt could belong only to the "merely private" sphere is precisely something that for Kristeva must mean much more. Where Arendt denounced the pervasion of the private into the public, forming the denigrated realm of modern society, Kristeva turns to a sense of revolt that indicates freedoms that may still lurk inside the "social" (2001, 162). We discover the reasons for her criticism of Arendt in her way of moving between psychoanalysis and modern writing. I believe this movement to be a highly suggestive and promising approach, which we explore here in some detail.

Why, then, turn to Rose for further elucidation of our problem, especially because she is so different, insisting on the philosophical comprehension of social and political experience through readings of Hegel after Marx and Adorno? We seem here to be a long way from Kristeva's placement of revolt in intimacy, the psychic realm. However, perhaps we can better understand Kristeva's equivocation over the worlds of action and revolt by seeing it also through other eyes. Here Arendt may serve as a bridge. Kristeva simultaneously appreciates and criticizes Arendt, yet her reading loses something of the concept of action, Arendt's political concept par excellence. This is for reasons that are cogent after their fashion but still leave an empty space requiring further thought. Rose retains the political while at the same time being critical of the central dichotomy of the social and political in Arendt. She focuses on Arendt's failure to develop her comprehension of the world of action. What is at stake between Rose and Kristeva on action and revolt are different views of the impasses of modernity, and of the motility that nonetheless remains to the modern subject. Arendt is the intermediary between the two in this paper but this does not allow us to settle the distinction or reveal the relation between action and revolt. What I do here is take the two critiques of Arendt to constitute a *chiasmus* in which the indefinite relation between action and revolt is thematized—conceptually figured rather than forgotten. To do this requires a reading of Kristeva on revolt and of Rose on action.

Kristeva on Revolt

Kristeva tells of a "new species of rebels (*révoltes*)" who are "discovering through their experiences that there is no answer to social, historic and political impasses without a radical inner experience; an inner experience that is demanding, unique, and able to appropriate the complexity of the past in order to approach the present and the future" (2014, 3). *Intimate Revolt* introduces an idea of *retrospective return* by affirming "the faculty of representation and questioning that specifies the human being" against their ceasing to think for themselves (Kristeva 2002, 6). To Kristeva, the suspension of retrospective return is itself "the suspension of thought," an Arendtian theme (ibid.). *Intimate Revolt* relates the impasses of modernity, above all, to the nihilism that shares in the suspension of thought.

> This is where we are: we can either renounce revolt by withdrawing into old values or indeed new ones that do not look back on themselves and do not question themselves or, on the contrary, relentlessly repeat retrospective return so as to lead it to the limits of the representable/thinkable/tenable. (Ibid., 7)

In connecting questioning to retrospective return, Kristeva invokes an Augustinian phrase that is, in fact, equally important to Arendt: *quaestio mihi factus sum*, "I have become a question to myself." To Kristeva, this means *se quaerere*, "going in quest of oneself," a return to the most interior (*intimus*). However, with modern man, retrospective return is other than "a simple reprise of the retrospective link that founds the innermost recesses of the Christian man, serene in his quest, which is completed by a return to the *summum esse*" (ibid.). Certain advances in the culture of the twentieth century have led retrospective return to the limits of the representable/thinkable/tenable: to *irreconcilable conflict* (ibid.). Arendt missed this. While she lauded the Augustinian "palace of memory," she did not recognize its complement, the Freudian one, in which the return to the innermost recesses of the psyche comes to the very limit of the energic/hermeneutic heterogeneity of the speaking being. Kristeva refers this limit—"an unfillable breach between drive and meaning—to Freud's idea of the *Zeitlos* (ibid., 27). The *timeless* in Freud appears first as the unconscious wish that is unaware of time (*The Interpretation of Dreams*) and later as the "death" drive in *Beyond the Pleasure Principle*, where the libidinal drive energy of the unconscious wish is reconceptualized as a binding drive in contrast with the "unbinding" death drive, whose significance there is absorbed into Freud's reflection on the psychical *compulsion* to repeat.

In Kristeva, the unbinding drive assumes a role in imaginary experience, "resuscitating rebellious potentialities in our innermost depths," and therefore plays a fundamental role in her notion of revolt (2002, 13). Her source in Freud for this development is the essay on "Negation," where the *simultaneous* instinctual binding and unbinding—the life of desire and the destructive drive—are situated in the very emergence of the faculty of representation. This faculty is established precisely, though not solely, on the basis of a distinction between psychical interiority and the external world. Prior to the emergence of this distinction, an interplay of the binding and unbinding drives makes up Freud's "original pleasure ego." In early sensorial experience, the introjection of what, under the promptings of the pleasure principle, "shall be in me" is in play with an instinctual repulsion and ejection (*Ausstossung*, *Verwerfung*) of what "shall be outside me" (Freud 2001c, 237). Freud called this interplay the language of the earliest life of the drives: "it shall be inside me or outside me (*es soll in mir oder ausser mir sein*)." The Freudian ego boundary is therefore formed and established through repetition in the form of the dual play of binding *and* unbinding drives. To Freud, then, a distinction between "inner" and "outer" in early ego formation underlies the more psychically developed one, in thought, between psychical interiority and an external world. "What is bad, what is alien to the ego and what is external are to begin with identical" (ibid.). That is to say, the unbinding drive is the forerunner of the more psychically developed appearance of what is *on* the outside (*draussen* in Freud). Like Lacan and Hyppolite before her, Kristeva discerns here the strange continuity of Freudian negation with Hegel, in whose philosophy the positing of the object belongs to the negativity of thought. Freud's drive repulsion and ejection are found to underlie this negativity of thought, so that desire in psychoanalysis—both re-finding and going beyond the object—is dependent on the primacy of the unbinding drive.

Further analysis of the intricate link between *Ausstossung* or *Verwerfung* and the negativity of thought led Kristeva to the notion of the rejecting drive, which, under certain conditions, becomes *symbolizing* negativity (2002, 9). Her notion of drive rejection may be contrasted with the changing shapes of consciousness and its object that rest on the negativity of thought in Hegel's *Phenomenology of Spirit*, for drive rejection implies a dislocation *and* recasting of consciousness and meaning. Kristeva will affirm the Freudian approach to death for the possibility it implies of taming death "by inscribing it immediately and simultaneously as instinctual force *and* unconscious representation, energy *and* psyche" (ibid., 32). This reading of Freud draws on Hegel's own breakthrough in thought—that "death lives a human life"—only at the same time to set Freudian death off from Hegel's philosophy, sometimes in criticism of the perceived reconciliation of the disunity of consciousness in Hegel's *Phenomenology of Spirit*. The Kristevan "inscription" maintains the unfillable breach of drive and meaning, which she calls the energic/hermeneutic heterogeneity.

Kristeva's own reorientation of Freud in relation to and departure from Hegel began early in her writings, with *Revolution in Poetic Language*, and has developed since. What *Intimate Revolt* adds to it emerges alongside both the writing of her intellectual biography of Arendt and a newly developing psychoanalytic and literary cultivation of theological and mystical writings. In proposing the thought of questioning as *retrospective return*, which calls back to an Augustinian motif, Kristeva suggests that the psychoanalytic "death drive" offers an unprecedented concept of time. The energic/hermeneutic heterogeneity in the psychic realm is grasped from the limits of a nontemporalizing "time outside time (*hors-temps*)" (Kristeva 2002, 25). To Kristeva, this "extrasubjective and extraexistential" temporality has certain affinities with Bergson and Heidegger. However, temporality in Freud is different than in philosophy. It "relies on the linear time of consciousness in order to inscribe a rift there, a breach, a frustration" (ibid., 29–30). The drive/meaning heterogeneity in the psychic realm is reallocated here to a breach of *time*: to time that does not temporalize (*zeitigen* from Heidegger). Kristeva finds an originality in Freud's *Zeitlos*:

> It seems to me to reside in an unconscious time that is not only not conscious time but encroaches on a prepsychical time and approaches the somatic. What's more, it is opposed to the advance or increase of consciousness, as well as of life, that characterizes all temporality . . . it is a matter of a detained temporality, at work through consciousness and the psychical. (Ibid., 31)

The movement in *Intimate Revolt* between psychoanalysis and modern writing turns on their respective and sometimes complementary modes of inscribing nontemporalizing time, which she calls the time of death or—given that death in Freud is unbinding—*unbound time*. Freud has given us three figures of the psychoanalytic timeless: unconscious memory, psychoanalytic working through (*Durcharbeitung*), and the dissolution of the transference (separation from the analyst) (ibid., 34–40). Each figure of the crossroads of time and the timeless presents psychical life *and death*, moving from the unity of meaning and the "symptom" of being-conscious, to the domain of images and the register of embodied speech, to the "other side" of this register, the prepsychical (ibid., 47). To Kristeva, these figures reveal the psychical capacity for "reuniting with affect through the metaphorical and metonymical rifts of discourse." Revolt *today* takes this psychical capacity to the border region of the speaking being—unbound time—and therefore endangers consciousness, risking the annihilation of the unity of meaning and the subject (ibid., 26). Kristeva concedes, then, that questioning and revolt have their own morbid impasses. However, for her, only relentlessly repeating retrospective return can counter both modern nihilism—the unquestioned positivity of values—and the eradication of thinking that she finds in Arendt's concept of evil: "the radical evil that would be the halting of thought and representation" (ibid., 10).

What psychoanalysis and modern writing have discovered, each in their own way, are the corollaries and the contrary of representation: from the corporeal and emotional *imaginary* register of "prerepresentation" to the *break* in the time of life and consciousness. Psychoanalytic thought composed the three figures of the crossroads of time and the timeless, developing them out of the psychoanalytic experience of repetition and return where the psychical capacity for and modalities of revolt were discovered. Modern literature engages the crossroads of life and death in writing, "finding its pulse in a realm that is no longer symbolic but semiotic." It is seeking "a language, a thought, a style" for a confrontation with the unity of meaning, "unfolding meaning to the point of sensations and drives" (ibid.). Modern writing takes the pulse of meaning in writing and literature to the border region of the speaking being where the indestructible drive—"extrapsychical" unbound time—enjoins, dangerously, the life of mind (thought and language). Modern writing therefore exemplifies the culture of revolt today. It traverses "evil" to accede to *jouissance* in an "experiment in psychosis." An experimental psychosis succeeds where psychopathological symptoms and structures, "appearing as various inabilities to integrate the atemporal," fail (ibid., 10, 31). This approach to modern writing and literature affirms *writing in revolt.*

To Kristeva, then, the question of what motility remains to the subject vis-à-vis the impasses of modernity is still a matter of what is most alive and promising in our culture, where life is not a value that renounces revolt, but is, rather, life that assumes the radical inner experience in which preverbal sensations and images sensorialize the life of mind. What is most alive and promising is the culture of revolt, relentlessly repeating retrospective return to the point of *inscription* of the breach in time.

Given these ways of moving between psychoanalysis and modern writing, Kristeva can affirm not only Arendt's life of the mind, seen as developing the philosophical tradition of interiority in Kant and Hegel, but also her concept of action insofar as its meaning must be put into a narrative. To say, then, that what Arendt missed is the Freudian "palace of memory," the domain of the unconscious, is to say a great deal. Arendt is still tied to a false "innocence of becoming" despite her loss of innocence on multiple fronts. For her, action is a new beginning that reveals the unique, distinct person, his or her living essence, and creates a new relationship in the web of human relationships. The storyteller is the one who then perceives the unique meaning of the action and puts it into a cogent narrative.[3] Kristeva's writer, by contrast, is more inwardly turned, more aware of the fractures and fault lines in the semiotics of the tale. This suggests that no easy transition between narrative and action, appearing in Arendt's political writings, is possible. Kristeva can thus affirm Arendt's "veritable politics of narration" but not any veritable politics of action.

Rose on Action

Kristeva's is not the only possible critique of Arendt. The other, offered by Gillian Rose in *The Broken Middle*, sustains the role of action, even in the face of what is broken or fractured. She does so by rejecting any fixed opposition of the social and the political. Arendt is criticized for having *justified* the separation of the social and the political that she had earlier *comprehended* in *The Origins of Totalitarianism*, thereby merely rejoining her thought to political theories that do not know their own situation. Rose's response lies in returning action to a historical and social problematic that enigmatically divides *moral agency* and *social action* in the modern subject. This view once again splits the self-identity of the subject, but does so differently than the psychoanalytic splitting in the heterogeneity of drive and meaning. I would like to argue that this splitting, too, has its importance and place, not as a substitute for but as a supplement to the splitting we have already attributed to Kristeva. The relation between the two cannot be directly represented, but it is not therefore to be abandoned. The view of action that comes with Rose's criticism of Arendt constitutes what I call a *chiasmus* with Kristeva on revolt.

Rose takes social and political experience to the *aporetic existence* of the modern subject split between moral agent and social actor, adopting Hegel's way of returning Kant's abstract dichotomy of autonomy and heteronomy to experience. Kant had recognized the simultaneous possession of inner morality and heteronomous public conduct, yet he arrested his recognition of history in the separation of appearances from their transcendental conditions. With Rose, Hegel maintains inner autonomy and outer heteronomy as—in Adorno's words—"torn halves of an integral freedom to which they do not, however, add up" (Adorno 1977, 123). She does not, therefore, read Hegel's philosophy as one uninterrupted development of spirit, as Arendt did. She enters, instead, into the two levels of Hegel's *Phenomenology of Spirit*: its dual movement of experiencing and philosophical consciousness. The former presents the inversions and despair of consciousness in losing its conception of itself and of the object, a loss that takes place in and through the very *experience* of the "object." The logical movement of "observing" philosophical consciousness presents philosophy as *witness* and *work*, which may be called the *way* of despair. However, while there is separation and convergence of the philosophical and experiencing levels, their relation is never resolved. On this reading, then, the "path" of experiencing consciousness is not one of dialectical contradictions and their reconciliation. Rather, we abide with the inversions that experiencing consciousness undergoes in Hegel's *Phenomenology of Spirit*. Because inversion is a movement in the mutual implication of the terms of an opposition, this does not abolish the dialectical treatment of experience, yet there is no resolution of the sundered unity of experiencing consciousness in either the usual sense attributed to Hegel or the Marxist sense. That is to say, the oppositions are not dialectical contradictions resolved in the concept: the triumph of logic over experience. Nor are they philosophical abstractions returned to social structures and their resolution in a future to come: what Kristeva has called the "singing tomorrows" in reference to the French Communist Party (Kristeva 2000, 50). These resolutions of the "splitting" come too quickly and are too easy.

With Rose, any too untroubled maintaining of the logical movement of Hegel's text at the level of philosophical consciousness is countered precisely by the inversions of experiencing consciousness. This allows her to read Hegel in terms of the *difficulties* of modern social and political experience. The difficulties of modernity are formed, for Hegel, in the works of his antecedents and contemporaries. In the *Phenomenology of Spirit*'s chapter on culture, the inversions of aristocratic values and of the noble and ignoble consciousness, which mark the end of the high confidence of aristocratic society, are given matchless form by Diderot in *Rameau's Nephew*. In the inversion from moral spirit to madness in the chapter on morality, Rose sees Goethe. Above all, returning Kant's abstract dichotomy of autonomy and heteronomy to experience intrigues the problem of the split in the modern subject between the inner autonomy of moral intentions and the outer heteronomy of public conduct. This appears against a background problem formulated by Marx in "On the Jewish Question."

> The perfection [*Vollendung*] of the idealism of the state was at the same time the perfection of the materialism of civil society. The shaking off of the [premodern] political yoke was at the same time the shaking off of the bonds which held in check the egoistic spirit of civil society. Political emancipation was at the same time the emancipation of civil society from politics, from even the *illusion* [*Schein*] of a "universal content." (Marx 1984, 233; cited in Rose 1992, 222)

That is to say, Marx's critique of the separation of civil society from new nation-state grasps the historical diremption of state and civil society *and* their mutual implication (Rose 1992, 219). Diremption is contrasted with contradiction in Rose.

"Contradiction" implies "resolution," whereas "diremption" may only be manifest as paradox; "contradiction" is a logical term, which implies the simultaneous assertion of A and not-A, while, as a term of political economy, it implies structural and developmental opposition of social functions and interests, capital and wage-labor, which becomes progressively polarized and conflictual; "diremption," on the other hand, implies "torn halves of an integral freedom to which, however, they do not add up"—it formally implies the third, *tertium quid*, implicit in any opposition qua sundered unity, without positing any substantial pre-existent "unity," original or final, neither finitely past or future, nor absolutely, as transcendent. (Ibid., 236)

The historical diremption and mutual implication of state and civil society is a prodigious source of both oppositions and the cultures of their overcoming. These oppositions or "contradictions" are reinterpreted by Rose in terms of diremption, an enigmatic actuality that "may only be manifest as paradox." The historical, political diremption is approached in authorships that discern paradox rather than positing contradiction. The authorship of "On the Jewish Question" belongs here. Marx discerned that the idealism of the new modern state is the illusion of a "universal content" appearing in the formal equality of legal persons, which mismatches and masks actual inequality, universal competition, and mutual exploitation in civil society. Rose appropriates this critical framework without, however, denouncing the social and then developing another "universal content" opposed to it. That is to say, she avoids the "ideal-typical" politics that she finds in Arendt's concept of action as a new beginning that opens up or maintains a public realm separated from the social.

Rose calls, instead, for the experience of the social and the political, *each in the other*, in conditions of the still-enigmatic actuality of the historical diremption and mutual implication of state and civil society. In these conditions, the subject is socialized into a split between inner moral autonomy, on the one hand, and, on the other, the outer heteronomy of public conduct in the institutions of civil society. Autonomy and heteronomy are the *inner and outer boundaries of the subject's self-identity*, which cannot be reconciled. Moral and social experience therefore takes the form of the inversions of experience. The subject traverses her boundaries, from inner moral motivation to social action and, in reverse, from social action to the inner autonomy of thinking and conscience, always only to discover that things never turn out as they were in the beginning. Rose calls this "the inversion of intentions and institutions." The inner autonomy of thinking and moral motivation *initiates action* in which the subject moves to her "outer boundary" in public conduct, only to discover her participation in heteronomous institutions in civil society, dominated by the means-end category. Her initiative, which began in moral intentions, turns into participation in the treatment of others and herself as means to the ends of private and civic interests. She is sent back to the inner boundary of her self-identity—to the freedom of thinking and moral motivation where the illusion (*Schein*) of a "universal content" is active. In these inversions, we discover that things never turn out to be as they were in the beginning, that we can find no satisfaction, that there is no place for subjective freedom as the autonomy of thinking, moral motivation, and action as beginning. The "actual self"—subjective freedom as act and actual existence—does not result. However, with Rose this does not mean u-topia: lack of a place and so idealized place. Rather, it is *a-poria*, "without a way," which is prelogical and "implies no exit from its condition" (Rose 1992, 201, 206). Yet the inversions of experience are multiple. Aporia is not without plasticity and motility.

Rose does not oppose the social and the political, then, but, rather, brings them together in aporetic existence that may critically recover, along with or in criticism of Marx, the problem of historical, political diremption. Rose finds this critical thought in the authorships of three German Jewish women spanning the late eighteenth to twentieth centuries: Rahel Levin/Varnhagen, Rosa Luxemberg, and Hannah Arendt (as the author of *The Origins of Totalitarianism*). Each authorship springs from the modern experience of the duality of exclusion from and emancipation into civil society. Rose accords to each of these women the "agon of authorship" that is both oppositional in relation to their culture and takes on the "anxiety of beginning." Anxiety of beginning acknowledges "the beginning of anxiety in the equivocation of the ethical (separation of civil society from new nation state)" (ibid., 198–99). By not avoiding the psychology of diremption—beginning of anxiety, anxiety of beginning—theirs is the "agon of authorship" that both struggles with their culture and *lets it be* (ibid., 207). Levin/Varnhagen is witness to the community separated ethically and politically from political life, but she avoids the position of the moral judgment that does not act. She both skirts and moves through civil society, using "the imagery of 'spraining' and 'lameness' to force the space for her difficult truth" (ibid., 193–94). Rose develops Luxemberg's critique of the diremption of reform and revolution in the shape of German social democracy and Russian Revolution. The diremption finds its witness and commentator in Arendt's *Origins of Totalitarianism*, after which Arendt failed her own recognition of the historical separation of state and civil society, for Rose.

The account of Luxemberg's critique is illuminating for our current purpose in resuming the split in the modern subject between inner freedom and outer unfreedom. Luxemberg expounds a critical relation to two "insinuated authorities" of her culture: revisionism and centralism; the trade unionism of German social democracy and the organization of the party in Russian Revolution. In one, Rose elaborates, the cultivation of moral judgment assumes that a beginning has been made in the transformation of social conditions, yet gradual reform does not act and only colludes with the hypocrisy of civic mores that it disdained. In the other, acting in the name of a collective will is substituted for a beginning. The organization of the party substitutes its own will for the collective will and, in the culture of terror, inadvertently revitalizes the corruption it sought to overcome (ibid., 200–10). Centralism is "a temptation of pure culture—destruction of the organization of the world in the name of the organization of the party" (ibid., 200). To Rose, then, Luxemberg struggles with the "insinuated authorities" of her culture: gradual reform and organization of the party. Each recognizes only one danger, opposing itself as moral judgment to political will or as political will to moral judgment that does not act. Both dangers stem from the failure to recognize the "double danger" of inner moral intentions and outer public conduct.

In bringing these authors into play for purposes of cultivating her problematic, Rose develops an ambiguity in the authorships she affirms. On the one hand, rather than erecting or falling in with the insinuated authorities of their culture, Levin/Varnhagen, Luxemberg, and Arendt discursively comprehend their culture—both struggle with it and let it be—in the "agon of authorship" that maintains the anxiety of beginning. The authorships renounce their knowledge of freedom and unfreedom by *forming* it in life and works. On the other hand, they also keep their knowledge to themselves in ways that, for Rose, mark failings of their authorship, when they substitute moral judgment that does not act for anxiety of beginning. Rose is especially concerned, then, with critiquing not only the problems of political will but also the danger that follows thwarted moral intentions: the withdrawal from action that intensifies the fatality of thinking and moral motivation (what Hegel called being-for-self). This withdrawal cuts the Arendtian "two-in-one" of thinking off from the bonds with the significations and values of the culture that it would question, thereby isolating it in impotent inwardness. Rose therefore affirms the inversions of experience over the danger of conscience-stricken *Innerlichkeit*. Her critical point is that an authorship inhibits recognition of history and arrests movement or motility when it substitutes either moral judgment that does not act or political idealism for *anxiety of beginning*. This is ultimately her criticism of the dichotomy of the social and the political in Arendt.

Rose will follow the inversions of intentions and institutions in this period to their most sinister conclusion. She is attentive to Arendt's report on the Eichmann trial, yet finds in that report that Arendt merged her judgment of Eichmann's crime with her discernment of the reason for it: *absence of thinking*. We find ourselves once more on ground that appeared in Kristeva as the modern nihilism that suppresses and is countered by revolt. For Rose, however, Arendt's moral judgment of the reason for Eichmann's crime forms the counterpart to a political idealism that, forgetting its own situation, reduced itself to an "ideal-typical" politics. Rose's view is this: Arendt *judged* the absence of thinking in human beings—their ceasing to think for themselves—rather than renouncing her knowledge by forming it in thought and writing. This inhibits recognition of history and arrests movement. Rose therefore separates the reason for Eichmann's crime—absence of thinking—from Arendt's judgment on not the deed itself, but this reason for it. To Rose, if the discovery in everyday experience of the cruelties of civil society can lead to an effort to maintain inner activity (thinking and conscience) in opposition to outer passivity in public conduct, this opposition is itself capable of the inversion that grasps the "ordinary man" argument from Hannah Arendt and Christopher Browning: that mass murder and routine "became one." Inner inactivity, the absence of thinking, accompanies outer activity, public conduct, in the performance of atrocities. In *Judaism and Modernity*, Rose finds that a dangerous thought now presents itself: "that it is 'morality' itself which has corrupted and continues to corrupt us" as one half of the diremption in our socialization into the simultaneous possession of inner freedom and outer unfreedom (Rose 1993, 35).

> To Plato, doing wrong could only occur if one lacked knowledge of what was right—one could not wittingly intend wrong; to Aristotle, it was possible to intend and act rightly but unwittingly to incur wrong—a dilemma, but not one of malicious foresight. To modernity, this dilemma of contingency acquires a systematic twist: for, it is possible to mean well, to be caring and kind, loving one's neighbor as oneself, yet to be complicit in the corruption and violence of social institutions. Furthermore, this predicament may not correspond to, and may not be represented by, *any available politics or knowledge*. (Ibid.)

Rose's short essay on "The Future of Auschwitz" in *Judaism and Modernity* shows how the double danger of conscience-stricken *Innerlichkeit* and colluding social action can be re-presented in the aftermath of atrocities, precisely at a "site" preserved for full acknowledgment of what happened. The child or adult visitor to the "site" of Auschwitz can be provoked by its arrangement into national pavilions to alternate between identifying him- or herself in infinite pain with the "victims" and intense self-questioning regarding the possibility of having counted among the perpetrators (ibid., 35–36). These identifications re-present what could be juxtaposed in the period that the "site" memorializes: the impotent inwardness of conscience and atrocities in public conduct. They repeat the morality that continues to corrupt us and cannot form a beginning. Visiting this "site" herself, in conjunction with the second meeting of a symposium on "The Future of Auschwitz" in 1992, Rose suggests that the inducement to these mute identifications be replaced by a question that would, instead, initiate discussion. *"How easily could we have allowed this to be carried out?"* (ibid., 36). The discussion would involve a questioning of European identities. "Are we Germans 'or' German-Jews, French 'or' French Jews, Polish professionals 'or' Polish Jews 'or' Polish peasants?" Rose proposes that such questioning might contribute to a change in awareness regarding "the *relation* between different oppositions—innocence and might, authority and force—between the inner and outer boundaries of our self-identity and lack of self-identity that turns us into *'strangers to ourselves'* as moral agents and social actors" (ibid., my emphasis).

Rose's question and this questioning did not reach beyond the symposium, however—it could not begin at the "site" of Auschwitz, on the grounds asserted by one participant, a specialist in Holocaust monuments and museums, that no curator could permit such a radical questioning of the visitors' agency (ibid.). For Rose, it is therefore philosophical comprehension that risks itself at this point, in the sense forwarded in her interpretation of Hegel.

> Philosophy's "grey in grey" was never intended to damage its endeavor: to keep it quiescent, modestly contemplative, servile or resigned. This subtle array, this grey in grey, would turn hubris not into humility but into motile configuration. Grey in grey warns against philosophy's pride of *Sollen*, against any proscription or prescription, any imposition of ideals, imaginary communities or "progressive narrations." Instead, the "idealizations" of philosophy would acknowledge and recognize actuality and not force or fantasize it. They act as the third, the middle, their own effectivity at stake between the potentiality and actuality of the world and engaging at the point where the two come into a changed relation: not *ex post facto* justification, even less *a priori* rejuvenation, but reconfiguration, oppositional yet vital—*something understood.* (Rose 1992, 185)

Following this, we might afford Rose the same recognition that Kristeva gave Arendt when quoting from the latter's *Essays in Understanding*. "Her unique passion remains: 'what is important for me is to understand' " (Kristeva 2001, 237). The vitality that Rose returns to philosophical comprehension in Hegel is maintained, for her, where philosophical reflection springs from encounter with the predicament of morality: our "implication in the activity and passivity of the ethical" (Rose 1992, 185). Rose therefore conjoins understanding to the discovery that the relation between our inner and outer boundaries turns us into *strangers to ourselves* as moral agents and social actors. From the encounter with sundered unity comes the "suspension of the ethical"—which does not abolish it—in the authorships that Rose affirms for their beginning in anxiety. Notably, she finds that to Luxemberg struggle is "the school of public life." It is ready to fail even rather than either forsake the critique of gradual reform that assumes a beginning in social transformation has been made *or* follow a law of history/consciousness that insists on the unity of struggle rather than its transmission. Luxemberg *conjoins* the revolution to the mass strike as "the transmission of struggle from one center to another" (ibid., 213).[4] This authorship does not therefore posit the revolution (revealed and known), but, rather, sees the factors of its origin as constantly changing. It is impossible to reckon on this changeable phenomenon with any degree of certainty. This moment in Luxemberg's critical writings corresponds most closely to the "agon" of authorship in the anxiety of beginning. To Rose, it is "facetious representation of something that cannot be represented" (ibid., 212). That is to say, Luxemberg's prose poem to the mass strike fails toward "unknown worlds." What this implies for the inversions of experience is that a *third* to philosophical and experiencing consciousness may appear in them, which cannot be posited as *tertium comparationis*—is not a position revealed or known. An "interstitial" existence comes out of and approaches the unknown third as a space between the potentiality and actuality of the world.[5] Interstitial existence engages and risks itself at the point where the potentiality and actuality of the world may come into a changed relation. Rose therefore puts the unrepresentable *unknown* at the heart of motility—lives and authorships that will not escape the inversions of experience, yet have sources in unknown worlds. This is political risk for Rose.

Revolt and Political Risk: Premodern Worlds

In answer to the question whether the political in Rose's thought can be brought together with Kristeva on revolt, it can be shown to do so in *premodern* worlds. For this, we turn to a digression on the "social" in Kristeva's intellectual biography of Arendt. To Kristeva, Arendt reduced the social to the "economic." She proposes that Arendt's approach to the body and her lack of attention to the psychic realm and intimacy neglect the plural and possible economies of prepolitical freedom that disclose the "social" (Kristeva 2001, 162). Kristeva marks the etymology of the term "economy," its meaning as *negotiation*:

> it is possible that the *oikonomia* that characterizes women and slaves is a ruse and a negotiation with immortality, an *oikonomia* that is different from a political outburst, of course, but that still allows for a softer approach to the invisible. The economy of *icons* (*eikōn*) was believed to be a divine incantation, which is how representation came to be accepted in the Christian world. (Ibid., 161–62)

To Kristeva, the Renaissance form of representation is "more worldly and political" than the Byzantine icon of the early Christian era, yet it did not eradicate the "economic" bond of images with "invisible eternity" (ibid., 162). I take Nicholas Poussin's *The Ashes of Phokion Collected by His Widow* (1648), a painting that engrossed Rose's thought on politics, for the image of Kristeva's intimate revolt of women and slaves in negotiating with immortality.

Poussin's work is a landscape painting based on Plutarch's first-century *Life of Phokion*, an Athenian general and politician. A model of civic virtue, remaining unchanged by a period of political ferment in Athens, Phokion was nonetheless accused by his enemies of treason and sentenced to die (Rose 1996, 22). His body was removed from the city for cremation and so denied the burial in Athens of a hero. Poussin's companion painting, *Funeral of Phokion*, shows this removal of his body by two slaves set against a background of the ancient city. In the landscape showing the second part of the story—*The Ashes of Phokion Collected by His Widow*—the ancient city is seen straight on, centered on the temple that climbs high in the background. Of the two figures in the foreground, the widow is bent to her task of collecting Phokion's remains, while the trusted companion stands tensely alert in direct line with the temple. If the light illuminating the temple links it to the foreground figures by throwing them into the shadows, where they carry out the secret task almost unnoticed, then Poussin's landscape has not eradicated the sense of the *oikonomia* of women and slaves, whose bodies in the ancient city are not, Kristeva suggests, "destined merely for an unhappy life of labor," but are negotiating with immortality. The burial of Phokion's unconsecrated remains, Plutarch tells us, cannot be in the tombs of his fathers. Thus it will not be in accordance with *megethos*, the greatness of his appearance in the *polis*.

There is *another* approach to the invisible divine: the burial of Phokion's remains at the hearth of his widow's home dedicates his soul to the household gods. With Kristeva, then, Poussin's landscape has not lost the softer approach to invisible eternity. It conveys intimate revolt in the negotiation of women and slaves with immortality. Moreover, with Rose, the fearful gesture of the standing figure in Poussin's painting expresses political risk in protest against arbitrary power (the tyranny that has overtaken classical political order), yet the painting does not oppose women and slaves to the *polis* from which they are exiled. They are not opposed to the *polis* as unjust power (ibid., 25–26). Rather, in this painting, it is in connection with them that the temple rises in splendor. Thus, finally, uniting Rose and Kristeva, the divine presence in the political realm rests on this *political risk* of the *oikonomia* of women and slaves. Intimate revolt is one with political act.

Modern Worlds: The Chiasmus

Modern representation cannot, however, achieve this unity. There is something uniquely problematic about modernity. We must therefore make good on the claim that the *chiasmus* is a good way to figure the relationship between Kristeva and Rose on difficult modernity. Chiasmus is a grammatical figure in which the order of words in one clause is reversed in the other clause. Because the words do not have the same meaning in the two clauses, the chiasmus is not a proposition of identity, nor can it properly form a contradiction. Rather, a seeming contradiction that is an overfamiliar abstraction is transformed, through the figure of chiasmus, into principles of social criticism. For purposes of illumination, we may take an example from Horkheimer and Adorno, who overcame the abstract contradiction of myth and enlightenment in the chiasmus: *myth is already enlightenment, and enlightenment reverts to mythology* (2002, xviii). In the first clause, myth is already a kind of rationality constituted by the strengthening of a self in mastering mythic powers (the cunning of Odysseus). In the second clause, enlightenment is not identified with the mythical world, but, rather, the enlightened world repeats the "irrational" powers that it sought to escape in pushing myth into the past. The repetition lies in the "rational" domination of the subject over nature. Horkheimer and Adorno's chiasmus formulates compulsion and repetition in a historical and social actuality. The chiasmus I propose for Rose and Kristeva is this:

> *In the life and consciousness of action we are already strangers to ourselves; strangers to ourselves, in revolt we advance to the break in life and consciousness.*

The chiasmus inhibits the abstract opposition of action and inaction that either banishes the interpretation of social and political experience or opposes psychoanalysis, art, and literature as inaction to action. It develops the equivocation over the "worlds" of action and revolt to the point where we can see their indefinite relation. The phrase *strangers to ourselves* is fleetingly an indeterminate moment that is pushed through to maintain the relation. That we are strangers to ourselves is common to both Rosean action and Kristevan revolt but cannot be held in common. In the first clause, the supposed stability of life and consciousness—unitary meaning in the "known" world of modern social and political experience—is already undone in the world of action. We are strangers to ourselves as moral agents and social actors. In the second clause, we are strangers to ourselves in the innermost depths of psychical life, the return to which may resuscitate our rebellious potentialities, keeping our *intimacy* in revolt (*en gardant ré-voltée notre intimité*) (Kristeva 2002, 13). The chiasmus therefore gives us a lens through which to see the different approaches of Rose and Kristeva to the impasses of modernity and the motility of the modern subject. It gives understanding its due as regards the indefinite relation between action and revolt.

Finally, we may call on an image for the chiasmus. The cover of Rose's *Judaism and Modernity* shows a maze design by Greg Bright. In an upper corner, the star of redemption releases threads that crisscross the tessellated paths separating and relating the public realm to the gates of the concentration camp. The star does not stand above social and political experience, for its shape is repeated in whole or part through the maze paths, and it yields to lack of a way. The configuration of star, gates, and world returns the idealized public realm to diremption and the inversions of experience. A third appears at a point where the potentiality and actuality of the world may come into a changed relation: a gathered arrow whose word

Figure 3.1. Maze design by Greg Bright.

is *whither*—what may be ventured. At the same time, points of darkness appear in the public realm, realities that might correspond to or foil the concentration of those at the gates of the camp: the eradication of thinking in human beings, "time unbound," and revolt engaging the crossroads of time and the timeless.

However, we cannot directly conjoin revolt and the discovery that underlies the gathered arrow: that we are strangers to ourselves as moral agents and social actors. The distinction and relation of the "worlds" of action and revolt cannot be grasped discursively. Rather than denouncing discursive comprehension, however, I have proposed that the relation between the modern "worlds" of action and revolt is indefinite but nonetheless maintained in the grammatical figure of chiasmus.

Notes

1. *"Ce n'est pas dans le monde de l'action . . . mais dans celui de la vie psychique . . ."* (Kristeva 2012, 28). In "New Forms of Revolt," the statement reads: "*not so much* in the world of action" (2014, 10). In *Intimate Revolt*, Kristeva writes "not exclusively (*pas exclusivement*) in the world of action" (2002, 11). The repetition and variations in the wording of this problematic across different texts show the importance and difficulty of the distinction between the two worlds in Kristeva's writings on revolt.

2. Arendt 1979a, chapter 3.

3. Arendt 1958, chapter 5.

4. See Luxemberg 1970, 181–82.

5. The notion of interstitial existence is introduced in Rose's discussion of Rahel Levin/Varnhagen (Rose 1992, 197).

Works Cited

Adorno, T. W. 1977. "Letters to Walter Benjamin." In *Aesthetics and Politics*. London: New Left Books.

Arendt, Hannah. 1958. *The Human Condition*. Chicago: University of Chicago Press.

———. 1978. *The Life of the Mind*. New York: Harcourt.

———. 1979a. *On Revolution*. London: Penguin Books.

———. 1979b. *Eichmann in Jerusalem: A Report on the Banality of Evil*. London: Penguin Books.

———. 1986. *The Origins of Totalitarianism*. London: Andre Deutsch.
———. 1994. *Essays in Understanding, 1930–1954*. New York: Harcourt Brace.
Browning, Christopher R. 1992. *Ordinary Men: Reserve Police Battalion 101 and the Final Solution in Poland*, New York: Harper Perennial.
Freud, Sigmund. 2001a. *The Interpretation of Dreams*. In *The Standard Edition of the Complete Works of Sigmund Freud*. Vols. 4 and 5. London: Hogarth Press.
———. 2001b. *Beyond the Pleasure Principle*. In *Standard Edition of the Complete Works of Sigmund Freud*. Vol. 18. London: Hogarth Press.
———. 2001c. "Negation." In *Standard Edition of the Complete Works of Sigmund Freud*. Vol. 19. London: Hogarth Press.
Hegel, G. W. F. 1977. *The Phenomenology of Spirit*. Oxford University Press.
Horkheimer, Max, and T. W. Adorno. 2002. *Dialectic of Enlightenment*. Stanford University Press.
Kristeva, Julia. 1974. *Revolution in Poetic Language*. New York: Columbia University Press.
———. 2000. *The Sense and Non-Sense of Revolt*. New York: Columbia University Press.
———. 2001. *Hannah Arendt*. New York: Columbia University Press.
———. 2002. *Intimate Revolt*. New York: Columbia University Press.
———. 2012. *L'Avenir d'une révolte*. Paris: Flammarion.
———. 2014. "New Forms of Revolt." *Journal of French and Francophone Philosophy* 22 (2): 1–19.
Luxemberg, Rosa. 1970. "The Russian Revolution." In *Rosa Luxemberg Speaks*. New York: Pathfinder.
Marx, Karl. 1984. "On the Jewish Question." In *Early Writings*. London: Penguin Books.
Rose, Gillian. 1992. *The Broken Middle, Out of Our Ancient Society*. Oxford: Blackwell Publishers.
———. 1993. *Judaism and Modernity: Philosophical Essays*. Oxford: Blackwell Publishers.
———. 1996. *Mourning Becomes the Law: Philosophy and Representation*. Cambridge University Press.

Part II

Imagining New Intimacies

Antiracist, Aesthetic, and Clinical Revolts

4

Revolt and the Lettered Self

Elena Ruiz

> I cried and I sang. The howling dogs chased the boys
> and the guards laid siege. I cried and harder as the bodies fell.
> Black and white I cried the song, the song to
> his disappeared love. I cried all my despair [. . .]
> I saw torture, I said as I opened my self [. . .]
> That's how I bled the wound and as it gushed red
> the song to their disappeared love started. All the letters were
> opening up like graves, the scream the country said no it didn't
> hurt.
>
> —Raúl Zurita, *Song for His Disappeared Love*

There are many ways of speaking, of making manifest, or of fitting together the range of meanings made possible by the sociohistorical communities we grow into. As individuals, we rely on the continuity of those communities to sustain the meaning of what we say, not only through words (as the speech-communicative paradigm is only one facet of language), but also through our moods, bodily gestures, rituals, caring practices, and art—to give only a few examples of the means with which we bear witness, with which we may *protest.* During times of great loss and distress, where words falter and the insufficiency of one resource of expression may give way to the creative employment of another, the heterogeneous, fluid, and dynamic nature of culture often provides apertures for alternative avenues of 'expression'—of 'giving voice' in particular ways. We turn to the paratactic, to poetry, to the syncopated off-beats of jazz, avant-garde art, or the abject tonality of a lone, echolaliac scream of mourning in the public square: "I cried all my despair," as Zurita says. We can turn to the fragmentary, to the preverbal morsels of bodily import that, together, try to signify what otherwise could not be said at the ideological level of official culture. From twentieth-century Central American murals and graffiti to Shostakovich's Eight Quartet, aesthetic narratives have served as alphabets of survival, as micropractices of resistance in times where the signifying economies recognized in the public sphere became hegemonic, smothering "the scream the country said no it didn't hurt." Under such circumstances, turning to the polyvalence of art to be able to speak, to stammer out names for what was not acknowledged *as existing* to be named, can be seen as the *ars poetica* of social movements and revolt because it rests on the premise that culture is indeed not static and monolithic—that, whether through participatory democratic processes or sudden cultural arrhythmia, another narrative *is possible.*

In this context, it is easier to see why, although today Kristevan scholarship in the Anglo-European academy has generally moved beyond the trope of polysemous signification (as an insurrectional cultural force rooted in the pre-predicative bodily motility and dynamism of the self as a signifying process), this early Kristevan framework still has salience in Latin America, where neoliberal signifying economies and cultural matrixes of power continue to hamper emancipatory, decolonial efforts at the structural level of culture. In particular, Kristeva's work on language (as it appears through RPL and her writings in the late 1960s and early 1970s) is an important framework of cultural analysis in politically hegemonic spaces because it shows precisely that *speech is always more than speech acts*, that the symbolic realm of signification is always already vested with semiotic drive charge and oscillating bodily motility that cannot be altogether foreclosed, and the symbolic is always under threat of a "reversed reactivation" by poetic language.

Given some of the theoretical prejudices associated with Kristeva's developmental account of language acquisition and textuality, which she inherits from the Greco-Roman semiotic tradition and her embeddedness in psychoanalytic discourse theory, it is also important to point out the limitations in applying her work to postcolonial, North-South contexts. Because one common concern in postcolonial and decolonial theory is the general applicability of European theories for articulating models of non-European (especially indigenous and Amerindian) resistance to neocolonial oppression, I take up these concerns by formalizing them in terms of cultural myopias and lacunas found in Kristeva's account of language acquisition and subject formation in RPL, especially at the thetic stage of the signifying process.

I show how Kristeva's novel approach to language is not novel at all if we consider the braided complexity, dynamism, and somatic richness of Native Amerindian linguistic practice as irreducibly ambiguous *nepantla* processes. By giving the history of Amerindian languages as polyvalent human practices forced into concealment by the imposition of alphabetic script and Western scribal technologies, including notions of literacy, I also show how Kristeva is not well attuned to North-South power dynamics in the form of Renaissance language policy (as a tool for domination) in the Americas. I take seriously the claims that while Kristeva's linguistic theories are helpful in rehabilitating static notions of language and subjectivity in structural linguistics and psychoanalytic discourse theory, they are still too indebted to Western developmental and linguistic frameworks and thus not well suited for addressing questions of hermeneutic rupture and social marginalization that arise out of the particularity of the Latin American experience with European colonization. However, I end by resituating the discussion in terms of Kristeva's overall project and the insurrectional models of signification she provides, arguing that our current historical embeddedness in histories of neocolonial and neoliberal domination give significant weight to the continued (strategic) salience of her theories in modern-day Latin America, especially in cases of aesthetic narratives of resistance to clandestine imprisonment and political disappearances.

The Lettered Self

In his acclaimed *The Darker Side of the Renaissance: Literacy, Territoriality, and Colonization* (1995), Walter Mignolo gives a detailed account of how European powers conquered vast Amerindian territories through the imposition of foreign categories of knowledge, of which the most important were Western literacy and the alphabetic technologies that supported it. For Mignolo, by colonizing Amerindian languages through a threefold process of alphabetization, orthographic systematization, and translation into European dictionaries, sixteenth-century missionary ethnographers displaced the primacy of speech and orality in Mesoamerican culture. They overlooked the fact that "speech and writing, in Amerindian societies, were not related and were not conceived in the same way that they were in Greece and in the construction of the Western tradition" (2004, 298). In light of this, the imposition of Greco-Roman alphabetic scripts as the basis for speech communication made it difficult for surviving Amerindians to express, to use one example, *embodied* relations of mutuality and interwoven reciprocity with their life-world, as these relations often had to be performed or sung and could not be reduced to the conventions of Western scribal technology. For instance, take the practice of narrative pictography, as seen in Nahua tacu (also amoxtli). These were accordion-like sheets of folded bark or deer-skin on which paintings conveying a story were recorded using (mostly) red and black ink drawn from plants and flowers. Tacu can be rendered (roughly, of course) as "the act of painting" or "design-making," yet it also had a second, equally important sense of attentive listening (or that one listens) (King 2004, 105, 127). This draws us to the reciprocal binary of giving/receiving that the practice of tacu, as a nepantla process, brought into balance. To write is to "rob flowers of their color," and so to maintain balance, one must reciprocate by listening to "the skin of the earth," which, because it is always transient, changing, and in flux, can only be (at most, dimly) conveyed by humans through the polysemous nature of song. This is why written Amerindian scripts, "as part of the earth," had to be sung and performed out loud.

Principles of interwoven reciprocity and embodiment were at the heart of Amerindian languages, such that, to use Lockhart's well-known example, at the level of spoken language, every Nahuatl noun "is at least potentially a complete equative (relational) statement in itself" with an internal subject and verb (2001, 11). Assigning a formal grammar to Nahuatl based on the logical operations of Western syntax obscures the fact that "the most basic words are, in Richard Andrew's term, 'sentence-words,'" with predicates already included in every substantive (Tomlinson, 29). Much of the grammatical ambiguity in classical Nahuatl and other contact-era Amerindian languages can be traced to the fact that reality itself was understood as "irreducibly ambiguous" (Maffie 2010, 13). European-trained ethnographers and grammarians, of course, had a radically different background understanding of language and reality. The fact that colonial orthography did not mark tone, breath, or even nasalization of Uto-Aztecan languages like spoken Nahuatl—forcibly recoding the highly polymorphous phonology through the single, fixed phonetic meanings assigned to each letter of the Roman alphabet—shows how western conceptual biases supported the imperial project in the Americas through *restrictive notions of linguistic practice.* Because of their rootedness in Greco-Roman semiotic and graphic traditions—which Kristeva inherits in her account of language—the modern Western pre-understandings of language could not accommodate the polysemous nature of Mixtec lexical structure or the related cultural understanding of subjecthood and language as a nepantla process—one that "places all things within a borderland, a dynamic zone of mutual interaction" and that conceives of the speaking subject as a complex, heterogeneous process that is always flexive and precariously positioned (Maffie 2010, 9).

Speakers of Indo-European languages have great difficulty grasping this braided complexity between spoken language and the proximate world. This is largely due to underlying Western assumptions about the nature of the world and the self that are, in turn, encoded in subject-predicate grammar. Thus, with the exception of Mayan hieroglyphs, by and large, modern Western linguists do not recognize *khipus*, *codices*, *tacu*, and textiles like *tocapu* as real scripts or "true writing," reducing them to simple "*aides-mémoire*" in cultures characterized by "primary orality" (Diringer 1953; Gelb 1963; Ong 1988, 83; Lounsbury 1989, 203). Mayan hieroglyphs, which currently date from as far back as the third century BC, have fared better on account of their logographic qualities; because they are made up of pictorialized logograms (with accompanying sets of phonetic clues in later glyphs), they resembled "embryonic" attempts at transcribing spoken language into fixed form and could thus, like Egyptian hieroglyphs, fit into the traditional classificatory schema for the development of Western writing (Houston 2004, 352).

The idea that Amerindian writing systems were at embryonic or early stages of chirographic development—which, given enough time and favorable conditions, might have blossomed into a robust semiotic system of standardized markings (with a fixed phonetic value and accompanying rule system for correct combinatorial use)—is an occidental prejudice, and a deep one at that. Kristeva's analysis of "Mayan texts" reflects such prejudices, noting how the "scriptural system" that "functions as ideograms" "does not seem to be able to mark/indicate sentences," despite the continuing "effort of several scholars" to completely decipher it (1981, 59–59). While Kristeva's astute understanding of language leads her to recognize an element of "multidimensionality" to "a number of nonalphabetic writings, as in Egypt or China, or among the Aztects or the Mayas," they are situated along a system-wide developmental continuum that begins with "pictograms" or "simplified ideograms" and ends with the modern science of language: "at whatever moment one looks at language—in most remote historical periods, among people said to be savage, or in the modern era, it presents itself as a most complex system," she writes (6). Kristeva's lack of attunement to the powerful ways language propagated the Imperial project in the Americas is most striking in her reading (by way of Russian linguists) of Fray Diego de Landa's (1524–1579) *Relación de las Cosas de Yucatan* (1566). Landa played a key role in the alphabetization of Amerindian languages by formally transcoding Mayan glyphs into letters in the Latin alphabet. Kristeva notes this in the context of social scientific analysis, whereby linguists "abandoned the hieroglyphic hypothesis" and "returned to the alphabetic hypothesis" of "the first decipherer of the Mayas" (59). Landa's manuscript, where he put forth his "alphabetic hypothesis," reads:

> These people [native Amerindians] made use of certain characters or letters, with which they wrote in their books their ancient matters and their sciences, and by these and by drawings and by certain signs in these drawings, they understood their affairs and made others understand them and taught them. We found a large number of books in these characters and, as they contained nothing in which there were not to be seen superstition and lies of the devil, we burned them all, which they regretted to an amazing degree, and which caused them much affliction. Of their letters I will give here an A,B,C, since their ponderousness does not allow anything more. . . . (169)

Landa's Eurocentric assumption that Mayan hieroglyphs had equivalences in the Roman alphabet (at least for A, B, C) was taken up by the Franciscan Diego Valdéz (1533–1589) in his monumental *Rhetorica Christiana* (1579), which served as a teaching tool for friars teaching Nahua speakers their own language back to them in Romanized form. But it was not enough to teach natives individual letters, for they might employ indigenous principles and habits to combine them in particular ways the Friars could not control. There needed to be an orthography to set out formal rules of usage and to ensure Amerindians "spoke as they wrote, and wrote as they spoke" (Nebrija 1517). To be a self, one had to become *a Lettered self.* Offering a critique of this framework is especially important given that, in the sixteenth century, even humanist "defenders" of Amerindian's rights held that "barbarians are those who lack a literary language (*qui literali sermone carent*) which corresponds to their mutual idiomatic language, as is Latin to us, and thus do not know how to express what they think" (Mignolo, 78, citing Fray Bartolomé de Las Casas [1484–1566]). Kristeva's model of language acquisition, as it is presented in *Revolution in Poetic Language,* also poses similar difficulties given its triangulation with psychoanalytic discourse theory.

Revolution in Poetic Language and the Colonial Thetic

As a revision to Lacanian theories of language acquisition that posit a unitary, self-conscious subject behind (post-oedipal) signifying activity, Kristeva's main thesis in RPL concerns the heterogeneity of the speaking subject, both prior to and after its entrance into the social realm. In dispelling the traditional Cartesian "notion of the judging subject as a fixed point" (118) in structuralist views of language—one that is disconnected from both pre-predicative bodily drives and desires and the affective dimension of speech (i.e., rhythms, tones, intonation)—Kristeva's aim in RPL is to show that, in fact, "the subject never is; the subject is only the signifying process and he appears only as a signifying practice" that is as fluid and dynamic as the processes that constitute him or her as a "subject" (215).

Historically, the psychoanalytic interest in subjectivity and its relation to language derives from Freud's psychological theories and his need, as a physician of nervous disorders, to develop a clinical model that could account for a range of somatic symptoms and conditions with no clear etiology in the material body (such as a brain lesion). As he describes in *The Interpretation of Dreams* (1900), his patients often presented an array of bodily symptoms that spanned from syncope, fatigue, and nausea, to "pains in the neck, abdomen, stomach," or even vomiting (93); to relieve his patients' suffering, a cure would have to be provided that medically linked these symptoms to abnormalities in processes originating within the individuals themselves, whether as organic conditions, biological processes, or some combination thereof. In other words, as a trained neurologist, Freud sought to stay within "the bounds of neuro-pathological interest" (ix) and the discursive paradigm of late-nineteenth, early twentieth-century neurophysiology, even when modifying its assumptions or adding to its diagnostic vocabulary through expansive notions of "psychic life" (466). Thus, for Freud, who viewed the brain as biological matter that functions through mind-dependent states that can be observed in their relation to human behavior, abnormalities in his patients' behavior such as "hysterical phobias, obsessions, and delusions" could be traced back to pathologies in the brain's activities—to process-driven "psychic structures" that form the basis for one's inner experiences of him- or herself (the "psychic life") via his or her product: thought (v). By attributing "pathologies" in behavior to psychic structures, Freud established a link between the mind (psyche) and the material body (soma) (hence the term "psychosomatic") that became deeply influential for twentieth-century neuropsychology. Psychosomatic symptoms were mentally induced symptoms. That is to say, they were brought on by a thought process that remained hidden from the sufferer's view. If they were not hidden and were instead transparent, then patients suffering from symptoms could, at least in theory, self-reflectively gain access to the source of their own maladies, demystify their origin, and potentially gain therapeutic relief by identifying the source of their suffering. Patients, of course, experienced these symptoms as acutely as organic illnesses.

To solve this predicament, Freud famously postulated the existence of a split psychological subject whose unity (as an "I") is generated through various inner struggles and conflicts taking place at differing levels of consciousness, thereby dividing the mind into "conscious" and "unconscious" parts. Using interpretive methods drawn from clinical models, the job of the psychoanalyst is precisely to try to analyze his or her patient's symptoms and behavior to establish a link to primary processes and motivations residing in the unconscious part of the mind, which the patient cannot him- or herself access but which can manifest itself through speech—through slips of the tongue, jokes, innuendo, double-entendre, or through dreams. However, to spot one of these slips or to know what his or her dreams are, the "analysand" (psychoanalytic patient) must first communicate them to the analyst. Hence, under the psychoanalytic framework, gaining access to the patient's mind relies on a view of language as a vehicle or medium—a diagnostic vessel, without which analysis of the psyche would prove impossible. As Kristeva explains:

> Psychoanalysis sees the patient's speech as its object. The psychoanalyst has no other means within his reach, no other reality with which to explore the conscious or unconscious functioning of the subject, than speech and its laws and structures . . . while the psychiatrist may look for a physical lesion as the cause of a disturbance, the psychoanalyst refers only to what the subject says . . . he discovers in his discourse first the unconscious, then the more or less conscious motivation producing the symptoms. Once he has discovered this motivation, all the neurotic behavior denotes an obvious logic, and the symptom appears as the symbol of this finally rediscovered motivation. (1989, 266)

The interest in subjectivity thus stems from the type of psychic structures the psychoanalytic therapeutic model must postulate to address phenomena in terms of the "inner" life or "psychic life" of patients. Given its roots in the medical sciences, which operates under a developmental model of the organic body, this interest led to theoretical speculation about the onset of the subject itself—its differentiation as an individual from the collective as well as its entrance into social structures like language and the family (i.e., kinship relations). For Freud as for his successor, Lacan, all subjectivity is "post-oedipal" because it is the end result of processes initiated in the early developmental life of a child. These processes are governed by the universal laws of the oedipal family drama, such as the fear of castration and the Law of the Father. They also provide the necessary motivation for humans to relinquish their reliance on the safe confines of the mother-child dyad and to begin speaking in terms of "symbolic" signifying structures like grammar. Thus, under psychoanalytic discourse theory, language acquisition goes hand in hand with the onset of subjectivity.

Specifically, for Lacan, subjectivity is initiated through the "mirror phase" that occurs between six and eighteen months of age; before that, the human child is an aggregate bundle of unorganized impulses and energy drives that make the child's experience of him- or herself disorderly, jumbled, and fragmentary at best. Lacan calls this stage the "imaginary phase." As Kelly Oliver explains,

> In the "imaginary" phase, the child has only fragmented experiences and no unified sense of self. In the mirror stage the child held in front of a mirror by an adult recognizes its image in the mirror. At first it confuses the image with reality. After some experimentation, it realizes that the image reflected is its own image and not just the adult's. Finally, it realizes the mirror image is not real. The mirror stage is the first recognition of the "I" . . . what is paradoxical in the mirror stage is that the realization that the child is unified comes through its doubling in the mirror. In a sense, it must become two (itself plus its reflection) in order to become one (a unified self). (1993, 20)

For Lacan, the mirror stage sets up the conditions for a child to enter into language (understood here as a signifying practice) on account of this representational doubling between itself and the image of itself in the mirror. Following Oliver's explanation, because the image is in fact a stand-in and performs the function of a symbol, "this substitution of the symbolic for the real body prefigures all subsequent development," including the child's shifting identifications with different protagonists in the family drama, as well as language use (ibid). The idea that this representational doubling *prefigures* language use, however, is built on the assumption that language is indeed a representational structure or modeled on subject/object principles. Lacan, who famously asserted that "the unconscious is structured like a language" (1977, 234), holds this view because it is consistent with his broader intellectual framework. That is to say, Lacan develops Freud's theories by further systematizing the unconscious through principles gathered from Lévi-Strauss's structural linguistics, and a representational view of language is the only one compatible with such a model of the unconscious.

For Kristeva, Lacan's theories "fail to articulate [the infant's] transitional link to the post-oedipal subject" accurately (22). Once the mirror stage is passed, Lacan assumes that the child is now a structured, unified self who is capable of conveying meaning through language. Although, on Kristeva's view, the onset of the subject does occur upon its entrance into language, it is never unified, unaffected by forces that existed prior to the mirror stage. Along with the post-oedipal subject, there is also a pre-predicative "psychosomatic modality of the signifying process" that continues to influence the developing infant even past its positing as a subject (28). For Kristeva, the onset of the subject is thus prefigured by a series of kinetic bodily processes that originate in the infant's relation to the maternal body, which she explores at length in RPL.

Kristeva's strategy in RPL is then to "reinvest language" with the full complexity and dynamism of prelinguistic drives while at the same time identifying the material body as already replete with all the pre-oedipal structures and primary processes necessary to initiate the onset of signification—to separate the developing infant from its reliance on the mother and usher mother and infant into the social practices and structures necessary to make speech "meaningful" in a culturally situated way (Oliver, 3–4). Because of the infant's preverbal bodily history, on Kristeva's view, speech is always more than speech acts and involves deeper laws and processes than those acknowledged in structural linguistics. She writes:

> Linguistic semiology generally shares the thesis that meaning is a "substance" preexisting in its "formation" in an expression—either a sentence or a sign (morpheme, lexeme, etc.)—assumed by the thinking subject . . . by contrast, in our view, one must distinguish language from other signifying systems and consider the linguistic sign (and the dichotomies it can give rise to: expression/content, etc.) as only one stage of the signifying process. (1984, 38–39)

To this end, in RPL, Kristeva conceives of language as the dynamic unfurling of a signifying process whereby meaning is produced through an oscillating tension "between two irreconcilable elements—separate but inseparable from the [signifying] process in which they assume asymmetrical functions" (82). She terms these two elements "the symbolic" and "the semiotic." The symbolic element is the one more familiar to us, as it is "imposed by the social realm" (48). It is what gives shape to language through an ordering principle [ordonancement] based "on socio-historical constraints, such as the biological difference between the sexes or family structure" (26, 29). It takes the child's random echolalias and organizes them based on social and cultural preunderstandings, so that what the child says becomes intelligible in a particular cultural matrix. As a source of boundaries and constraints, it manifests itself most powerfully in syntax and grammatical categories, which impose further limits on what kinds of utterances one can say and how one can say them. The symbolic thus "appears in propositions" (41); the difference for Kristeva is that, while structural linguistics (and, by proxy, Lacanian psychoanalytic theory) took this to be the fundamental factor in shaping the child's utterances after the mirror stage, she views this as only one element of a larger signifying process. It is the tip of the iceberg rather than the base of the mountain, albeit a point without which one could not speak in any meaningful way at all.

By contrast, the semiotic is Kristeva's contribution to psychoanalytic discourse theory. With it, she goes beyond structural linguistics and reinvests language with motility and bodily dynamism. The term, she writes, is taken from the Greek word *semion*, meaning "distinctive mark, trace, index, precursory sign" (25). It consists of prelinguistic drives and desires that are "articulated by a flow and marks" and "energy transfers" below the level of consciousness (40). Following Freudian drive theory, Kristeva believes that "the human body is also a process. It is not a unity but a plural totality" that constitutes the "place where the drives are applied" (101). That is to say, for both Freud and Kristeva, "discrete quantities of energy move through the body of the subject who is not yet constituted as such"; consequently, it is replete with energy drives that, when discharged, motivate (in the literal sense of initiating movement) organic processes like digestion and metabolic functions. However, for Kristeva, these drives always "connect and orient the body to the mother" by way of gestational links—the vibration in the womb from the mother's voice is one example (27).

Thus, by semiotic, Kristeva means "the effects of meaning that are not reducible to language," such as the child's echolalias, "the play of colors in an abstract painting or a piece of music that lacks signification but has meaning" in the broader sense of an inarticulable weight or import on us (1996, 21). If signification were only semiotic, however, our speech would manifest itself in meaningless babble or psychotic drivel. This means there is no one without the other: "because the subject is always both semiotic and symbolic, no signifying system he produces can be either 'exclusively' semiotic or 'exclusively' symbolic, and is instead necessarily marked by an indebtedness to both" (24). The semiotic makes it possible for Kristeva "to disclose a fundamental stage—or region—in the process of the subject, a state that is hidden by the arrival of signification" (40). This is the preoedipal maternal realm Lacan neglected as a significant source of influence in the constitution of the subject. As Kristeva contends, before the onset of subjectivity in the mirror stage (followed by its completion in the Freudian stage of castration), the child's body is invested by a series of energy "waves" and "stases" that can be compared with the primary processes of condensation [*Verdichtung*] and displacement [*Verschiebung*] in Freud (60). This continuous rhythmic flow of energy transfers undergo "stases" when it is "checked by the constraints of biological and social structures," in other words, by the symbolic (28). In prenatal life that is not yet subject to the symbolic realm of signification, the repetition of these drive charges produces stases that allow the rhythmic flow to remain dynamic (27).

This oscillating process of charges and stases—and not simply a Freudian fear of castration or the Law of the Father—are what motivate the subject to relinquish the attachment to the mother's body and initiate symbolic speech on their own. In this way, they "produce" the subject (27). Kristeva refers to this dialectical process of semiotic drive charges and stases as "negativity" to distinguish it from Hegelian "negation, which is the act of a judging subject" (28). Negativity describes the temporal axis of the pre-oedipal, insofar as it is used to describe a process and an activity. For the metaphysically ambiguous pre-oedipal spatial dimension, Kristeva borrows the term *chora* from Plato's *Timaeus*. According to Kristeva, the chora is the place where the oscillating process of charges and stases (negativity) can take place (28). It is an "essentially mobile and extremely provisional articulation constituted by movements and their ephemeral stases" (25, my emphasis). That is to say, its existence as a "nonexpressive totality" is a theoretical prerequisite for understanding the processes that follow it: "the chora is generated in order to attain to this signifying position" that follows the mirror stage, and for this reason it must theoretically precede and underlie all figuration (the symbolic) (26, my emphasis). Put otherwise, one cannot order space without the theoretical positing of precreation space. The chora performs the theoretical role of precreation space. Thus, while the symbolic "orders" [ordonancement] the semiotic elements of signification, the chora is the preverbal semiotic space where regulating process [*réglemmentation*] may occur. This is why the chora is associated with the mother's body: because its processes of motility in gestation are pre-oedipal and presymbolic. Because the mother's gestational body already contains all the logic necessary to initiate the later processes Freud and Lacan ascribe to the mirror stage and castration, "it is therefore what mediates the symbolic law organizing social relations and becomes the ordering principle of the semiotic chora" (27).

Kristeva also refers to "the signifying process as a thetic negativity" (55). According to her, the "thetic" is a stage in the constitution of the subject that "marks the threshold" between the semiotic and the symbolic (48). We can think of the thetic phase as a crucial moment of transition between "heterogeneous realms" brought about by negativity (that is, by the oscillating tension between prelinguistic drive charges and their stases). It is a formal break or scission that ushers one into the symbolic realm of signification, "which is always that of a proposition or judgment, in other words, a realm of positions" (43). Its counterpart in the mother-child dyad is the moment of separation from the maternal body during birth. For Lacan, this separation would be total and complete. Instead, Kristeva's semiotic realm ensures that, even past the thetic phase initiating the child into the symbolic order, an umbilical link remains that challenges this order. The thetic phase requires the child to "take a position," to think of herself as a self in order for "the possibility of enunciation" to materialize (44). In this way, Kristeva writes, "the thetic is the precondition for both enunciation and denotation" in the formal sense (53).

Here is where Kristeva's developmental, though dynamic, view of language acquisition and subjectivity begins to pose limitations for applications to Amerindian and postcolonial settings, where, historically, "language" has come to mean something different that is perhaps obfuscated by Kristeva's model. We find this difficulty most strikingly in the thetic stage of the signifying process. According to Kristeva, "even if it is presented as a simple act of naming, we maintain that the thetic is already propositional (or syntactic) and that syntax is the exposition of the thetic" (54). This alone would not be problematic, as, by including "syntactic" in the description, Kristeva allows for grammatical formations that are not necessarily propositional. She follows this statement, however, with the claim that "the subject and predicate represent the division inherent in the thetic" (ibid). Again, to say something is inherent does not mean it will necessarily lead to its expression. Yet, she insists, both in RPL and in the course of later writings of the 1970s, that the grammatical structures of "subject" and the "predicate" are "indissociable from the thetic process" (54). If syntax is the exposition of the thetic, as Kristeva seems to suggest, then the polysemous syntax of Nahua lexical structure posits a very different kind of speaking subject than Kristeva's thetic seems to allow for—a speaking subject that is always already constituted by a semiotic-like state of in-betweenness and change that is not propositional. Structurally, Kristeva needs to posit a symbolic realm that is characterized by subject-predicate grammar because only in this way can (semiotic) poetic language break up or destabilize the symbolic, whether through avant-garde art or the paratactic lexical structures of poems that displace the expectation of meaning in a text. Yet the problem with the colonial legacy in Latin America is that it obfuscated the ways in which the symbolic realm was always already invested with semiotic drive force, to use Kristeva's terms. *It was already vested* with "drive, sensation, prelanguage, rhythm, melody, and so on" that Kristeva finds to be her novel contribution to theories of linguistic practice. Were it not for the fact that Kristeva's psychoanalytic model commits her to basic claims about the universal nature of her project—that the model of language acquisition and subject constitution she presents is true at the species-wide level—it would be far less of a problem for theoretical applications in North-South contexts because it would have no direct bearing on Amerindian experience.

Reinvesting Revolt

On September 11, 1973, the day General Augusto Pinochet took power in Chile though a CIA-backed coup-d'état, several hundred students and professors from the Universidad Federico Santa Maria were arrested under suspicion of subversion and secretly jailed in the hull of a military ship. The culture of terror that preceded and continued after the coup rested, in large part, on the ability to haunt Chileans with a constant, panoptical threat of violence through the specter of the disappeared body. Because most kidnappings occurred at night and many bodies were unrecoverably strewn across the natural landscape, it was almost impossible to prove a crime had been committed. Without writs of habeas corpus to challenge official military narratives of missing family members as defectors, exiles, and left-wing dissidents who willfully abandoned their families, everyday life took on surreal qualities. While documentary realism prevailed in the twentieth-century photographic journalism of officially recognized wars like Vietnam, in Chile the opposite inclination emerged toward denunciatory surrealism, as seen in Eugenio Dittborn's dreamlike pastiches of Chilean life.

Among those kidnapped on the morning of September 11 was an engineering student, Raul Zurita. Zurita, who survived the torture and extralegal imprisonment, took up poetry in the period leading up to the dictatorship because, for him, it was "the only thing that told me that I wasn't crazy, that I wasn't living in a nightmare" (2010, 1). In the twentieth century, Latin American state terrorism created a powerful rift between the narrative processes that allow social beings to meaningfully recode experiences structured by narrative *dis*continuity and violence into cohesive cultural narratives of, for example, genocide or illegal torture—specific understandings of historical memory that allow one, in turn, to take a stand on past events as *political* agents seeking public redress of wrongs. This spurred the unprecedented rise of political art action groups like CADA (Colectivo de Acciones de Arte) in response. From the murals of revolutionary Nicaragua to the insurrectional social narratives produced by CADA, poetic language served to challenge the destabilizing effects of terror on individual narrative identities and, at the level of culture, the discursive construction/distortion of collective memory by official government accounts of history. This carries through to contemporary times: the mass kidnapping of forty-three students from the college of Ayotzinapa in Guerrero, Mexico, in 2014 has spurred a critical mass of political art and aesthetic narratives of dissent. As Julia Kristeva explains, poetic language enters into the social debate by confronting static signifying economies (*Bedeutung*) and questioning the very principle of the ideological, but it does so "with all meaning, and hence all enunciation produced by a positing subject" . . . and it is thus, she writes, that "the signifying process joins social revolution" (RPL, 61).

If we recognize the historical provenance of Kristeva's thought and problematize what it means to be a "positing subject" as contextually dependent, in large part, on powerful cultural asymmetries that privilege the enunciative life of some speakers over others, we can reinvest the salience of her insurrectional hermeneutics in the service of social movements and revolt. Understanding the historical context and embeddedness out of which philosophical bodies of work emerge can help ease the burden of having to reject large parts of philosophical frameworks one otherwise finds empowering or useful for one's projects on account of applicability. We can bring this approach to Kristeva's work on language by noting that Kristeva, from the beginning, is primarily a scholar who is interested in texts and textual practice. She is an interpreter of Western literature, writes on literary genius, and considers "Rabelais, Swift, Sade, Lautréamont, Kafka, and Bataille" as marginalized voices "on the fringe of official culture" (1983, 86). Although one can cherish such High Renaissance and modern European writers for their transgressive narratives in Western literature, they may certainly fail to capture what it means to be "on the fringe of official culture" for subaltern, postcolonial peoples who cannot even include literacy as a category unencumbered by historical oppression. This is not to fault Kristeva for her positions, but rather to show how historical backdrops inform those positions, creating blind spots in areas our respective histories allow us to take for granted. Kristeva is not attuned to the ways literacy, textuality, or even the alphabet can be a source of oppression because she identifies with a Western European cultural context that is Byzantine:

> I learned from Bulgaria the importance of culture. Bulgaria is the country in which the Slavonic alphabet was created. It was two Bulgarian brothers, Cyril and Methodius, who gave the Slavonic alphabet to the world—it is now the alphabet that the Russians use. There is in Bulgaria a Feast of the Alphabet, probably the only one in the world. Every year on May 24, children parade through the streets of Sofia, each displaying a letter on their fronts, so we are identified with the alphabet. (1997, 160–61)

So indeed, recalling Mignolo's thesis that the alphabet served as an European *weapon of war* in the Americas, we can see how, at least through these examples, Kristeva's work as a whole is simply not well suited for applications in North-South contexts. Yet, despite the disconnect, in social locations where material strife and structural oppression dominate, methods of analysis ought not be foreclosed in advance of their possible deployment, especially in creative, tactical, strategic, and critical ways. After all, when asked why establishing the semiotic element of communication is important to the study of language, Kristeva replied that it is vital "so as to recognize the phenomena that are so common in the daily life of subjective experience . . . where signification disintegrates, arriving at lower thresholds of meaning that do not coincide with normal communication, if not a total eclipse of signification" (1996, 22). This could prove helpful—simply as one resource among many—for beings whose lived-experience of signification "disintegrates" in the wake of trauma, as in the case of political disappearances and clandestine imprisonments in Latin America.

Works Cited

Diringer, David. 1962. *Writing*. St. Louis: McGraw-Hill.

Dittborn, Eugenio. 1993. *Mapa: The Airmail Paintings of Eugenio Dittborn 1984–1992*. London: Institute of Contemporary Arts.

Gelb, Ignace. 1963. *A Study of Writing*. Chicago: University of Chicago Press.

King, Mark B. 2004. "Hearing the Echoes of Verbal Art in Mixtec Writing." In *Writing Without Words: Alternative Literacies in Mesoamerica & the Andes*, edited by Walter Mignolo and Elizabeth Hill Boone. Durham: Duke University Press.

Kristeva, Julia. 1984 [1974]. *Revolution in Poetic Language*. New York: Columbia University Press.

———. 1989. *Language, the Unknown: An Initiation into Linguistics*. New York: Columbia University Press.

———. 1996. *Julia Kristeva: Interviews*. New York: Columbia University Press.

Landa, Diego de. 1941 [1566]). *Relacion de Las Cosas de Yucatan*. Cambridge: Harvard University Press.

Lockhart, James. 2001. *Nahuatl as Written: Lesson in Older Written Nahuatl, with Copious Examples and Texts*. Stanford: Stanford University Press.

Lounsbury, Floyd. 1989. "The Ancient Writing of Middle America." In *The Origins of Writing*, edited by W. Senner. Lincoln: University of Nebraska Press.

Maffie, James. 2010. "Pre-Columbian Philosophies." In *A Companion to Latin American Philosophy*, edited by Susana Nuccetelli, Ofelia Schutte and Otávio Bueno. Oxford: Wiley-Blackwell.

Mignolo, Walter D. 2004. "Signs and Their Transmission: The Question of the Book in the New World." In *Writing without Words: Alternative Literacies in Mesoamerica & the Andes*, edited by Walter Mignolo and Elizabeth Hill Boone. Durham: Duke University Press.

———. 2003 [1995]. *The Darker Side of the Renaissance: Literacy, Territoriality, and Colonization*. 2nd ed. Ann Arbor: University of Michigan Press.

Oliver, Kelly. 1993. *Reading Kristeva: Unraveling the Double-Bind*. Bloomington: Indiana University Press.

Ong, Walter J. 1988. *Orality and Literacy: The Technologizing of the Word*. London: Routledge.

Tomlinson, Gary. 2007. *The Singing of the New World: Indigenous Voice in the Era of European Contact*. New York: Cambridge University Press.

Zurita, Raul. 2010. *Song for His Disappeared Love*. Translated by Daniel Borzutzky. Notre Dame: Indiana University Press.

5

Extimate Trauma, Intimate Ethics

Kristevan Revolt in the Artwork of Kara Walker

Amy Ray Stewart

> the madness that remembers
> the madness that howls
> the madness that sees
> the madness that is unleashed
>
> —Aimé Césaire, *Notebook of a Return to the Native Land*

In the closing remarks of his *Introductory Lectures on Psycho-Analysis*, Freud (1917) claims that "if a knife does not cut, it cannot be used for healing either," thereby affirming not only an intimate relationship between the analytic encounter with traumatic phenomena and the capacity for psychical healing, but also the unsettling experience that working-through demands (463). Advancing Freud's assertion, this chapter examines how the abject images that constitute the trauma aesthetic of Kara Walker's contemporary artwork enact a visual return to the cultural repressed. By cutting into the extimate traumas of racial, sexual, and cultural violence, Walker's revolting artwork incites a purposeful return to what Cathy Caruth (1995) terms an "impossible history" of psychical and social rupture characterized by repetition, repression, and inaccessibility (5). Walker's artwork thus stages an intimate return to an extimate trauma to prompt thought, remembrance, and perpetual questioning. Cultivating an artistic "madness that remembers," Walker's howling inscriptions of race and sexuality, trauma and *jouissance*, and power and displacement provoke a witnessing and working-through of the unspeakable so as to "give meaning to suffering" (Kristeva 2002a, 24). In this way, Walker's trauma aesthetic initiates an experience of intimate revolt, a continuous psychical process of anamnesis and interrogation that Kristeva (2002a) defines as a perpetual "questioning and displacement of the past" (5) through which there emerges a "potential for making gaps, rupturing, [and] renewing" (2002b, 85). Working through Kristeva's psychoanalytic formulation of intimate revolt as a retrospective interrogation of being and transformation of meaning at the threshold of the psychical and the social, this chapter emphasizes the ethical and political possibilities of Walker's trauma aesthetic through which pain is redressed and meaning is renewed in a time and space of intimate revolt. This chapter argues, then, that Walker's return to the repressed legacies of racial, sexual, and cultural trauma initiates an intimate ethics of aesthetic revolt that makes possible not only the rebirth of psychical life, but also the future of meaning altogether.

Cutting into Kara Walker's Trauma Aesthetic

Since her debut in 1994, Kara Walker has become one of the most prominent and controversial African American woman artists working in the United States. Curating an intimate return to the repressed, Walker's contemporary artwork figures a trauma aesthetic through which revolting inscriptions of identity, power, and violence intersect and implicate their spectator, thereby resurrecting and calling into question the traumas of history, memory, and subjectivity. Imagining haunting tableaux of antebellum slavery, Reconstruction, and Jim Crow, Walker assembles unsettling depictions of slavery and plantation life, racial stereotypes and cultural displacement, decapitation and dismemberment, sexual assault and lynching violence. With each wretched landscape, equally abject and ambiguous, Walker uncovers the repressions of racism and violence specific to the racial histories of the United States. Cutting into this "impossible history" of cultural trauma and racial violence, Walker thus summons the fraught realities of racism and racial history through a calculated use of fantasy. Indeed, "the most misunderstood part of Walker's work," Kevin Young (2013) explains, is that "she traffics in fantasy, rather than some version of reality or even protest" (45–46).

Nevertheless, the abject fantasies that constitute Walker's trauma aesthetic are always already emerging from the traces of a tangible reality of cultural pain and suffering, as is evidenced especially in her visual rememory of plantation life and lynching violence.

Although Walker's artwork routinely employs graphite and gouache, she is best known for her galleries of cut-paper silhouettes that beckon the spectator to witness unspeakable scenes of subjection. Walker's intimate return to the legacies of racial, sexual, and cultural trauma is constructed with little more than plain black paper and the handiwork of a craft knife, materials from which she carves out fantastical figures and landscapes agglomerated within a chaotic space devoid of borders or time. Her cut-paper silhouettes thus offer a purposeful semblance of simplicity while riddling both the scene and the spectator with an unsettling sense of undecidability. Walker's revitalization of the silhouette form is an artistic—even ironic—return to the eighteenth-century technique of "shadow portraits" that captivated the same cultural milieu that endorsed and perpetuated the peculiar institution of slavery. Central to Walker's fashioning of her silhouettes is a cathartic act of retort and creation whereby she initiates a witnessing and working-through of the "impossible history" of racism and cultural trauma. Cutting out sketches culled from the racist imaginaries of history, literature, and memory, Walker physically removes and repositions her silhouettes onto the gallery wall, leaving behind the emptied doubles of each figure. Through this act of double negation, in which her paring away at "the surface of this black thing" uncovers a hollowed void left behind from the excised silhouettes, Walker accomplishes the art of "creating a hole," thereby exposing the inarticulable wound and void of trauma itself (Walker 2003, 8:55 min). Once affixed to the gallery wall, Walker's revolting silhouettes summon the spectator into an ostensibly simple space in which unconscious imaginaries of race and sexuality, power and violence, are unleashed, projected, and encountered. In this way, the silhouettes that form Walker's trauma aesthetic reflect the shallow and arguably cartoon-like structure of stereotypes overdetermined by racist fantasies.

If Walker's trauma aesthetic performs a visual return to the cultural repressed, an artistic "madness that remembers," then it is because her artwork accomplishes the rememory of an "impossible history" of trauma and suffering (Césaire 2001, 18). "Through visual utterance," Gwendolyn DuBois Shaw (2004) explains, Walker "commands the return of the repressed, the seeing of the unspeakable" (52). Indeed, Walker's purposeful conjuring of a past inextricably linked to the present reverses, as it were, the

Freudian structure of the return of the repressed, which traditionally posits that the repressed returns through "substitutive formations and symptoms" (Freud 1915, 154). Walker's artwork thus effects an intimate return that not only uncovers the repressed legacies of racial and sexual abjection, but also implicates the spectator into these repressed legacies to prompt thought and self-questioning. Walker (2003) clarifies of her artwork, however, that the "illusion is that it's about past events, the illusion is that it's simply about a particular point in history and nothing else" (3:48 min.). Walker indicates, then, that her return to and rememory of an "impossible history" of cultural trauma works through an intentional illusion of the past to interrogate its impact on the present and future. Walker's return to the repressed thus performs an inscription, if not articulation, of inarticulable devastation, rupture, and loss, thereby shaping her trauma aesthetic as an intimate act of redress, which Saidiya Hartman (1997) describes as an "exercise of agency directed toward the release of the pained body, the reconstitution of violated natality, and the remembrance of breach" (76–77). This is to say that Walker's visual "articulation of loss" serves as an act of cultural redress through which racial, sexual, and cultural traumas are given meaning in an aesthetic space of intimate revolt (Hartman 1997, 77).

Walker's visual return to the cultural repressed therefore enacts a psychical process of "return/turning back/displacement/change" that Kristeva (2002a) identifies as intimate revolt (5). According to Kristeva (2002b), intimate revolt—be it "psychic revolt, analytic revolt, artistic revolt"—"refers to a state of permanent questioning, of transformation, change, [and] an endless probing of appearances" (120). Tracing its etymological evolution, Kristeva stresses intimate revolt as "return, returning, discovering, uncovering, and renovating," in addition to "rupturing, renewing," for revolt, Kristeva maintains, "is not simply about rejection and destruction; it is also about starting over" (2002b, 85, 123). Intimate revolt, which Kristeva also connects to experiences of transgression, imagination, and sublimation, thus makes possible the rebirth of psychical life and the future of meaning inasmuch as revolt, on Kristeva's account, remains not only our recourse against cultural ossification, but also our remedy for what she diagnoses as the "new maladies of the soul" (1995, 9). Walker's trauma aesthetic therefore centralizes the rupture, recovery, and redress of racial violence in a sublimatory space of intimate revolt through which an articulation of the inarticulable is made possible.

Revitalizing not only the silhouette technique, but also the grand form of the cyclorama, Walker's (1997) *Slavery! Slavery!* (figure 5.1) stages a revolting panoramic inscription of an antebellum Southern plantation in which the

Figure 5.1. Kara Walker, *Slavery! Slavery! Presenting a GRAND and LIFELIKE Panoramic Journey into Picturesque Southern Slavery or "Life at 'Ol' Virginny's Hole' (sketches from Plantation Life)" See the Peculiar Institution as never before! All cut from black paper by the able hand of Kara Elizabeth Walker, an Emancipated Negress and leader in her Cause* [detail], 1997. Cut paper on wall. Installation dimensions variable; approx. 144 × 1,020 inches (365.76 × 2,590.8 cm). Installation view: *Kara Walker: My Complement, My Enemy, My Oppressor, My Love.* Hammer Museum, Los Angles, 2007. Photo: Joshua White. Courtesy of Sikkema Jenkins & Co., New York.

borders between reality and fantasy collapse. Notably constructed as an abject resignification of Eastman Johnson's (1859) *Old Kentucky Home—Life in the South (Negro Life at the South)* and reminiscent of late nineteenth-century panoramic paintings more generally, Walker's *Slavery! Slavery!* is a cyclorama installed in a large, circular room with only one threshold that functions simultaneously as the entrance and exit. Although the panoramic structure of *Slavery! Slavery!* offers only a semblance of narrative intelligibility, Walker's nonlinear installation gives "meaning to suffering" through the intimate redress of cultural trauma (Kristeva 2002a, 24). Indeed, Kristeva (1996) indicates in *Time and Sense* that "the fantasy makes the unconscious into a narrative. As a result, when the outside-time of the unconscious is named and recounted, it acquires meaning, a goal, and a value" (326). As a new form of revolt, *Slavery! Slavery!* thus captures Walker's efforts to bear witness and give meaning to the unspeakable traces of racial, sexual, and cultural trauma.

As a panoramic installation, *Slavery! Slavery!* presents a nonlinear agglomeration of silhouettes that not only resists a coherent narrative structure, but also obscures any fixed locus of power, agency, or identity among the tumultuous landscape. Throughout Walker's fantastically rendered chaos of Southern plantation life, bodily excretions such as vomit, feces, semen, and blood abound amid the subtly interconnected and purposefully ambiguous scenes of violence and desire: from sexual assault to sexual stimulation, from dancing to decapitation, from racial stereotypes to violent revenge. The singular and simultaneous entry/exit wound that functions as the physical interstice of *Slavery! Slavery!* importantly severs the small wagon (visible on either side of the threshold) that is pulled by a young woman hunched forward with an infant strapped to her back. Walker's decisive splitting of the wagon, which carries another woman and child concealed underneath its thick straw (not visible in the above frame), signals the manner in which the wagon is always in motion, regardless of the position from which the spectator gazes. In short, the severed wagon, which might also signify the pathway toward freedom, thus indicates that the entire landscape of *Slavery! Slavery!* is an abject cycle of trauma and ecstasy that is always already impossible to escape.

What is significant about Walker's installation of *Slavery! Slavery!* as a silhouette cyclorama is that it actively lures the spectator into the nightmare of a nonlinear narrative that has neither a beginning nor an end. Not unlike Walker's wider oeuvre, *Slavery! Slavery!* resists being read in any single direction or from any singular point of view and therefore refuses any totalizing interpretation. Instead, Walker's use of the cyclorama implicates the spectator into the scene such that one encounters oneself within the landscape alongside the silhouetted figures. Catching the spectator in a potentially disorienting experience that collapses fantasy and reality, *Slavery! Slavery!* signals the nonlinear nature of trauma. Indeed, Walker's nonlinear constellation of silhouettes inscribes not only the timelessness of the unconscious, but also the psychical structure of trauma as that which retroactively orbits within the ruptured space of the psyche.

As an unsettling landscape of trauma and *jouissance*, an abject fantasy always already riddled with ambiguity, *Slavery! Slavery!* nevertheless holds the gaze over its spectator. *Slavery! Slavery!* therefore functions as an abject spectacle that simultaneously beckons and disturbs its spectator, inaugurating an experience of looking awry such that the spectator is "caught, manipulated, captured, in the field of vision" and is "literally called into the picture" (Lacan 1998, 92). In this way, the captivating enclosure of silhouettes that constitutes *Slavery! Slavery!* signifies what Kristeva (1982) describes as "a deep well of memory that is unapproachable and intimate" (6). Walker's visual return to the cultural repressed therefore positions the spectator to not only conjure the repressed and ostensibly "unapproachable" histories of racial trauma, but also question those histories through an introspective experience of intimate revolt. In *The Sense and Non-Sense of Revolt*, Kristeva (2000) articulates the revolutionary impact of artwork, specifically the installation:

> An installation invites us to tell our story, to participate, through it and our sensation, in a communion with being. It also produces an unsettling complicity with our regressions, for when faced with these fragments, these flashes of sensations, these disseminated objects, you no longer know who you are. You are on the verge of vertigo, a black hole, a fragmentation of psychical life. (11)

Kristeva's account of the powers and possibilities of artistic installation emphasizes the necessary disruption that artwork enacts on its spectator. For Kristeva, these unsettling sensations of rupture and redress that artwork performs reveal the capacity of aesthetic forms, such as art and literature, to produce experiences of intimate revolt that may indeed bear ethical and political consequences for the rebirth of psychical life and the future of meaning.

Unlike the elaborate landscapes of abject fantasy that shape installations such as *Slavery! Slavery!*, Walker's (1998) *Cut* (figure 5.2) presents a plain,

Figure 5.2. Kara Walker, *Cut*, 1998. Cut paper on wall. 88 × 54 inches (223.5 × 137.2 cm). Courtesy of Sikkema Jenkins & Co., New York.

albeit riveting, quasi–self-portrait. Constructed in response to a photograph of herself by Noe DeWitt that appeared in *Interview* magazine the same year, *Cut* exposes the struggles that Walker faces as an African American woman artist working in an art world dominated largely by white men. In *Seeing the Unspeakable*, Shaw (2004) writes that *Cut* is an image of "grotesque self-mutilation and ambiguous ecstasy [that] speaks [to] the self-creation of Walker's artistic persona and her attempts to control the discourse around her work" (125, 127). *Cut* visualizes the particularities that Walker experiences as a woman of color whose artwork directly challenges the racism and sexism that filters not only her profession, but also her social and cultural milieu. *Cut* therefore epitomizes the psychical and existential tensions of identity, trauma, and desire that define Walker's oeuvre more generally.

Cut depicts the suspension of a silhouetted young woman—presumably a recasting of Walker—caught somewhere between a leap of ecstasy and a fatal descent. In a fantastical redoubling of authorship, Walker assumes the agency of cutting herself up to stage her spectral image as having been incised by her own hands. Indeed, the contradictory signification of the clicking of heels and the slitting of wrists captures precisely the inarticulable experience of trauma and *jouissance* that defines the artwork. *Cut* thus articulates the very condition that renders the image abject: ambiguity. By visualizing the impossibility of discerning where Walker's unashamed silhouette ends her ascension and begins her descension, *Cut* signifies the undecidability of her silhouette-specter as framed in facticity or transcendence, suppression or liberation. On the one hand, the fatal descent signals Walker's relationship to her facticity and the traumas of racism and sexism that make up her lived situation and its traces in memory. On the other hand, the leap of ecstasy signals Walker's relationship to her transcendence and the intimate revolt that catapults her into a future of meaning, desire, and redress. In this way, Walker recasts her public image as one of abject ambiguity that, not unlike the nature of trauma and *jouissance*, resists any totalizing symbolization.

Inasmuch as *Cut* renders visually the concurrent relationship between rupture and renewal, Walker's silhouette outlines for its spectator the intimate revolt, the rebirth of meaning. *Cut* thus emphasizes how Walker's trauma aesthetic serves as a working-through that incites a desire for meaning over a destructive thoughtlessness. The calculated and cathartic nature of Walker's artwork as a new form of revolt is perhaps best articulated in the following passage from Kristeva's (2012) *The Severed Head* in which she describes the experience of the woman artist:

> It is easy to cut up a woman's body if you're a woman. You know it so well! . . . You know how to set it about, which flap of skin to lift off, which joint to go for, which bit of cartilage to destroy. You know what shame to awaken, what suffering to revive, what susceptibility to trample on, what jealousy to exacerbate, what longing to thwart, what desire to frustrate, what death to repeat—to go on repeating endlessly, not letting the pain ever ease. You're attacking yourself, but from a distance. You protect yourself and survive while the other dies, disappears into the void to which she seems always to have belonged. You yourself are reborn, set off again. (119–20)

Kristeva's account of curating the powers of horror reflects precisely the artistry with which Walker forms her trauma aesthetic, though Walker's exactitude captures and cuts up the particularities of not simply the sexed body, but the body schematized intersectionally to stress race, gender, class, and age as well as sex. Not unlike the images of decapitation that Kristeva analyzes in *The Severed Head*, Walker's unspeakable scenes therefore serve as an intimate "flight of thought" and sublimatory act of revolt that bears the capacity for psychical rebirth (Kristeva 2012, front matter).

If *Slavery! Slavery!* implicates its spectator into a haunting landscape laden with the memories of cultural trauma, then *Cut* bears witness to the intimacy of psychical suffering and revolt through which redress is made possible. Together, Walker's two installations inscribe the racial, sexual, and cultural traumas that reside at the threshold of the psychical and the social, for *Slavery! Slavery!* stresses the social ruptures and traces of trauma in our shared world, while *Cut* reveals the psychical ruptures and subsequent struggles particular to the curation of the self. In *Revolt, She Said*, Kristeva (2002b) maintains that "the artist's role is not to make a faithful copy of reality, but to shape our attitude towards reality" through an "act of creation" and revolt that "is not about domination or concealment, but about the interstice, about appropriating and being possessed, about the resonance between the self and the world" (122). Indeed, what links Walker's intimate return to the repressed and her creation of an aesthetic space of revolt is precisely what resides in the threshold, or what acts as the "interstice," between the realities of cultural trauma and the fantasies of artistic imagination: pain. In *The Body in Pain*, Elaine Scarry (1985) contends that "pain and imagining are the 'framing events' within whose boundaries all other perceptual, somatic, and emotional events occur" (165). In the interstices of the interior and the exterior, the psychical and the social, the self and the world, pain thus pulsates as a driving force of Walker's artwork.

Walker's trauma aesthetic therefore cuts into the pains and memories of an "impossible history," effecting a visual return to the cultural repressed through which the spectator is drawn into an intimate space of rupture, redress, and revolt. Kristeva (2000) affirms that "we all need an experience" of "something unknown, surprise, pain, or delight," for it is through such experiences of "impact"—of rupture and recovery—that psychical life may be refashioned (11). Moreover, Kristeva acknowledges that "there is an urgent need to develop the culture of revolt starting with our aesthetic heritage," which is why artwork such as Walker's has ethical and political import (2000, 7). Walker's artwork thus presents the unpresentable, inciting not only an unsettling encounter with the impossible, but also an intimate revolt into perpetual thought and questioning.

Witnessing the Extimate Trauma of the Real

The visual return to the cultural repressed that constitutes Walker's trauma aesthetic is an intimate cultivation of remembrance and redress through which our bearing witness to the "impossible history" of psychical and social traumas are made possible. To be sure, the power of Walker's intimate and aesthetic revolt lies in her capacity to articulate visually what Caruth (1996) expresses generally as "unclaimed experience"—the inarticulable or unspeakable memories of trauma—such that legacies of racial, sexual, and cultural violence are given meaning and the capacity for redress. By cutting into the extimate traumas of an "impossible history," Walker's intimate revolt thus serves not simply to unearth the continued cultural repressions of racism and racial oppression, but also to cultivate aesthetic spaces for witnessing, rememory, and redress.

At the heart of Walker's trauma aesthetic lies the Real, which Lacan (1991) describes as "this something with which all words cease and all categories fail" (164). The most elusive and inarticulable register of Lacan's tripartite schema, the Real is that which escapes language and persists as a traumatic trace within the psyche. Lacan regularly conceptualizes the Real in relation to trauma insofar as the Real underpins psychical life as a trace of immemorial loss and rupture. As an absent center of psychical life, the Real is also characterized by Lacan (1997) in *The Ethics of Psychoanalysis* as "extimate," which signals not the opposite of intimate but, rather, the quality of being both inside as well as outside (139). The Real therefore resides as an extimate trauma of subjectivity that is at once the most intimate and internal as well as the most opaque and external. Walker's intimate revolt vis-à-vis an "impossible history" of subjection thus captures the extimate traumas specific to the legacies of slavery and racial violence more generally. Although Walker's trauma aesthetic cuts deeply into the "vanished instant" of the Real, this is not to say that Walker's artwork achieves any clear representation or reproduction of the Real onto the gallery wall, for a direct encounter with the Real—as that which is opposed to the Imaginary and beyond the Symbolic—would cause an utter collapse of meaning altogether (Lacan 2013, 42).

What is encountered through Walker's artwork, then, are the rememories of extimate trauma specific to the legacies of racial, sexual, and cultural violence that continue to shape our shared world. According to Caruth (1995), trauma "does not simply serve as record of the past but precisely registers the force of an experience that is not yet fully owned" (151). Indeed, Caruth's account of trauma, indebted to the Freudian model of *Nachträglichkeit*, suggests that it is not the originary experience of the traumatic event that is wounding but, rather, the belated experiences of the initial event that return through repetition and rememory to constitute the trauma as such. Moreover, Caruth's (1996) reading of Freud in *Unclaimed Experience* reveals that trauma is "the story of a wound that cries out, that addresses us in the attempt to tell us of a reality or truth that is not otherwise available" (4). Traumatic experience, for Caruth (1996), is thus an "unassimilated" wound that "remains unknown in our very actions and our language" (4), hence Freud's (1914) analysis of the patient who "does not *remember* anything of what he has forgotten and repressed, but *acts* it out" (150 emphasis in original). In this way, Caruth's (1995) exploration in trauma and memory reveals a parallel to Lacan's account of extimacy:

> the apparent split between external and internal trauma in psychoanalytic theory . . . would all be a function, in Freud's definition, of the split within immediate experience that characterizes the traumatic occurrence itself. It is the fundamental dislocation implied by all traumatic experience that is both its testimony to the event and to the impossibility of its direct access. (9)

Caruth's articulation of an "apparent split" and "fundamental dislocation" in experiences of trauma uncovers, then, the extimacy of traumatic experience inasmuch as trauma is at once both intimate and inaccessible, intrusive and opaque, experienced and unassimilated, such that the psychical impact and "impossible history" of traumatic experiences are "largely inaccessible to conscious recall and control" (1995, 5, 151). Walker's trauma aesthetic and the intimate encounters that it curates therefore initiate what Caruth (1995) describes as a "new kind of listening, the witnessing, precisely, *of impossibility*" (10, emphasis in original).

Perhaps Walker's most controversial piece of artwork to inscribe the eruptive force of extimate trauma is her (2010) *The moral arc of history ideally bends towards justice but just as soon as not curves back around toward barbarism, sadism, and unrestrained chaos* (figure 5.3), a large graphite and pastel drawing that was put on display at the Newark Public Library in November 2012. Only five days after its installation, however, the artwork was concealed by a black and white cloth and symbolically repressed, thereby repeating perhaps ironically not only Walker's purposeful disruption of racial binarism, but also the way in which psychical trauma, for Lacan, lies just behind a thin veil. As its swift censorship evidenced, the installation of Walker's artwork thus forced

Figure 5.3. Kara Walker, *The moral arc of history ideally bends towards justice but just as soon as not curves back around toward barbarism, sadism, and unrestrained chaos*, 2010. Graphite and pastel on paper. 72 × 114 inches (182.9 × 289.6 cm). Courtesy of Sikkema Jenkins & Co., New York.

an intimate, albeit unsettling, encounter with the psychical and social horrors of extimate trauma in a public space nevertheless reserved for questioning and the "flight of thought" (Kristeva 2012, front matter). On a psychoanalytic level, then, it is clear that Walker's *moral arc of history* provokes an intimate encounter with the Real. "The moments of encountering a Real," Slavoj Žižek (2014) notes, "are the moments when, under its traumatic impact, the symbolic protective network disintegrates and we are exposed to the raw impact of the Real" (132). Although Walker's artwork was eventually unveiled after invited public discussion over its censorship and the cultural legacies of racism, featuring the participation of Walker herself at an open forum held at the Newark Public Library, this unsettled public encounter with the extimate traumas of racial, sexual, and cultural violence reveals the ethical and political import of bearing witness to such an "impossible history."

Like peering into a haunting nightmare or constellation of repressed trauma, Walker's *moral arc of history* depicts an agglomeration of abject horrors that swell from an "impossible history" of racial terrorism and sexual violence that, in part, defined the social milieu of Reconstruction and Jim Crowism. Walker's chaotic rememory includes the gathering of Klansmen underneath a large burning cross; the lynching and burning of a black body that starkly resembles a lynching photograph from 1919 depicting the burning corpse of William Brown (see plate 97 in James Allen, 2000); the chasing of a naked black man—clinging to an amorphous figure—by white men whose aggressive desire is signaled by an assailant's lynching rope and protruding tongue; and the violent sexual assault of a young black girl, whose face is forced onto a white man while her hand is held by a tall mammy figure. In the midst of Walker's unspeakable constellation is a rendering of President Barack Obama at a lectern, whose "speechifying" on race—which, Walker (2013) indicates on the dust jacket of *Dust Jackets for the Niggerati*, "never leaves the past alone"—simultaneously conjures up and is obscured by the surrounding inscriptions of racial, sexual, and cultural trauma that consume the nightmarish landscape.

The unrestrained chaos illustrated in Walker's *moral arc of history* captures visually the psychical and social ruptures of cultural trauma, which Ron Eyerman (2001) describes as a "dramatic loss of identity and meaning, a tear in the social fabric, affecting a group of people that has achieved some degree of cohesion" (2). Indeed, the unsettling energy of Walker's installation evidences the extimate traumas of racial and sexual violence that are at once both intimate and inaccessible, both internalized and inarticulable. Walker's *moral arc of history*, including the public controversies it provoked, therefore serves as a working-through of the repressed pains and memories of cultural trauma, demonstrated by Walker's subtle and sarcastic scrawling of "thanks for the memories" on the far left edge of the artwork. Conjuring the abject affects and repressed memories of racial, sexual, and cultural trauma, Walker thus transposes the spectator into an intimate and sublimatory encounter with the impossible through which the capacity for bearing witness, working-through, and thought as such becomes possible.

Enacting an eruption of extimate trauma, Walker's artwork therefore initiates an aesthetic "*encounter with the real*," an intimate encounter that Lacan (1998) terms the "*tuché*," whereby the spectator is drawn into an unsettling confrontation with the Real (53 emphasis in original). Derived from Aristotle's rendering of a "brush with" chance or fortune, Lacan (1998) interprets the *tuché* as a kind of "brush with" the Real. Sarah Kay (2007) further indicates that the origins of Aristotle's *tuché* refer to "the unthought within thought" and that which "takes place in the gaps" and "is 'outside reason' and unaccountable" (145–46). According to Lacan (1998), however, the *tuché*—as a "brush with" the Real—is an encounter that is essentially "missed" (55). Walker's artwork thus functions as an aesthetic, albeit traumatic, space of controlled chaos in which the spectator encounters the Real as essentially "missed," or perhaps only in tiny bits. In this way, Walker's artwork provokes a disturbance in the spectator that beckons a perpetual questioning and working-through of an "impossible history" of racial, sexual, and cultural trauma. To be sure, the working-through central to Walker's trauma aesthetic is never simply completed in the sense of overcoming the past but, rather, is an endless retrospective process of bearing witness and questioning, of anamnesis and revolt, that is indispensible for the renewals of psychical life and the future of meaning. Not unlike Caruth's (1995) efforts to "examine how trauma unsettles and forces us to rethink our notions of experience," Walker's curated encounter with the Real invites a rememory and redress of trauma that may be conceived, on Kristeva's interpretation, as acts of sublimatory revolt (4).

Walker's visual return to the cultural repressed is therefore achieved through the intimate work of sublimation, which Kristeva (2000) describes as a psychical process of recovery and representation that is "indispensable and subjacent to the thought process in every speaking being" (57). For Kristeva, sublimation founds the psyche "through and through," serving as an intimate link to not only creation, but also connectivity with otherness, for "it is the capacity of *signifiance* (representation-language-thought) based on sublimation that structures all other psychical manifestations" (2000,

56). Kristeva (1996) maintains, then, that artistic sublimation is "bound up in a displacement of this tempting wound," thereby creating a "sheltering space of an elocution that offers meaning, pleasure, and pain" (185–86). In this way, Walker takes up a transformative relation to extimate trauma to "remake nothingness . . . for the sake of someone else" and to recover psychical life for the future of meaning (Kristeva 1989, 99).

Sublimation thus effects an uncovering of extimate trauma and a recovering of memory and meaning through an intimate psychical process akin to the analytical model of working-through, which Elaine Miller (2014) defines as a "form of nonidentical repetition, in which a repressed memory, perhaps of a traumatic event, that has been repeating itself through neurotic symptoms is remembered and repeated in a way that is fundamentally modified by interpretation" (130–31). Walker's trauma aesthetic thus cultivates a revolutionary space of sublimation, performing not only what Sara Beardsworth terms a "recovery of 'the lost,' " but also the "sublimations of the corporeal and affective aspects of subjectivity that correspond to a confrontation with limit situations in individual and cultural life" (2009, 135). Faced with an "impossible history" of extimate trauma, works of art such as Walker's open up an aesthetic space of intimate revolt in which "sublimated *jouissance* replaces violence toward self and others," Kelly Oliver (2009) writes, and "representations of sacrifice and human vulnerability replace literal sacrifice" (60). Inciting "tiny revolts," Walker's artwork therefore opens up a sublimatory space for rememory and redress, for witnessing and working-through, to secure the rebirth and future of psychical life (Kristeva 2002a, 5).

Walker's trauma aesthetic thus emerges as a sublimatory inscription of intimate revolt. In doing so, Walker's artwork enacts a cutting into the extimate traumas of the Real by working through the level of the Imaginary to "give meaning to suffering" in the Symbolic (Kristeva 2002a, 6). "The artist performs the 'right' kind of violence," Kristeva (2002b) argues, for "by appropriating what lies outside [her], [she] achieves a balance between the self and the world. This very delicate alchemy, whose value we often underestimate, is an act of creation that takes place precisely at this interstice between the individual and the world" (122). Through a revolutionary engagement with imagination, Walker performs this "delicate alchemy" of sublimatory "creation" within the interstices between the self and the world, between the interior and the exterior, such that racial, sexual, and cultural trauma may be remembered, recovered, and redressed. If, as Oliver (2005) suggests, "trauma is what is unrepresentable as a result of the inability to assimilate the meaning of the traumatic experience into the social," then Walker's artwork opens up an aesthetic space of imagination and resistance in and through which intimate revolt unfolds as "necessary for meaningful experience" (79). Walker's sublimatory return to the extimate traumas of the Real is therefore achieved through the "transformative power of witnessing" and the intimate ethics of aesthetic revolt that together make possible the rebirth of psychical life and the future of meaning (Oliver 2001, 106).

The Intimate Ethics of Aesthetic Revolt

Walker's visual return to the cultural repressed serves as an intimate ethics of aesthetic revolt that not only incites a recovery and witnessing of the traumas of history, memory, and subjectivity, but also inscribes a revolutionary space of "permanent questioning," thereby revitalizing our psychical capacity for rememory, resistance, and rebirth (Kristeva 2002b, 120). Through her efforts to remember and redress artistically the "impossible history" of racial, sexual, and cultural trauma, Walker fashions the Imaginary as a sublimatory space of intimate and aesthetic revolt through which the psychical sutures of these extimate traumas and their repressions might begin to come undone. Indeed, the affective movements of rupture and recovery central to Walker's trauma aesthetic bear a profoundly ethical impact insofar as it is through the intimate renewals or "tiny revolts" of psychical life that meaning and social connectivity become possible (Kristeva 2002a, 5). The veritable powers of horror that shape Walker's artwork are therefore transformed into a creation of meaning such that her aesthetic practice of "sublimation enabled by representation translates violent impulses into creative life" (Oliver 2009, 60). This is to say that Walker's efforts to articulate the inarticulable through sublimations of trauma and *jouissance* produce significant ethical and political possibilities, for it is through the intimate processes and cultivation of recovery, redress, and revolt that our links between subjectivity and otherness may become realized.

Throughout her trilogy on *The Power and Limits of Psychoanalysis*, Kristeva (2000) stresses that intimate revolt makes possible a "renewal of the psychical space" (28). Moreover, Kristeva (2002a) wagers that "the future, if it exists, depends on" intimate revolt, for it is the endless returns, the loving recoveries, and the transformative rebirths of psychical life that grant a future for meaning and subjectivity (5). As a "displacement of the traumatism, a progressive, incessant, and perhaps even interminable displacement," intimate revolt is experienced as a perpetual return to and recovery of an "impossible history" that nevertheless calls for response (Kristeva 2000, 29). If, as Kristeva (2000) suggests, intimate revolt "is an antidote to the threat of lost memory that certain contemporary artists seem to perceive," then Walker's trauma aesthetic may be interpreted as an intimate ethics of revolt through which the future of meaning and the capacity for regeneration are made possible (16).

Walker's (2007) *Somebody Call an Ambivalence* (figure 5.4) renders precisely the ethical and political import of recovering the "impossible his-

Figure 5.4. Kara Walker, *Somebody Call an Ambivalence*, 2007. Paper collage, gouache on wood panel. 24 × 17.125 × 1.25 inches (61 × 43.5 × 3.2 cm). Courtesy of Sikkema Jenkins & Co., New York.

tory" of extimate trauma. In this unsettling collage that perhaps achieves a visual inscription of the timelessness and spacelessness of trauma itself, Walker signals the loss of meaning in the context of racial suffering and death. The spectator is drawn to the upper right corner of the paper and gouache collage, where Walker reproduces unmistakably the December 1961 lynching in McDuffie County, Georgia, of David Jackson, who is no longer tangled within the southern trees from which he was hanged, but is now left suspended by the perpetual pull of a dead time and space (see plate 19 in James Allen, 2000). In the foreground below Jackson's corpse is the silhouette of a woman who appears to be walking across the ostensible nothingness. It is impossible to pinpoint the emotion or purpose with which the silhouetted woman moves across the collage (is she marching defiantly or striding blithely?) or to determine exactly how or to what extent she interacts with Jackson's body, which further supports the titular ambivalence of the work. Among the diverse and undecidable significations that compose *Somebody Call an Ambivalence*, Walker's attention to ambivalence reveals not only the struggle for recognition and response, but also the reality in which traumas of racial, sexual, and cultural violence have largely been repressed or lost to an ambivalent culture estranged from the psychical and social capacities for intimate revolt.

As a call for the remembrance and redress of extimate traumas, Walker's *Somebody Call an Ambivalence* signals a deepening crisis in meaning that Kristeva (2000) affirms may be remedied through various forms of intimate revolt. Kristeva (2002a) declares that "psychical life knows that it will only be saved if it gives itself the time and space of revolt: to break off, remember, refashion" (223). In this way, Walker's aesthetic revolt inaugurates an intimate politics of cultivating sublimatory spaces of rupture, redress, and rebirth through which meaning and subjectivity are renewed. To be sure, the ethical and political import of Walker's trauma aesthetic is that she does, in fact, "break off, remember, refashion" through an imaginative process of seeing the unspeakable. "The limits of representability must protrude in the visible spaces that surround us," Cecilia Sjöholm (2005) argues, for "if it does not, the society of images becomes a threat to the possibilities of politics. When negative and nihilating functions are no longer allowed we are run over by 'images without imagination,' killing consciousness and the capacity to think and feel" (122–23). That Walker's artwork incites a return to and recovery of repressed traumas through the negativities of sublimation reveals, then, the ethical and political urgency of her wider oeuvre. Walker's trauma aesthetic therefore serves as an intimate ethics of revolt inasmuch as her witnessing of and responding to racial, sexual, and cultural violence illustrates new forms for revitalizing our capacities for thought and self-questioning.

Demonstrating the social, political, and arguably ethical dimensions of intimate revolt, Kristeva (2000) states that revolt "appears as a continuous necessity for keeping alive the psyche, thought, and the social link itself" (144). This is to say that the capacity for psychical life and the connectivity between subjectivity and otherness necessitates the processes of intimate revolt, for, as Kristeva (2000) urges, "the very possibility of culture depends on our response," that is, our capacity for rememory and revolt (7). In *Intimate Revolt,* Kristeva (2002a) acknowledges that "cultural revolt intrinsically concerns public life and consequently has profoundly political implications. In fact, it poses the question of another politics, that of permanent conflictuality" (11). The ethical and political import of Kristeva's wager on the link between intimate revolt and the rebirth of psychical life is illuminated in Oliver's (2002) remarks on the powers and possibilities of resistance:

> Resistance not only brings people together to create meaning for themselves but also begins to provide the social space necessary for empowered psychic space. Creating the social space for resistance to racism and sexism provides the social support necessary to reverse and deter the process of internalization or epidermalization of oppressive values . . . Social revolt and psychic revolt, what Kristeva calls intimate revolt, go hand in hand; one is not possible without the other. (63)

Oliver's contention is that there is a constitutive relation between psychical and social revolt such that spaces of resistance, including Walker's trauma aesthetic, are indeed grounded on the link between psychical and social revolt. The ethical and political import of Walker's artwork is thus revealed in its capacity to incite the rebirth of psychical life and the recovery of social ties.

Resistance indeed shapes the intimate ethics of revolt at the heart of Walker's trauma aesthetic. In *Hatred and Forgiveness*, Kristeva (2010) declares that "the subject must be allowed to revitalize *all of his/her own resources*: of binding and *unbinding*, of love and *hate*, or trust and *aggressiveness*. Analysis becomes a *space of revolt*, and, if it does not become that, psychical life cannot be reborn" (154 emphasis in original). Kristeva emphasizes here the experiences of "unbinding," "hate," and "aggressiveness" that are central to the psychical process of intimate revolt. Replicating the analytic setting, Walker's trauma aesthetic serves as an intimate space through which rupture, rememory, and renewal are not only made possible, but are indeed necessary for achieving what Kristeva (2010) terms "healing" or "psychical rebirth" (154).

Conjuring the traces of racial and sexual trauma through her visual return to the cultural repressed, Walker therefore establishes an intimate ethics of rememory and revolt. As an intimate space of resistance and revolt, Walker's trauma aesthetic cultivates what Kristeva (2012) describes in the front matter of *The Severed Head* as "*the flight of thought* [and] *the wandering of the imagination*," which are linked not only to questioning, but also to freedom (emphasis in original). Walker's rememory and recovery of repressed trauma and *jouissance* reveal to us, then, the ethical and political possibilities of intimate revolt through which impossible histories of racial, sexual, and cultural rupture may be redressed, thereby granting a rebirth of psychical life and a future of meaning. "Faced with the invasion of the spectacle," Kristeva (2002a) writes, "we can still contemplate the rebellious potentialities that the imaginary might resuscitate in our innermost depths" (13). It is finally within these unsettling imaginaries, within the intimate spaces of aesthetic revolt, that Walker prompts us to think. If Walker's artwork takes us from the extimate traumas of social rupture to the intimate ethics of psychical life, then it is precisely out of the hope that, as Kristeva suggests, we may never cease to think, to witness, to question, to revolt.

Works Cited

Allen, James. 2000. *Without Sanctuary: Lynching Photography in America.* Santa Fe: Twin Palms Publishers.

Beardsworth, Sara. 2009. "Love's Lost Labors: Subjectivity, Art, and Politics." In *Psychoanalysis, Aesthetics, and Politics in the Work of Julia Kristeva*, edited by Kelly Oliver and S. K. Keltner. New York: State University of New York Press.

Caruth, Cathy, ed. 1995. *Trauma: Explorations in Memory.* Baltimore: Johns Hopkins University Press.

———. 1996. *Unclaimed Experience: Trauma, Narrative, and History.* Baltimore: Johns Hopkins University Press.

Césaire, Aimé. 2001. *Notebook of a Return to the Native Land.* Translated and edited by Clayton Eshleman and Annette Smith. Middletown: Wesleyan University Press.

Eyerman, Ron. 2001. *Cultural Trauma: Slavery and the Formation of African American Identity*. Cambridge: Cambridge University Press.

Freud, Sigmund. 1911–1913. "Remembering, Repeating and Working-Through." In *The Standard Edition of the Complete Psychological Works of Sigmund Freud*. Vol. 12. Translated and edited by James Strachey, 147–56. London: Hogarth Press.

———. 1914–1916. "Repression." In *The Standard Edition of the Complete Psychological Works of Sigmund Freud*. Vol. 14. Translated and edited by James Strachey, 146–58. London: Hogarth Press.

———. 1916–1917. "Introductory Lectures on Psycho-Analysis, Part III. General Theory of the Neuroses." In *The Standard Edition of the Complete Psychological Works of Sigmund Freud*. Vol. 16. Translated and edited by James Strachey, 243–463. London: Hogarth Press.

Hartman, Saidiya V. 1997. *Scenes of Subjection: Terror, Slavery, and Self-Making in Nineteenth-Century America*. New York: Oxford University Press.

Kay, Sarah. 2007. *The Place of Thought*. Philadelphia: University of Pennsylvania Press.

Kristeva, Julia. 1982. *Powers of Horror: An Essay on Abjection*. Translated by Leon S. Roudiez. New York: Columbia University Press.

———. 1989. *Black Sun: Depression and Melancholia*. Trans. Leon S. Roudiez. New York: Columbia University Press.

———. 1995. *New Maladies of the Soul*. Translated by Ross Guberman. New York: Columbia University Press.

———. 1996. *Time and Sense: Proust and the Experience of Literature*. Translated by Ross Guberman. New York: Columbia University Press.

———. 2000. *The Sense and Non-Sense of Revolt: The Power and Limits of Psychoanalysis*. Vol. 1. Translated by Jeanine Herman. New York: Columbia University Press.

———. 2002a. *Intimate Revolt: The Power and Limits of Psychoanalysis*. Vol. 2. Translated by Jeanine Herman. New York: Columbia University Press.

———. 2002b. *Revolt, She Said*. Translated by Brian O'Keeffe. New York: Semiotext(e).

———. 2010. *Hatred and Forgiveness: The Power and Limits of Psychoanalysis*. Vol. 3. Translated by Jeanine Herman. New York: Columbia University Press.

———. 2012. *The Severed Head: Capital Visions*. Translated by Jody Gladding. New York: Columbia University Press.

Lacan, Jacques. 1991. *The Seminar of Jacques Lacan Book II: The Ego in Freud's Theory and in the Technique of Psychoanalysis*. Translated by Sylvana Tomaselli. New York: W. W. Norton.

———. 1997. *The Seminar of Jacques Lacan Book VII: The Ethics of Psychoanalysis*. Translated by Dennis Porter. New York: W. W. Norton.

———. 1998. *The Seminar of Jacques Lacan Book XI: The Four Fundamental Concepts of Psychoanalysis*. Translated by Alan Sheridan. New York: W. W. Norton.

———. 2013. *On the Names-of-the-Father*. Translated by Bruce Fink. Cambridge: Polity Press.

Miller, Elaine P. 2014. *Head Cases: Julia Kristeva on Philosophy and Art in Depressed Times*. New York: Columbia University Press.

Oliver, Kelly. 2001. *Witnessing: Beyond Recognition*. Minneapolis: University of Minnesota Press.

———. 2002. "Psychic Space and Social Melancholy." In *Between the Psyche and the Social*, edited by Kelly Oliver and Steve Edwin. Lanham: Rowman and Littlefield Publishers, Inc.

———. 2005. "Revolt and Forgiveness." In *Revolt, Affect, Collectivity: The Unstable Boundaries of Kristeva's Polis*, edited by Tina Chanter and Ewa Płonowska Ziarek. New York: State University of New York Press.

———. 2009. "Meaning against Death." In *Psychoanalysis, Aesthetics, and Politics in the Work of Julia Kristeva*, edited by Kelly Oliver and S. K. Keltner. New York: State University of New York Press.

Scarry, Elaine. 1985. *The Body in Pain: The Making and Unmaking of the World*. New York: Oxford University Press.

Shaw, Gwendolyn DuBois. 2004. *Seeing the Unspeakable: The Art of Kara Walker*. Durham: Duke University Press.

Sjöholm, Cecilia. 2005. *Kristeva and the Political*. New York: Routledge.

Walker, Kara. 2003. "Stories: Kara Walker." In *Art in the Twenty-First Century, Season 2*. PBS Art 21 Video. September 9, 2003. Accessed October 31, 2014. http://www.pbs.org/art21/artists/kara-walker.

Walker, Kara. 2007. *My Complement, My Enemy, My Oppressor, My Love*. Minneapolis: Walker Art Center.

———. 2008. *Bureau of Refugees*. New York: Charta Books Ltd.

———. 2013. *Dust Jackets for the Niggerati*. New York: Gregory R. Miller & Co.

Young, Kevin. 2013. "Miss Pipi's Blue Tale." In *Dust Jackets for the Niggerati*. New York: Gregory R. Miller & Co.

Žižek, Slavoj. 2014. "A Staged Real." In *lacanian ink 43/44*, edited by Josefina Ayerza. New York: Lacanian Ink.

6

Patient Interpretation

Kristeva's Model for the Caregiver

Melinda C. Hall

In this chapter, I use Julia Kristeva's work in *Hatred and Forgiveness* to encourage new thinking in medical ethics. My discussion pertains to the relationship between medical professionals and patients in clinical practice. Medical ethicists, especially those engaged in phenomenology, emphasize the importance of patient experiences and seek to reintroduce the lived body into the clinic (Rothfield 2005). At the same time, ethicists and those working in the medical humanities recognize that patients contend with issues of identity and the collapse of meaning as a result of the disruptions of illness (Laranjeira 2013; Little et al. 2000; Schultz and Carnevale 1996). Some medical humanists suggest that medical professionals should practice tolerance for imperfection and see themselves in their patients to better care for the patients who are tangled in these experiences (Shapiro 2008). In their practices, medical professionals seek to bridge the gap between themselves and their patients in precisely this way, yet they struggle to identify with their patients and can even be disgusted by them or experience the desire to reject them (Little et al. 2000; Shapiro 2008).

A dialogical, rather than a projective, model is needed in professional care practices by which the medical professional can interact with the patient on a level other than the merely somatic or diagnostic. Kristeva can teach medical professionals to be "patient interpreters" (a term I explore below) engaged in a dialogical narrative building that would improve caregiving. As many have noted, healing is not just a matter of the body and its functions; for Kristeva, healing involves the work of rebuilding one's identity: "Healing? Yes, provided we do not forget that healing involves psychological rebirth . . ." (2010, 158).

In what follows, I describe the medical humanities and link it to narrative medical ethics. Then I use Kristeva's discussion of Pierre, an angry patient, to build the model of patient interpretation and show how it can relate to the work of medical professionals. I compare Kristeva's model of patient interpretation with a competing model derived from Aristotle's virtue of *phronesis* and show that Kristeva's patient interpretation is more successful on both explanatory and ethical dimensions. Finally, I describe how the benevolent listening and postmodern forgiveness advocated by Kristeva can create a space of intimate revolt for patients as they build new meaning and identity from within experiences of illness and disability. This intimate revolt has social potential.

The Medical Humanities and Narrative Ethics

The medical humanities is a growing field of interdisciplinary concern. Through reflections on cultural artifacts of all kinds, including art, novels, archival ephemera, and poetry, academics and medical professionals seek supplements, or even alternatives, to the diagnostic discourse of medicine. These reflections are meant to bridge gaps between medical professionals and patients (Gordon 2008, 420). The medical humanities attempts to bring the "arts" back into the "medical arts" and to understand medicine in a fuller sense as a complex healing practice (Peterkin 2008). Dr. Allen Peterkin, assistant professor of psychiatry at the University of Toronto, believes the medical humanities can provide an antidote for "near-worship at the altar of evidence-based medicine" by "creating a space for creative reflection and for thinking and feeling" (2008, 648). Peterkin reminds his readers that medicine is not the only field that deals with suffering, and in consequence medical professionals can learn much from other fields—including the fine arts, writing, and history—that will help them treat patients. Peterkin writes:

> We work every day with patients who struggle to find new meaning in the face of illness. They expect us to offer guidance. True healers have always used images, music and poems to help find

> the way. Little by little, these and many other creative tools are finding their way back into our black bags. (2008, 648)

The medical humanities is therefore a route toward "compassionate patient care" (Gordon 2008, 420). Ideally, this compassionate patient care would take the suffering of the patient, and the patient's search for new meaning after accidents, diagnoses, and other disruptions, seriously as an integral part of healing or caregiving.

Experiencing the disruptions of illness and searching for new meaning will involve narrative building for the patient. Increasingly, "narrative ethics" has taken up the question of the role of stories in moral life (Lindemann Nelson 1997). For philosopher Hilde Lindemann Nelson, there are several narrative approaches relevant for medical contexts. Primarily of use in the medical humanities is the practice of reading stories. Reading stories can result in a kind of moral education—drawing "one's attention to the rich and subtle particulars of the narrative—the moral, intellectual, emotional, and social nuances" (1997, x). But narrative ethics also involves telling stories. In that light, it is illuminating to read the bioethics case presentation as storytelling. Indeed, Tod Chambers argues that the bioethics case, with its particular plot points and resolutions, is its own genre (1997). Meanwhile, the established bioethical practice of casuistry, which compares bioethics cases and establishes paradigm and analogous cases, can be read as a type of narrative ethics. Narrative ethics can also amount to literary analysis, a practice that would vary based on what is taken as the text—the patient, the case, and the illness are a few examples. Finally, there is the common bioethical practice of invoking stories to make philosophical or moral points (Lindemann Nelson 1997, xi–xii).

For the purposes of this chapter, I use a multifaceted narrative approach. I seek to highlight the patient's need to construct new meanings in the face of the disruptions of illness. I characterize the patient as a text in need of interpretation. This is a shift in genre; I depart from the bioethics case, which is told in monologue after a case is "closed," in favor of listening and shared storytelling as a core process of care. In this way, I combine the concerns of the medical humanities and narrative ethics, while at the same time pointing to how Kristeva would describe an opening for caring and healing in a fuller sense—one that is both psychical and somatic and refuses to reify "the primary dualism" of the "body/soul" (2010, 157).[1] I therefore also engage in the most primary form of narrative ethics in the medical humanities—I read Kristeva's stories from her psychoanalytic practice to enrich the medical profession by introducing her model for caregiving.

Dialogical storytelling is a key part of "compassionate patient care," but the medical humanities and narrative ethics are both greatly in need of a nuanced model to follow. In Julia Kristeva's discussion of "patient interpretation" in *Hatred and Forgiveness,* I find a promising model. In describing this model, I invoke two meanings of the phrase "patient interpretation."

Kristeva's Hatred and Forgiveness

In *Hatred and Forgiveness*, Kristeva discusses links between cancer and depression and expresses, as those working in the medical humanities do, a wish for an "era when doctors could write, like Chekhov or Céline" (2010, 155). This is desirable because, as Kristeva claims, now, more than ever, doctors need to meet their patients' psychical needs. According to Kristeva:

> More and more, slowing the progression of cancer—which has been achieved over the past few years—and stopping it have led medical professionals to become involved in the psychical context of illness: to assist the patient in overcoming the depression that has either preceded the appearance of the cancer or developed after its appearance. (2010, 153)

She wryly notes that medical professionals are "encroaching" on psychoanalysis, but seems to not altogether dislike the idea (2010, 155). For Kristeva, the "cared for/caregiver" dyad necessarily involves transference and countertransference (ibid.). But Kristeva rightly worries that medical professionals are not trained to deal with this and so will not be able to provide what the patient needs, that is, what Kristeva calls the "space of revolt" where the patient can go about "reestablishing ties" such as the "narcissistic image" and "erotic ties" (154). Transference should be "contained and oriented toward a specific psychotherapy, and Kristeva wonders: "how do we prepare medical personnel for this goal?" (ibid.).

Without an answer to that grander question, she prescribes "benevolent listening" in cases of terminal illness; she writes: "the dying person expects not so much a response as to be heard" (2010, 155–56). She does not want doctors to behave as if they were psychoanalysts, but wants them to practice "psychical availability" (156). She would direct doctors, "at the very least, to read novels" (2010, 156).

In this way, Kristeva joins the chorus of those working within the medical humanities and narrative ethics. But how, beyond reading novels, can one develop benevolent listening in the clinic? What exactly is benevolent listening? To venture an answer, I turn to Kristeva's discussion of Pierre, whose paranoid hatred led Kristeva to write *Powers of Horror*, her close reading of abjection, and to reflect on her psychoanalytic practice in *Hatred and Forgiveness* (2010, 190). In her roles as analyst and writer, Kristeva "reads" the stories of her analysands by listening and goes on to both tell and invoke these stories in her writings. Pierre's story, and Kristeva's subsequent reflection, can provide a model of benevolent listening of great use in medical contexts. There is no need to limit the practice of benevolent listening to terminal illnesses; the disruptions of illness and diagnosis to one's identity are enough to necessitate benevolent listening.

Of her experiences with her patient, Pierre, Kristeva writes:

> Pierre was a difficult patient I hesitated taking on. His raging hatred, which would one day necessarily be turned against me, scared me less than his narcissistic close-mindedness: it made his "insights" . . . superficial, bookish, and insignificant in fact—clever defenses that prevented any questioning of the self. At times he hated himself as much as he hated others, but *he never questioned himself*. (2010, 188, emphasis mine)

Kristeva notices that Pierre "solicited" her through transference to be both "abject mother" and "oedipal father" (190). The multiple roles Kristeva was called upon to play in this context must match, in intensity, that of the role of the caregiver who is treating a dying patient. Indeed, Kristeva portrays Pierre as almost drowning; he was "pouring out torrents of pure hatred" against those he perceived to be persecuting him with hatred (188). She describes herself as unsure of what to do and also somewhat overtaken by his hatred:

> I felt persecuted in turn: not only did Pierre end up convincing me of the ugliness of "people" and of the world in which we lived, but his wife had already made the interpretations that were on the tip of my tongue! Did he come to consult me in order to prevent me from speaking, out of hatred of analysis? Or else was he revealing the unbearable truth of the speaking being whose hatred uncovers what was concealed? (2010, 189)

Much as the medical professional is reminded of mortality through working with a dying patient, Kristeva is here reminded of original repression (cf. 2010, 183–86). Both deal with the limitations of subjectivity and, ultimately, abjection, which is covered over and constitutes repression.

For Kristeva, hatred like Pierre's is built on abjection (2010, 190, cf. 184). We need abjection to confine our subjectivity; that is, abjection is the first step toward subjectivity (184). Of abjection and subjectivity, Kristeva writes: "The abject and abjection are my guardrails, the beginnings of my culture, my beginning of culture" (187). In a "psychosomatic avant-garde of the future oedipal revolt," the subject is "driven to expel my progenitors and in this way I begin to create my own territory, bordered by the abject" (186). But the "inaugural abjection" of the subject can go badly wrong, subverted by hatred, a void, or perhaps phobias—and can imprison the subject or perhaps end in "paranoid hatred" like Pierre's (186).

But Pierre is, eventually, able to speak with Kristeva about his shame, begin painting as an outlet, and eventually terminate analysis. Kristeva notes that his hatred did not disappear but became, over the course of treatment, "less invasive" (2010, 190). How did Kristeva help him accomplish these results? Kristeva tells Pierre's story not only to explicate and invoke a life lived in paranoid hatred but also to describe her response to it, a response she claims helped her outline her conception of psychoanalysis (191). She explains that she did not respond with love, or hate, but instead gave a gift of "*patient interpretation* of the psychical movements subjacent to his 'state of war,' broke the chain of persecutions in which his psychical negativity had been stuck and inserted it into the openness of psychical time—the gift of a new way of being" (ibid., emphasis mine). This patient interpretation, provided at a kind of remove, gave Pierre access to his own psychic temporality. She calls this gift the pardon of interpretation and paints interpretation "as a postmodern version of forgiveness" (ibid.). Her response to Pierre—the forgiveness of psychoanalysis, her patient interpretation—is the model of benevolent listening for use in patient care I seek.

Kristeva's postmodern forgiveness is an essential ingredient of benevolent listening. Kristeva posits that forgiveness was initially offered by religion. But religion rewrote hatred as sin and offered forgiveness only through godly authority (2010, 191–92). In other words, forgiveness was tied to an external law or prohibition. Regardless, she writes, "through forgiveness, time for vengeance is suspended, allowing a rebirth . . . before the metamorphoses of abjection begin again" (191). Psychoanalysis, for Kristeva, replaces religion's forgiveness by way of authority with a new version; it offers forgiveness without calling hatred sin and without referring to an absolute power (191–92).[2] She claims that the "Freudian revolution" offers "the interpretation of variants of hatred that feed a symptom, invented to stop the time of judging in the name of the dogma of love (of God or our fellow man)" (192–93). Religion (and now psychoanalysis) "corresponds to a vital need in the speaking being: that of opening up psychical time" (193).

Again, interpretation can open up psychical time because it constitutes a "postmoral" "forgiveness" that "renews the unconscious" (Kristeva 2010, 193–94). Ultimately at issue is "meaning beyond judgment, without transference and counter-transference . . . the analytical experience leads us to the borders of thought" (2014, 10). This description of attending to or building meaning at the borders of thought will lead us to Kristeva's conception of revolt and the psychic renewal attendant upon revolt. I return to the question of revolt, both intimate and social, below.

Using Kristeva's reaction to Pierre, I now turn to draw an analogy between what Kristeva does for her analysands and what a medical professional might do for her patient. I follow Kristeva in thinking that medical professionals, unless trained, should not engage in psychoanalysis; however, they can engage in benevolent listening derived from psychoanalytic practice. Given the intimacy of the relationship between caregivers and the cared-for, this seems more than appropriate—in fact, responding to patient needs requires it. Further, given Kristeva's description of the benefits of benevolent listening, the opening it affords us for renewal is quite wide indeed despite not meeting the specific criteria of a psychoanalytic approach.

Patient Interpretation: Kristeva's Model for Patient Care

Kristeva "hesitated" to take Pierre as an analysand, taken aback by his narcissism and his hatred, and in the same way physicians can recoil from their patients. Medical humanist Johanna Shapiro writes: "When someone is sick, disabled, in pain, hurt, or dying, medicine expects an altruistic impulse from the physician" (2008). But this altruistic impulse is rarely the first response. With reference to Kristeva's concept of abjection, Shapiro writes: "the impulse to 'draw closer,' to become engaged and connected with the suffering other, is far from automatic . . . we have an equal, if not stronger, and opposite impulse to draw back, detach, and separate from the contamination of illness" (2008). Illness calls up abjection, placing our leaky boundaries and borders in sharp relief and issuing an unsettling challenge to the exclusions required by subjectivity (1982, 2).

In a discussion of dignity in the context of treatment for colon cancer, Miles Little noted that an instance of abjection interfered with caring practices. One patient experienced a refusal by nursing staff to irrigate his colon. The nurse exclaimed: "I don't want to look up an old man's bum!" (Little et al. 2000, 229 and 240). As a result of this attitude, the man did not receive regular treatments. Another patient with colon cancer described her own feelings of revulsion: "I am revolted by [the ileostomy] . . . it has to be emptied 8 times a day . . . you sort of think this is the pits, your head in the toilet half the day" (239). Abjection threatens to overwhelm us and unmake our subjectivity in the clinical encounter, whether we are ill or those we care for are ill. To heal, we need a psychical as well as a somatic intervention. The destruction and dissolution of our boundaries requires a kind of reconstitution of the self—and it seems that we might achieve this through storytelling. But this storytelling requires openness on the part of the caregiver.

As Kristeva points out, those who are ill—including the terminally ill—want to be heard. Kristeva speaks of "psychoanalytic listening to vulnerability" (2010, 44). Phenomenologists such as Richard Zaner have noted that there is a fundamental asymmetry among those who encounter each other in the clinic (2000, 266). The physician is powerful and the patient is vulnerable. Kristeva describes the dynamic this way: ". . . the attending physician is invested with the supreme power of the *subject supposed to know* . . . amorous transference then passes to a new power: the doctor is the possessor of life and, therefore, of the mystery of death" (2010, 155). I posit that the medical professional, the caregiver, must allow the patient, the cared-for, to speak, even against the master discourse of diagnosis and the physician's own desire to recoil. More than that, the caregiver must provide patient interpretation the way Kristeva did for Pierre, that is, not a response of love or hate, but rather a nonjudgmental, continuous acknowledgment of the utterances of the patient—benevolent listening. This is an iterative practice that takes place across time.

Benevolent listening is both "patient interpretation" in Kristeva's original sense of generously giving time and "patient interpretation" in a second sense—that is, hearing the patient speak and interpreting that speech as a text, which is desirable if it is achieved through benevolent listening. While this practice cannot be taught, only modeled, it is a skill medical professionals can enact and develop. Benevolent listening in the clinic, like psychoanalysis, can open up "psychical time" and allow space for the patient to be cared for.

Patient Interpretation Compared

There are many other models that seek to improve the relationship between medical professional and patient and thereby improve caregiving. In this section, I touch on one that competes with patient interpretation, "clinical phronesis" (Schultz and Carnevale 1996). I choose it because it is inspired by Aristotle's virtue ethics, a frame that is influential in medical ethics. Also, it articulates many of the same concerns Kristeva has in clinical contexts; in fact, this particular articulation of the model refers explicitly to creating a space for the patient to "express anything that was significant," and the model is described as dialogical (195, 200). Finally, clinical phronesis builds on the principalism that pervades bioethical literature—that is, the idea that several core ethical principles (for example, on Beauchamp and Childress's model, autonomy, beneficence, nonmaleficence, and justice, 2001) must be adjudicated by the caregiver, who must weigh and apply principles to a particular case.[3]

Dawson Schultz and Franco Carnevale claim that "engagement and suffering" along with one's patient "are essential aspects of responsible caregiving" (1996, 192). They seek to connect the patient and medical professional across the gap that illness seems to create, and worry about relying on "formal decision schemes" that would "correctly" rank principles and values to make "morally valid" clinical decisions (ibid.). But they argue that this mechanistic image of caregiving is impoverished and that ideally "moral imagining, perceiving, recollecting, and especially feeling" would be involved in moral decision making on the part of the caregiver in the clinic (ibid.).

For Schultz and Carnevale, clinical phronesis involves "alertness, receptivity, and acquiescence to an engaged approach to clinical decision-making" (1996, 195). This engaged approach is "realized only through respectful, truthful conversation and dialogue"—that is, it is achieved dialogically (ibid.). In addition to this truthful conversation, there is also an emotional reciprocity, a "felt reciprocity that exists between the affliction suffered by the patient, and its reflection mirrored in our experience by the images, metaphors, and symbols that comprise clinical discourse" (ibid.). These elements are finally interpreted by the clinician who exhibits phronesis in order to make decisions regarding therapies (197).

The authors provide an example of clinical phronesis by referencing the case of a young Inuit boy named Jimmy who was flown hundreds of miles to receive treatment for major burns (1996, 199–200). The treatment was extremely painful, and sessions of cleaning the wounds and re-dressing them would last for hours at a time. Schultz and Carnevale stated that their aim was to "establish a non-threatening relationship with Jimmy wherein he could feel free to express anything that was significant to him . . . and try to help establish a 'safe space' in which he could dwell" (200). This would assist him in dealing with the pain of the treatment and his isolation (he was far from his family).

The authors focused on relaxation and meditation, but turned a corner with him when they began reading Inuit stories to Jimmy:

> I offered to read a couple of Inuit stories to him. At that point, his entire face lit up with approval. These were short folk tales of children successfully overcoming adversity. Jimmy focused attentively on the illustrations in the books and seemed fully engaged in the stories. The stories seemed to enable him to escape to a more familiar, more comfortable place. After the stories, Jimmy and I "spoke" for several minutes about his home life. We established a method of discourse whereby I could easily read Jimmy's facial expressions. (1996, 200)

After these encounters, they began helping Jimmy give voice to his pain by lending their voices when his facial expressions seemed to warrant it during treatments. As these relationships developed, they spoke of "knowing" him and feeling a high sense of sympathy for his pain and pleasure when they brought him comfort (202).

To take a momentary broader view, the application of abstract principalism often expressed in bioethical literature is a top-down narrative discourse that is informed, but not ultimately transformed, by listening. Narratives that subvert abstract principalism may be rejected or overlooked, which threatens the practice of benevolent listening and, therefore, patient interpretation. Like casuistry, which involves matching new cases to paradigmatic past cases and is typified in the monologic narrative of the bioethics case, abstract principalism risks unexamined implications that likely shrink the patient's space for expressing and rebuilding identity and experiences. Looking closely again at the model at hand, Aristotelian clinical phronesis, Schultz and Carnevale appear to make a similar mistake. The Inuit stories that comforted Jimmy were existing narratives. What if existing images and narratives need to be questioned for healing to take place?

I claim that Kristevan patient interpretation provides a better frame for understanding the needs of the patient (not just comfort, but also rebuilding identity), so it is more explanatory and has greater ethical import in that it can make room for critique of the "images, metaphors, and symbols that comprise medical discourse" (1996, 195). I turn now to this issue through a discussion of the speaking subject and revolt.

Patient Interpretation and the Space for Revolt

Earlier, I set aside the "grander question" that Kristeva evades in *Hatred and Forgiveness*—that is, the question of whether or not medical professionals can provide a space of revolt for their patients through patient interpretation. She specifically worries that medical professionals are not trained to help patients "reestablish" the "narcissistic image" and "erotic ties" the way psychoanalysts are (2010, 154). But this concern can be resolved by looking more closely at Kristeva's discussions of the speaking subject and revolt. I turn now to tackle the question, then, by considering these discussions and the deeper movement of benevolent listening in the medical context. I suggest that, in fact, the best forms of care fostered by patient interpretation make precisely this kind of space by creating room for discordant, multiple, and subversive meanings and understandings of illness, death, and disability. Unlike Kristeva in *Hatred and Forgiveness*, I am ready to afford medical professionals the ability to create space for revolt—that is, intimate revolt. This intimate revolt may even highlight avenues for social revolt. In defending this claim, I complete my discussion of patient interpretation and what it involves.

For Kristeva, the speaking subject is suspended between two realms—the semiotic (the discharging of drives through the flesh by way of rhythm and tone without referents, associated with the mother) and the symbolic (referential language, organized within grammar) (Oliver 1997, xiv). In the process of building meaning by representing experiences through symbols, a person translates the semiotic into the symbolic and understands the symbolic through the semiotic (McAfee 2004, 105; Oliver 1997, xv). The connection between the two realms, that is, the dynamic charges between them that the subject actively knits together, makes it possible to speak. Kelly Oliver calls the connection a "dialectical oscillation" and writes:

> Without the symbolic element of signification, we have only sounds or delirious babble. But without the semiotic element of signification, signification would be empty and we would not speak, for the semiotic provides the motivation for engaging in signifying processes. We have a bodily need to communicate. The symbolic provides the structure necessary to communicate. Both elements are essential to signification. (1997, xv)

Kristeva argues that the subject, to begin speaking, needs to believe in the love or openness of the other, one who listens. She poses the father (who loves the mother) as the one the child believes in (Kristeva 2014, 10). As Sarah Hansen puts it, the subject believes in an "accepting space for love, drives, and affect in the site of meaning" (2015, 59). The father who speaks has accepted the mother, who is linked to experiences of the flesh (Kristeva 2014, 10).

But crises and problems can challenge the dialectical tension between the semiotic and the symbolic; meaningful signification is threatened or severed when one realm or the other is overemphasized or forgotten. On the one hand, modern culture prefabricates symbols through circulating images and commodities that capture our attention and draw us away from our semiotic experiences. This causes a loss of meaning and the loss of the psychical space of inner experience (McAfee 2004, 106). Symbols no longer have meaningful reference. On the other hand, psychosis results when the semiotic is overemphasized and the subject fails to represent experiences through symbols (105). Kristeva frames the subject as a subject-in-process; however, it seems that subsumption by the symbolic threatens to suspend the subject by processing her and eliminating psychical space, while subsumption by the semiotic threatens to stave off symbolic processing through the refusal of the symbolic (the cordoning off and deflation of psychical space) (ibid.). Noëlle McAfee writes of the balance necessary: "Even as semiotic charges disrupt her attempts at being a self-identical, stable subject, she must carry on as if she were one. In other words, speaking beings have to keep the semiotic *chora* intact but at bay" (ibid.).

For my purposes in this section, I focus on the first problem—that is, the subsumption of the subject by the symbolic. McAfee traces Kristeva's discussion of the loss of the semiotic alongside the work of Guy Debord, whose society of the spectacle becomes Kristeva's culture of the show (2004, 108–09). The proliferation of images and narratives disconnected from the dialectical oscillation between the semiotic and symbolic become replacements for meaningful signification. Along with signification, the space for inner experiences is reduced. Writes Kristeva: "The conditions of modern life—with the prevalence of technology, image, speed, and so forth, all inducing stress and depression—tend to reduce psychical space and to abolish the faculty of representation" (Kristeva 2014, 10).

Kristeva's commentary here lends itself easily to analyzing medical contexts, especially those relevant to experiences of disabilities. In medical contexts, surgery and medicine are the relevant *technologies*; diagnosis, stereotypes, and preexisting narratives of illness and even death are the *image*; and finally *speed* can be understood as the warping of the time of illness by way of diagnosis. I consider each of these issues briefly by way of an example.

The use of a variety of technologies—surgical, diagnostic, and otherwise—have contributed to a feeling of disconnection and disembodiment. Women report this with regard to the use of reproductive technologies. Some feminist groups, along with the Roman Catholic Church, an odd bedfellow, have rejected these technologies "for reasons connected to worries about treating procreation as an out-of-the-body laboratory production" (Lauritzen 1995, 322, cf. Corea 1985). Disconnection from enfleshed drives and, therefore, the semiotic is also a risk with regard to preexisting narratives and images connected to diagnoses and death. Jeffrey Bishop argues that "the medical study of life originates with a decontextualized dead body; the body of the dead cadaver represents the bodies of the living" (Bishop 2012, 14). This image impacts medical treatment and how patients view themselves through the medical lens; Bishop argues that the dead body is normative for medicine. Bishop also claims that medicine deploys normative images of grief through empirical study:

> what is a normal period of grief, and what is an abnormal grief? These are the sorts of questions that medicine and psychiatry attempt to answer empirically, or expertly. Once the questions are answered, the whole of the discipline's power—disciplinary power, in Foucault's sense of the phrase—can be brought to bear on the person who is grieving. (2012, 14–15)

The pacing of grief imposed by a logic articulated in a discourse of power leads me to the final point: speed. The "time" of illness is warped in diagnostic practices. Diagnoses, when shared with patients, will radically alter self-conceptions in a sudden way. One must then catch up.

As a psychoanalyst, Kristeva provides attentive, benevolent listening, thereby becoming a stand-in for this father-who-loves-the-mother and rupturing time to open space for meaning-making (2014, 11). This meaning-making can reconnect the semiotic and symbolic on the level of the intimate, rebuilding inner experiences. Medical professionals are thrust into this role as well, and can subvert the monological diagnostic authority they represent by attempting benevolent listening. They can make room for a patient to speak, write, and otherwise artistically describe his or her experiences, all actions increasingly called for in the medical humanities. In this way, patients have the opportunity to begin subverting the narrative stagnation and lacunae attendant upon technology, image, and speed in medical and social contexts by expressing their own narrative-building and meaning-making while in the presence of the medical professional as authority, an authority that can legitimate these expressions of revolt by listening. This action subverts the reinforcement of the top-down narrative of the bioethics case.

I turn now specifically to revolt, which Kristeva describes as moving to the "limits of the representable/the thinkable/the bearable" (2014, 6). For her, a culture of revolt, a place for permanent revolt, is a "questioning of the self, of everything and of nothingness, which no longer seems to have any place to occur" (3). The subject in revolt is one who questions him- or herself (recall that Pierre never questioned himself when he began treatment, as noted above), but now that the culture of revolt has been snuffed out, Kristeva calls for an intimate revolt. The revolt she seeks is in "psychical life and its social manifestations (writing, thought, art)" (10).

If medical professionals engage in benevolent listening, and encourage writing, thought, and art that knits meaning by rekindling the connection between the semiotic and the symbolic, they are opening a space for revolt in their practice of patient interpretation. The patient in revolt will be revolting, that is, abject—a subject in process. But if postmodern forgiveness can suspend the desire on the part of the medical professional to reject the patient, the work of patient interpretation can begin. Hansen makes a parallel suggestion for teachers, who can engage in a pedagogy of intimate revolt through a loving listening; this listening opens a "space of loving acceptance in language" (2014, 60).

Kristeva suggests that intimate revolt can prepare the way for social revolt. We must be able to represent our traumas and inner life, believe in the possibility of someone listening, and use that interpersonal space for translating our utterances into language. Subversion against the master discourse of diagnosis in the clinic can be translated into a vulnerability or disability politics. This would involve an intimate but also a social and political forgiveness, in which we allow those around us to be other than symbolized through prefabricated images and stereotypes and allow them to be abject or in progress. To complete this thought, I close with a look to Kristeva's work on disability and commentary on John Cadigan, a schizophrenic man who was the subject and purported co-director of a 2003 documentary titled *People Say I'm Crazy* (2006).

Kristeva claims that disability is fundamentally accompanied by reminders of mortality, both for people experiencing it and for those who encounter them (2013, 225). Meanwhile, Kristeva argues that death accompanies life biologically, from the moment of conception, and death lies at the heart of life for all of us—this is true despite the fact that we may not be aware of this accompaniment (225). This thought echoes her claims elsewhere that vulnerability accompanies disability, yet we are all significantly vulnerable; in fact, human identity generally, for Kristeva, is paradoxically constituted by "destructivity, vulnerability, and imbalance" (2010, 42). That Kristeva sees disability as having features both shared and unshared is obvious in her insistence on resisting the formulation "we are all disabled" while at the same time pointing to the "essential vulnerability of the speaking body" (2013, 224 and 2010, 41, respectively). In her discussion of Cadigan, she clarifies that while every person is vulnerable, only persons with disabilities are irreparably vulnerable (2006, 224).

She seeks to add a fourth term, then, to the classic liberal formulation of liberty, equality, and fraternity: that is, vulnerability (2006, 222). But she is suspicious of "integration" of persons with disabilities without "interaction"—that is, subsumption into language and authority without a space of listening. After viewing Cadigan in *People Say I'm Crazy,* she described the film as an attempt to "heal" and "integrate" Cadigan. His sister, an amateur filmmaker, wanted to share his art, and so the "madman" "became a disabled artist" (220). This prefabricated role and set of meanings unsettled Kristeva:

> I had been witness to a *process*, perhaps even to a procedure, but not to a *rebirth*—to an integration, but not to an interaction. The disabled person was indeed supported, but this was done in order to facilitate the insertion of his produced objects into the circuit of consumption, where success was measured by the bringing of his story to the screen. The subject in his entirety was absorbed by his objects and his psychical life taken as cured since it had quite simply disappeared from sight. (2006, 220, emphasis mine)

The attempt to process a subject, rather than accepting a subject in process, has deadened and tightly circumscribed psychical life for Cadigan. Of his art, she writes:

> Not a word or an interpretation accompanied John's dramatic depictions of the brains and stomachs swarming around with abject flora and fauna . . . Perhaps he could not speak? Perhaps no attempts had been made to let him speak? Perhaps he would try to speak after the making of the film? Who knows? (2006, 220)

The speaking subject has been eliminated in a subsumption by the symbolic. She goes on:

> it is true that the adventure has pushed him to produce and exhibit objects that will even be put up for sale, or at least it is hoped so. What a success! It is obvious, he is cured. What more could be wanted in the benign society of the spectacle other than good disabled people? It suffices that the patient has only to become a producer and/or an object of the "show." An immense sadness restrained my unreserved applause. (2006, 220)

Here we see the enormity of the problem related to the culture of the "show," which cares more for production and objects than subjects in process and only accepts a multiplicity of images if they are simply for sale rather than heard.

Intimate revolt can become social revolt. In the clinic, medical professionals can open up a space through benevolent listening accomplished by way of patient interpretation. This space for self-questioning, new understandings of illness and disability, and new self-understandings can subvert the culture of the show and be part of a social and political revolt that challenges ableist formulations such as the "madman" and the "disabled artist." The speaking subject is a subject in process, not a processed subject. Kristeva's insightful commentary in reaction to the depiction of John Cardigan in *People Say I'm Crazy* illustrates the point.

Conclusion

Medical ethicists and medical humanists have noted the importance of bridging the gap between medical professionals and patients, and phenomenologists focus on bringing embodiment back to the center of clinical practice. Many note that a caring practice must articulate the concept of healing in a full sense and not consider healing a merely somatic issue. As Kristeva puts it, "there is no life without psychical life" and no somatic healing without psychical healing (2010, 157). Illness, disability, and diagnosis disrupt self-understandings and identities and leave patients searching desperately for meaning. So, it seems, new narratives must be built. Yet medical professionals can be disgusted by patients, and patients are not heard by those who are caring for them. In these circumstances, it is difficult to build meaningful narratives and knit together the semiotic and symbolic in a practice of meaningful speech.

I suggest that Kristeva's patient interpretation be taken as a model for new practices of reflection and care that could foster patient expression and recognize multiple sources of meaning while simultaneously breaking the stranglehold of the authoritative master logic of diagnostic criteria and purely somatic understandings of disease. Kristeva's work helps make new sense of medical encounters and brings a fresh lens to the medical humanities by offering a model of listening—benevolent listening to vulnerability that opens itself up to patient utterances and builds the background conditions for patient storytelling in dialogue. This storytelling, in turn, can support and stimulate intimate revolt in the Kristevan sense and—perhaps—even support and stimulate wider forms of revolt.

Notes

1. Kristeva is hesitant in her use of the word "healing" because it implies that an end state of "health" will be achieved once and for all (2010, 154). Her worry is well founded, and so I refer primarily to caregiving practices in this chapter.

2. Notice here the similarity between Kristeva's postmodern forgiveness and the unconditional forgiveness beyond sovereignty posed as an ideal and impossibility by Jacques Derrida. Derrida writes: "What I dream of, what I try to think as the 'purity' of a forgiveness worthy of its name, would be a forgiveness without power: *unconditional but without sovereignty* (2001, 59).

3. The principles are typically left unranked when articulated and when applied are given priority in a manner that depends on the facts of the case.

Works Cited

Beauchamp, Tom, and James Childress. 2001. *Principles of Biomedical Ethics*. New York: Oxford University Press; 2001.

Bishop, Jeffrey P. 2012. *The Anticipatory Corpse: Medicine, Power, and the Care of the Dying*. Notre Dame: University of Notre Dame Press.

Cadigan, John, and Katie Cadigan. 2003. *People Say I'm Crazy*. Documentary. New York: HBO/Cinemax.

Chambers, Tod. 1997. "What to Expect from an Ethics Case (and What It Expects from You)." In *Stories and Their Limits: Narrative Approaches to Bioethics*, edited by Hilde Lindemann Nelson. New York: Routledge.

Corea, Gena. 1985. *The Mother Machine*. New York: HarperCollins.

Derrida, Jacques. 2001. *On Cosmopolitanism and Forgiveness*. New York: Routledge.

Gordon, J. Jil. 2008. "Humanising Doctors: What Can the Medical Humanities Offer?" *Medical Journal of Australia* 189 (8): 420–21.

Hansen, Sarah. 2014. "Pedagogies of Revolt, Politics of the Self." *Journal of French and Francophone Philosophy* 21 (2): 56–61.

Kristeva, Julia. 1982. *Powers of Horror: An Essay on Abjection*. Translated by Leon S. Roudiez. New York: Columbia University Press.

———. 2001. *The Sense and Non-Sense of Revolt*. Translated by Jeanine Herman. New York: Columbia University Press.

———. 2002. *Intimate Revolt: The Powers and Limits of Psychoanalysis*. Translated by Jeanine Herman. New York: Columbia University Press.

———. 2006. "At the Limits of Living: To Joseph Grigely." *Journal of Visual Culture* 5: 219–25.

———. 2010. *Hatred and Forgiveness*. Translated by Jeanine Herman. New York: Columbia University Press.

———. 2013. "A Tragedy and a Dream: Disability Revisited." *Irish Theological Quarterly* 78 (3): 219–30.

———. 2014. "New Forms of Revolt." *Journal of French and Francophone Philosophy* 22 (2): 1–19.

Laranjeira, Carlos. 2013. "The Role of Narrative and Metaphor in the Cancer Life Story: A Theoretical Analysis." *Medicine, Health Care and Philosophy* 16 (3): 469–81.

Lauritzen, Paul. 1995. "Whose Bodies? Which Selves? Appeals to Embodiment in Assessments of Reproductive Technology." *Theology and Medicine* 6: 113–26.

Lindemann Nelson, Hilde, ed. 1997. *Stories and Their Limits: Narrative Approaches to Bioethics*. New York: Routledge.

Little, Miles, Christopher F. C. Jordens, Kim Paul, Emma Sayers, and Dhananjayan Sriskandarajah. 2000. "Face, Honor and Dignity in the Context of Colon Cancer." *Journal of Medical Humanities* 21 (4): 229–43.

McAfee, Noëlle. 2004. *Julia Kristeva*. New York: Routledge.

Oliver, Kelly. 1997. *The Portable Kristeva*. New York: Columbia University Press.

Peterkin, Allen. 2008. "Medical Humanities for What Ails Us." *Canadian Medical Association Journal* 178 (5): 648.

Rothfield, Philipa. 2005. "Attending to Difference: Phenomenology and Bioethics." In *Ethics of the Body: Postconventional Challenges*, edited by Margrit Shildrick and Roxanne Mykitiuk. Cambridge: MIT Press.

Schultz, Dawson S., and Franco E. Carnevale. 1996. "Engagement and Suffering in Responsible Caregiving: On Overcoming Maleficence in Health Care." *Theoretical Medicine and Bioethics* 17 (3): 189–207.

Shapiro, Johanna. 2008. "Walking a Mile in their Patients' Shoes: Empathy and Othering in Medical Students' Education." *Philosophy, Ethics, and Humanities in Medicine* 3 (10).

Toombs, S. Kay. 1992. *The Meaning of Illness: A Phenomenological Account of the Different Perspectives of Physician and Patient.* Boston: Kluwer.

Zaner, Richard M. 2000. "Power and Hope in the Clinical Encounter: A Meditation on Vulnerability." *Medicine, Health Care and Philosophy* 3 (3): 263–73.

Part III

Language and Narrative in Kristeva

7

Language as *Poeisis*

Linguistic Productivity and Forms of Resistance in Kristeva and Saussure

Beata Stawarska

> *Faire de la langue un travail—poiein—*, oeuvrer dans la matérialité de ce qui, pour la société, est un moyen de contact et de compréhension, n'est-ce pas se faire, d'emblée, étranger a la langue? . . . Etrangement proche, intiment étrangère a la matière de nos discours et de nos rêves, la "littérature" nous parait aujourd'hui être l'acte même qui saisit comment la langue travaille et indique ce qu'elle a le pouvoir, demain, de transformer.
>
> —*Semeiotike: recherches pour une sémanalyse*, 9

In her work dealing with linguistics and poetics, Kristeva distinguishes between two alternative approaches to language, both derived from the work of Ferdinand de Saussure. The first one is a *scientific semiology*, which seeks to study language as a structured system of signs—a static, closed and autonomous system dissociated from any notion of the speaking subject (*Desire in Language*, 24); this approach has been programmatically adopted within the structuralist tradition in philosophy and the human sciences. The second approach is an open, *paragrammatic semiotics*, which draws on Saussure's unorthodox studies of poetic language from the *Anagrams* (published in *Words behind Words*); this approach emphasizes that language is an infinite, free play without closure, which accommodates multiple intra- and intertextual relations and functions therefore as an open web of connections (*Semeiotike: recherches pour in sémanalyse*, 144; see also *Desire in Language*,

69; 128). Kristeva thus both advances a critique of the scientific semiology associated with Saussure's general linguistics and locates resources for overcoming the closure and stasis of a scientific semiological approach to language within Saussure's own, less publicized, work. She uses his subversive (and not recognizably scientific) texts to destabilize the structuralist (and poststructuralist) doctrine and to support her own conception of poetic language in particular and of open semiotics in general. In this chapter, I propose to expand on the subversive dimension of Saussure's work in light of the recent developments in Saussure scholarship to expose a greater than previously acknowledged alliance between Kristeva's and Saussure's projects. I draw on materials from Kristeva's early work in linguistics and poetics, including untranslated essays from the collection *Polylogue* (1977) as well as from the better known *Semeiotike* (1969),[1] and on materials from Saussure's *Nachlass*, some of them recently discovered and published in *Writings in General Linguistics* (2006), to argue that this alliance needs to be extended beyond a narrow focus on poetics to include language study more broadly. In extending their alliance in this way, I seek to shed light on the intrinsic productivity of language, as found both within the poetic process narrowly construed and within social contestation of linguistic norms. I argue that linguistic productivity, thematized broadly as *poiesis* in the etymological sense of the word (*travaille* in the French, or *work*), offers a strategy of resistance and revolt against normalization within individual and social life and reveals the extraordinary side of the so-called ordinary language.

Linguistic Objects, Poetic Subjects: Saussure and Kristeva

It is still little known, in the philosophical circles at least, that scholarly research on Saussure's linguistics of the last five decades has radically shifted the ways in which his intellectual heritage is interpreted. In response to the documented discrepancies between the edited version of Saussure's linguistics from the posthumous redaction of the *Course* by his presumed "disciples" and the source materials (autographed writings by Saussure, the student lecture notes from his courses on general linguistics at the University of Geneva from 1907 to 1911), as well as the recently discovered and published autographed writings by Saussure (*Ecrits de Linguistique Générale*, 2003/*Writings in General Linguistics*, 2006), and in light of the revelations from the recently published correspondence between the main stakeholders in Saussure's estate (the two editors of the posthumously published *Cours de Linguistique Générale*, 1916/*Course in General Linguistics*, and Saussure's students and colleagues), contemporary scholars are shifting from the so-called *first* to *the second editorial paradigm of Saussure's general linguistics*.[2] In other words, Saussure scholars are gradually abandoning an earlier (the *first*) research paradigm, which consisted primarily of a critical comparison between the 1916 posthumous redaction of the *Course on General Linguistics* and the source materials. While this approach helped to locate the manuscript sources of the editorial redaction of general linguistics (and also to establish a lack of manuscript evidence for some of the central claims made in the *Course*), it inadvertently maintained the status of the *Course* as central reference in Saussure scholarship, its documented shortcomings notwithstanding. In their passage to the *second* editorial paradigm, Saussure scholars are largely abandoning the *Course* and its structuralist legacy and working solely with historically authentic texts.[3]

Philosophical scholarship has lagged behind these scholarly developments, with the *Course* still serving as the official version of Saussure's linguistics in scholarly publications and college-level pedagogy alike. It is therefore still common to identify Saussure's linguistics with *scientific semiology*, but this view profoundly distorts Saussure's philosophical and reflective approach to language, with its concomitant critique of scientific methods. In fact, when studied based on the texts from the *Nachlass*, his project exhibits productive and mutually enriching parallels with Kristeva's open semiotics, as discussed next.

The familiar doctrine associated with the book of the *Course in General Linguistics* (1916) includes a set of oppositional pairings between the signifier and signified, *la langue* and *la parole*, and synchrony and diachrony. These paired notions are organized according to a logic of violent hierarchies wherein the signifier towers above the arbitrary signified content, synchronic arrangements between the signs circulating within a structured system are elevated above diachronic differences, and *la langue* is elected as the proper object of scientific study, independently of the contingent processes related to speaking (*la parole*). This hierarchical and dichotomous taxonomy has been adopted within structuralism as part of an effort to study human reality (social arrangements, neurotic symptoms, literary genres) with scientific rigor; it may in fact constitute a hallmark of structuralist activity, one that distinguishes it from the other traditions of inquiry (Barthes, *Critical Essays*,

1972, 213). Structuralism can therefore be defined as direct application of the "Saussurean doctrine" to the many fields within the human sciences as well as philosophy.

The validity of this Saussurean/structuralism doctrine has come under increased scrutiny in the last decades, but, writing in the 1960s, Kristeva understandably accepts the received view of Saussure's linguistics in her work. She therefore charges Saussurean structuralism with an intrinsic shortcoming of privileging stasis and ahistoricism, which makes it impossible to account for literary productivity (*Semeiotike*, 113). Within the structuralist (and poststructuralist) economy, language appears as a finished product, as a set of formalized utterances cut off from the activity of the body and the subject, as archeological remains from a bygone era, as a fascinating fetish (*Revolution in Poetic Language*, 13).

Because of its narrow focus on language as a finished product, scientific semiology expels the speaking subject from its field of work:

> as soon as linguistics was established as a science (through Saussure, for all intents and purposes) its field of study was thus hemmed in (*suturé*); the problem of truth in linguistic discourse became dissociated from any notion of the speaking subject." ("The Ethics of Linguistics," *Desire in Language*, 24)

Recall that in Saussure's linguistics as presented in the *Course in General Linguistics*, the general task is to define the "integral and concrete" object of study: *la langue* or language understood as a semiological system. This task is pursued without considering the methodological question of what the status of an object really is within the emerging science of language, and, as a result, unexamined normative categories derived from formal logic are simply assumed as being valid. Language is construed as a formal and relatively autonomous system of signs that can be studied with disengaged objectivity. As a result, the complex reality of language becomes modeled according to two opposed but related categories: "the 'object' language is confronted with a metalanguage that projects its own structures upon it—as if language were split into two, language as 'object' and language as 'instrument' " (*Polylogue*, 298, translations are my own). The epistemic relation between metalanguage at the subject end and language as object of study depends on a paradoxical process whereby the former is but a part of the latter but is also seemingly able to recover it in toto, and without a remainder (ibid). The speaking subject is therefore split between the positions of a participant in linguistic process and an observer from afar; the subject is both implicated in and separated from language by the subject-object bar, which needs to remain in place if the epistemic relation in linguistics is to remain recognizably scientific. Hence the complicated position in which this subject finds itself: on the one hand, the subject is the site in which language is understood as a living process sustained by the libidinal body works, and on the other hand, it becomes an object of theories about this productive process arrived at by projecting systematic categories of knowledge onto it as onto a distant other (299).

How will scientific linguistics negotiate this tension of the subject position in linguistics? Through a foreclosure or a suspension of the *speaking* subject in favor of a *scientific* one. Modern linguistics will construe language as a monolithic, logical system, and "it will reduce language without a subject to a pure system of classification devoid of any productivity" (302). As a result, the subject in linguistics can direct attention to the "objective" relations between the signifier and the signified, and the value relations between signs; the linguistics of speech and syntax will be neglected because they depend on the subject (ibid). Kristeva acknowledges the existence of references to the unconscious within Saussurean linguistics, which could suggest an opportunity to tie the signifying process to the libidinal body, as theorized especially by Freudian psychoanalysis. However, she notes that the references to the unconscious processes in language only mark a limit to scientific knowledge—they do not suggest an alternate libidinal logos coexisting with conscious rationality, the "other scene" of the Freudian unconscious (ibid). They effectively function therefore as gestures of its foreclosure or exclusion from out of the subject, following the principles of scientific objectivity and its inherent laws.[4] The knowing subject is not itself unconscious but a site of metalinguistic rationality; the knowing subject is not a *speaking* subject who lives language as a mobile process in the manner of a poet (*Polylogue*, 306). The knowing subject has set up a bar between him- or herself and the linguistic unconscious, with its bodily force. While the poetic subject lets the unconscious enter into his or her productive process, the scientific subject wants to know nothing about what conditions his or her own knowledge (ibid). In sum, there is an irreconcilable tension between the subject position in language approached by way of a poet *through* whom language speaks and the meta-stance assumed by a scientist who seeks to speak *about* language without being claimed or moved by it in turn. Kristeva can therefore argue that the speaking subject must be placed in opposition to Saussure's linguistics and its philosophical offspring ("Speaking Subject," *Structuralism*).

The split between the scientific and the poetic/speaking subject runs in Kristeva's view across Saussure's work and creates tension between an objectified, frozen conception of language from general linguistics on the one hand and an alternative understanding of poetic language from his studies in poetics on the other. She writes:

> The immense bloc of Saussure's *Anagrams* crashes with all its weight the *Course* which it contests; it provides striking evidence of the contradiction at the limit of knowledge that the speaking subject attains when confronting the signifying material which makes him. (*Polylogue*, 305/6)

In sum, in Kristeva's reading, Saussure's project in general linguistics is corrupt because of its unexamined commitment to a scientific ideology of objects coupled with a metalinguistic stance, and it can only be surpassed via a turn to poetics with its alternative view of language and subjectivity. The *Course* is crashed by the *Anagrams* like scientific rationality by a direct surge from the Unconscious. Saussure's poetics emerges therefore as a much-needed alternative offering a more complex approach to language.

Recall that in his studies of the *Anagrams*, Saussure sought to establish the presence of an anagram or a guiding "theme-word" (such as a god's name) in Hindu, Greek, and Latin poetry. The anagram would have been decomposed into its component parts (syllables and phonemes) and dispersed or disseminated throughout the poem to create an internal echo in its vocal chain. Saussure writes to Meillet that in the Saturnine Latin, "all phonic elements without exception are coupled with one another. . . . Each Saturnine passage is but a swarming of syllables or phonic groups which echo one another" (1964, 110, my own translation). For example, in the Latin line *ibi manens sedeto donicum videbis*, the *de* of *videmis* echoes the *de* of *sedeto*, the *bi* of *videbis* that of the opening *ibi* (Utaker, *La philosophie du language*, 160). The repeated syllables thus instill a rhythm into the poetic verse, endowing it with an identifiable beat that facilitates the recitation of the poem and its retention in public memory. Poetic verse is equipped with a discernible structure that operates both at the vocalic level (the rhyme, rhythmic repetition) and at the level of the basic linguistic units (syllables, phonemes); Saussure can thus credit the poets with being the first phoneticians who developed an analysis of words by attending to their vocal form (Utaker, 153). This analysis is relevant at the level of both linguistics and poetics: it deploys an operative understanding of linguistic structure, that is, the articulation of vocal chain into sequential units (which need not yet have been explicitly theorized by the writers themselves), and it puts this structure in the service of poetic creativity. The anagrammatic process includes therefore both the dispersal of component parts of the presumed word-theme within the verse and the corresponding echoing between repeated sounds that resonate one with another.

One may be suspicious on empirical grounds of Saussure's attempt to identify a hidden anagrammatic theme within poetic verse—an attempt that inspired Kristeva's semanalysis as well as Derrida's "dissemination"[5] but was largely condemned within the linguistic community as a "long and sterile quest" (Godel 1960, 6), "an absurd pastime" (Amacker), and "an unhappy, misguided attempt" (Redard) (cited in Fehr 2000, 190). Still, the quest after the enigmatic anagram forms part and parcel of his study of language structure (which may be located elsewhere than in the compact word); this structure is available not only to the scientist but also, and perhaps more practically and concretely, to the poet for whom the play of structured elements translates into the felt rhythm of the verse and affords its memorization and oral reproduction; as a result, from the poet's perspective, these structured elements are tied to the position of the speaking subject and related to practices of usage. I am therefore in agreement with Utaker when he writes that Saussure "succeeds insofar as he thinks through [the anagrams] as a linguist, which renders his reflection on language more profound . . . he fails insofar as he cannot be sure of the real existence of the anagrams he found" (161). For the latter always turn up either too few or too many to settle the question of an operative word-theme in any definitive way.

In her engagement with Saussure's *Anagrams*, Kristeva is interested especially in the hidden (but discernible) interrelations between the textual elements disseminated throughout the poem insofar as they seem to obey a unique logic—one that is distinct from the logic operating at the level of the signifier. She will call this alternative textual logic *paragrammatism*. In its paragrammatic functioning, poetic language does not put signifiers in the service of a referential function but rather of unbounded semiological play. Kristeva writes that in the *Anagrams*, the Saussurian sign (signifier/signified) introduces "the heretofore unrecognized possibility of envisioning language as a free play, forever without closure" (*Desire in Language*, 128). In fact, she argues, the very concept of the sign with its vertical/hierarchical distinction between the signifier and the signified can no longer be regarded as a self-standing unit within poetic language. Instead, the minimal linguistic unity is "at least double," and includes a dialogical relation played out between the variously combined and paired textual elements, both within the space of an individual text as well as in the space between the texts that respond to and summon one another (*Desire in Language*, 69).[6] Drawing on the *Anagrams*, this means that each sign is irreducible to the signifying relation playing out within it; it is also a site of the "other scene" of linguistic play organized around the presumed word-theme and its permutations within a text. Each word is therefore both itself and a host for another word (or word-parts) echoed within it. Kristeva can conclude therefore: "The double would be the minimal sequence of a paragrammatic semiotics to be worked out starting from the work of Saussure (in the "Anagrams") and Bakhtin" (*Desire in Language*, 69). Kristeva's *paragrammatic* conception of poetic language as free play and an open-ended web of relations (*Semeiotike*, 114) thus develops and draws theoretical implications from Saussure's *anagrammatic* project. Saussure emerges therefore as a possible ally in her own semiotic venture—but only as long as his reflections are stripped of any aspirations to scientific rigor and objectivity. Kristeva apparently does not consider the possibility that Saussure pursues a linguistic (albeit not recognizably scientific) inquiry when studying phonetic dissemination within poetic language; however, if we allow that dissemination at the level of sound and syllable operates within poetic language and language *tout court*, then the choice between linguistics and poetics should not be made too hastily.

Speaking Subjects: Saussure's Linguistics Revisited

It is usual to associate Saussure's linguistics with the view that language (*la langue*) constitutes a static, closed, and autonomous system of signs dissociated from any notion of the speaking subject. However, in the materials from the *Nachlass*, Saussure emphasized that language and speech stand in a reciprocal relation. In the third course of lectures on general linguistics, he instructs the students to take down verbatim the following remark:

> There is nothing in *la langue* which has not entered <directly or indirectly> through speech (*parole*), that is through the sum

> total of speech acts received (*des paroles percues*), and, reciprocally, there is no speech possible before the development of this product called *la langue*, which supplies the individual with the elements for the composition of his speech. (*Saussure's Third Course of Lectures on General Linguistics [1910–1911]*, 1993, 91)

Saussure's conception of language is not therefore opposed to speaking practice; it results from it and informs it in turn. Furthermore, any contemporary arrangement of signs within a system is not opposed to its temporal development or diachrony. For example, in Saussure's manuscript notes, the famed game of chess analogy is used to underscore the inseparability of diachrony and synchrony, in agreement with an emphasis on the dual nature of language. Commenting on this analogy in the "Notes for an Article on Whitney" (Saussure, *Writings*, 2006, [203–16]; 140–51), Saussure observes that the game of chess analogy has been used before him, but in a different and misleading manner:

> Theorists of language before the foundation of the discipline and adepts of linguistics since Bopp always considered the language system (*la langue*) to be ONE chess POSITION of the chess game with nothing *before or after* it, and have wondered about the respective value, power of the pieces, in this position. (Saussure, *Writings*, 2006, [207]; 143)

In other words, linguists like Bopp mistakenly thought of language as nothing but a rule-governed system, thus failing to give justice to its temporal dimension ("with nothing before or after" a given position in a given arrangement of pieces). The notion that language should be construed as, ideally, a static and subjectless system is, pace Saussure's manuscripts, *an abstraction attributable to Bopp*; it is not endorsed but rather dismissed. Importantly, this abstracted view ties to Bopp's failure to see language as a *phenomenon*, in relation to the speaking subject (Saussure, *Writings*, 2006, [129–30], 85/6). Language (*langage*) as a phenomenon is indissociable from particular language acts (*actes de parole*) as performed by the speakers. *La langue* is the ensemble of concordant forms this phenomenon assumes in a collectivity of individuals at a given time. However, it must not be regarded outside of the speaking subjects—isolating *la langue* as a system from the phenomenal reality was the mistake made by Bopp and his school:

> The misunderstanding that the school founded by F[ranz] Bopp fell victim of was to assign to languages (*les langues*) an imaginary body and existence outside of speaking individuals. An abstraction relative to language (*langue*), even if made for good reasons, is in practice susceptible of limited application only—it is a *logical* device—and being at the mercy of this abstraction, endowed with a body, was an even greater impediment. . . . (Saussure, *Writings*, 2006, [129], 85)

In the first course of lectures on general linguistics, Saussure thematizes language (*langage*) in terms of the so-called linguistic analogy, that is, as an interconnected web of innovative or creative linguistic expressions made by the speakers in analogy with established expressions. For example, an author writing in the French may coin a new term, such as *répressionnaire* (in analogy with *mission: missionaire = répression: X*), or an adjective *firmamental /firmamentaux* (from *firmament*; in analogy with *fin—final/finaux*) (*Saussure's First Course of Lectures on General Linguistics [1907]*, 1996, 62). Similarly, a child may generate a (nonexistent) formation *venirai* (from *venir*, to *come*) on the model of similar-sounding verbs, like *punir* or *choisir*, whose first-person singular reads *je te punirai* and *je choisirai*. This novel form is grammatically incorrect (the correct one being *viendrais*), but there is a logic to the child's inventiveness—it perceives and puts to work the manifest regularities within and between individual words. It does not simply grasp any of the individual words (like *punir*, *choisir*, *venir*) in isolation, and it does not regard the similarities between them as based solely on their physical physiognomy. It detects and deploys the grammatical relations connecting the individual terms like a spider web and does so in a consistent (albeit socially unsanctioned and historically nonsedimented) fashion. Such inventiveness is true to the deep grammar of language while violating surface correctness: "There is nothing more consistent, nor more logical and more accurate, than the reasoning that leads to *venirai*" (Saussure, *Writings*, 2006, [160]; 107). These seemingly simple examples count as instances of veritable linguistic creation because the novel form does not replace or modify a preexistent one (there was no akin term prior to the innovation), and yet the novel form does not emerge ex nihilo either but is guided by the established pathways connecting nouns for states and participants, nouns and adjectives, the singular and the plural forms of the nouns, and so forth. Such analogical innovativeness can be found within any literary, artistic creation (*Saussure's First Course of Lectures on General Linguistics [1907]*, 1996,

62), and is therefore directly relevant to the creative usage of language in literature. It constitutes also the driving force behind linguistic change: if accepted as part of shared social convention, the novel expressions become written into linguistic code.

The analogical innovation is not a specialized process confined, for example, to the literary usage of language. In agreement with the Neogrammarians, it is both a principle underpinning any individual speaking activity, not matter how habitual and mundane, and a vehicle of linguistic innovation where the already established associative links point the way to novel forms of usage.[7] Analogical innovation pertains to language *in actu*, where grasping linguistic meanings, ideas, and their relations enables unprecedented yet understandable instances of usage in ordinary speech. In sum, analogy offers a window onto the language of literature and the language of ordinary life, insofar as it harbors a potential for inventive expression. This is in agreement with Kristeva's point that the paragrammatic logic belongs to any reflected productivity and includes the medium of "prose" as well as the so-called ordinary language—even though it may be best captured within poetic discourse narrowly construed (*Semeiotike*, 144/5; 115–16). Importantly, however, poetic language ceases to be isolated as a mere "ornament," a superfluous or anomalous practice associated with a narrow and exclusive group within a hierarchical society (115). Poetic language becomes a marker of a general linguistic productivity and a capacity of social resistance to normalization.

As she writes:

> Within this perspective, literary practice emerges as an exploration and a discovery of the possibilities of language; it is an activity which liberates the subject from certain psychic and social structures; a dynamism which breaks the inertia of linguistic habits and offers to the linguist a unique possibility of studying the becoming of signification of signs. (*Semeiotike*, 117–18)

We find a similar emphasis on linguistic dynamism and productivity in Saussure's conception of language. Contrary to the linguists before him (from Bopp to Schleicher, from 1816 to 1870–75), for whom change is a historical error and a mistake against language, Saussure argues that it is both a normal and permanent condition. In enumerating the main errors committed by the linguists before him, Saussure lists insufficient attention to "the incessant <daily> creation within the language [*la langue*]; I mean analogy" (*Saussure's Second Course of Lectures on General Linguistics [1908–1909]*, 1997–86). This lack of attention accounts for the fact that linguists used to regard it as a violation of language in its original state (ibid).[8] In sum, "The language (*la langue*) was . . . not allowed to use analogy; it seemed to be a kind of license, infraction, whereas it is the normal way for a language to renew itself" (ibid, 86). Saussure issues a plea to recognize this "continual work of renewal" (*Saussure's Second Course of Lectures on General Linguistics [1908–1909]*, 1997, 93); as he put in a motto-like phrase: "language always works (*la langue travaille tout le temps*); this work is analogy" (Ibid, 160). This motto is echoed in Kristeva's opening lines in *Semeiotike* (9), where she writes that language should be treated as work (*un travail*), as in the Greek term *poiein*. The emphasis on poetic language should not be understood in a narrow and purely ornamental sense of "poetic" as distinct from the "prosaic" or "ordinary" language, but rather in the broadest possible sense of an incessant productivity of language insofar as it is put to work by the speaking subjects.

It should also be noted that Saussure's emphasis on analogical innovation applies to language as a whole and can therefore be counted as one of the principles of general linguistics. The linguist goes as far as to equate the totality of language with the processes and products of analogical work:

> any language at any moment is nothing other than a vast web of analogical formations, some very recent, others dating back so far that one can only guess them. Asking a linguist to name some analogical formations is therefore like asking a mineralogist to name some minerals, or an astronomer some stars; I say this at the outset so as to avoid any misconceptions concerning the value given to these facts: they are neither exceptional nor anecdotal, neither curiosities nor anomalies; rather, they are the most clear substance of language everywhere and at all time, its everyday history and the history of all times. (*Writings*, 2006, [161]; 107–08, translation revised)

Such overt emphasis on linguistic productivity and play, made within a series of reflections on general linguistics, subverts the received view of language as a static and ahistorical sign system. This emphasis is only strengthened by the fact that in the student lecture notes, unlike in the posthumous redaction of the *Course*, linguistic analogy is used to introduce the distinction between the synchronic dimension of *la langue* on the one hand and the diachrony of *la parole* on the other. In the official presentation in the *Course*, "analogical formations are mentioned as providing historical evidence (CLG, 227) for a distinction [between *langue* and *parole*] already established on a priori grounds" (Harris, *Saussure and His Interpreters*, 2003, 30). The distinction can therefore figure as an axiom within a deductive system—rather than a double axis helping to map out a complex phenomenon whereby established patterns give rise to novel expressions. Insofar as most scholars uncritically accept the editorial presentation of the *la langue/ la parole* distinction in the *Course* and its structuralist uptake, they are unlikely to trace its provenance in the lectures notes: "Today it is still probably true that the majority of scholars who discuss "Saussure's" distinction between *langue* and *parole* are completely unaware of its original emergence from the doctrine of analogy" (ibid, 30). The majority of scholars would therefore be hard-pressed to appreciate that its original emergence from the doctrine of analogy complicates the assumed logic of vertical dichotomies associated with the distinctions between *la langue* and *la parole*, synchrony and diachrony, semiological system and speaking subjectivity. In sum, the distinction between synchrony and diachrony is not a vertical hierarchy of the properly scientific and merely contingent linguistic facts; it is rather a distinction between linguistic products (the synchronic states) and linguistic processes (diachronic speech), which continually act upon one other. Even though developed within Saussure's general linguistics, which Kristeva's categorized as objectivating scientific semiology, this conception of linguistic productivity deployed by speaking subjects fits broadly into Kristeva's alternative program of paragrammatic semiotics.

Saussure's linguistics and Kristeva's semiotics also share a commitment to linguistic duality as being more primary than a focus on an individual sign standing on its own. It is usual to regard Saussure's conception of language as being based on the distinction between the signifying and the signified facets of an individual sign, and therefore as being wedded to the traditional notion of *signatum* (Derrida, *Of Grammatology*, 1998, 12–13).[9] However, this conception is chiefly a product of the editorial misrepresentation of the source materials, which confuses the received view of language as a nomenclature critiqued by Saussure and his own proposed view of language as a complex web of intersecting relations (see chapter 1, Stawarska, *Saussure's Philosophy of Language as Phenomenology*, for development). Referring to the famed diagram picturing the concept (such as "tree") and the auditory image (such as the Latin word *arbor*), which suggests that "the signification is the counterpart of the auditory image and nothing else. The word appears or is taken as an isolated and absolute whole" (ibid, 135), Saussure observes: "A trap (*piège*) awaits us in this view as in a cave (*caverne*)" (ibid, 135). The trap has to do with this: how can signification ever be engendered within any individual sign if it is also contingent on the mediating relations to other signs in the language system? (ibid, 135). The response to this paradox is to adopt a systemic or textual view, rather than that of an individual sign, from the start (ibid, 137). That means that a sign is defined not only in terms of signification, but also by its *value*—a category relative to the given term's relations with other surrounding terms. To use the classic example, the French *mouton* does not have the same value as the English *sheep*, because the former refers to the animal both "on the hoof and on the table," while the latter to the animal but not to the meat (*mutton*) (ibid, 136). This simple lexical fact illustrates the far-reaching philosophical idea that a word such as *sheep* cannot rise to the task of labeling a preexistent natural kind grasped by means of a universal idea, because the ideas are shaped by what could be termed the *semiological halo* or *horizon* of any individual word. This semiological horizon is not simply external to the individual word, circumventing a clearly delimited, bounded being; according to the notes, signification and value overlap in part, even though they cannot be collapsed.

Saussure dismantles therefore the nomenclature view of language, which posits a series of seemingly disconnected and self-standing terms. He writes that "the real configuration is: *a-b-c*, outside of any knowledge of a functional relationship such as * - *a*" (*Writings*, 2006, [230], 162), where * stands for an object knowable in advance. The "real configuration" is therefore an at least double relation between signs, rather than an individual sign linking up with a referent. Saussure's reflections on signification from general linguistics are therefore broadly compatible with Kristeva's commitment to the double as forming the minimal sequence of paragrammatic semiotics, even though they are developed within a broad reflection on general linguistic principles and not on poetic language in the narrow sense.

It is also significant that Saussure considers a purely "objective" understanding of language in terms of value relations between signs to be abstract, mainly because the focus is on the sign and the language system (*la langue*) considered as an object dissociated from speech (*parole*). According to the student lecture notes, such partial focus is problematic because "that would only be language (*la langue*) apart from its social reality, and unreal (because comprising only one part of its reality). For there to be a language, there must be a body of speakers using the language. The language . . . is located in the collective soul right from the start" (*Saussure's Third Course of Lectures on General Linguistics* (1910–1911), 1993, 101). This social fact is part of the definition of *la langue* (ibid, 101); in fact, this weight of the community would give language a center of gravity (ibid, 97). Saussure reaffirms this point in the autographed notes for the course: language (*langue*) divorced from social reality (*réalité sociale*) becomes unreal (*irréelle*); a speaking collectivity (*masse parlante*) is part of the "very definition" of language itself (Saussure, *Writings*, 2006, [334], 238). The *socius* is the therefore necessary *subject* of language, and language itself is not purely linguistic but rather enabled and reinforced by social conventions of usage that have been transmitted from mouth to ear and from one generation of speakers to another. Language is an ongoing contract within a speech community that endures and is relatively resistant to change. This receptive stance and acknowledged passivity of the language user before the sign removes any remnants of voluntarism from language, considering that historically sedimented social practice largely constrains individual free choice in language use:

> The power of time constantly holds in check the power we may call arbitrary <free choice>. Why do we say *man, dog*? Because before us people said *man, dog*. The justification lies in time. (*Saussure's Third Course of Lectures on General Linguistics [1910–1911]*, 1993, 97)

Even though the received view of Saussurean linguistics suggests that that the speaking individual is to be evacuated from the language system, the source materials state that an individual *alone* is powerless to effect lasting change; what is needed is the sanction and consecration of a community. As a collectively sanctioned medium, language is therefore amenable to a social analysis and social critique; it figures as a vehicle of traditional values, which can be both empowering and oppressive for the individual (see also Thibault, *Re-reading Saussure*, 1997, 216). While Saussure does not develop an approach geared specifically at such critical analysis, his notion that linguistic signification and value must bear the stamp of collective approval exposes their contingency and opens up possibility of language practice creating a nontraditional set of values. Differently put, as a socially constituted medium, language is open both to the possibility of transmission and revision through the evolving practices of usage. For example, according to contemporary proponents of the reclamation strategy of responding to harmful language like racial slur and sexist speech, social groups are empowered to negotiate what words signify and what effects they produce; in a felicitous case of reclamation like that of the term *queer*, an expression that previously carried the force of exclusion and contempt shifts to a celebratory term of self-affirmation within the gay group.[10]

The process of reclamation can be deciphered with the help of Saussure's general linguistics. Signification is, in agreement with Saussure, *arbitrary*, that is, constituted by the many vicissitudes of social convention—and not a capricious play of signifiers among themselves. For arbitrariness does not imply simply an absence of external motivation by a natural law or divine decree; in the materials from the *Nachlass*, it is defined rather as a positive category whereby the speaking community determines signification by means of historically sedimented (but revisable) linguistic habits (see Stawarska, chapter 1, *Saussure's Philosophy of Language as Phenomenology*, for development). Saussure's general linguistics can therefore shed light on the intrinsic *mutability* of language and help to decipher the otherwise perplexing fact that language carries the weight of historically sedimented norms *and* tolerates novel expressions and violations of the norm. It may be that the cardinal principles from general linguistics, such as linguistic arbitrariness and immutability/mutability, are best studied within social movements that make a renewed claim to linguistic meaning.

The Poetics of Revolt

Kristeva's conception of the speaking subject offers an alternative to the metalinguistic stance in linguistics; it also provides a site of resistance and revolt against established linguistic (and other social) norms enacted especially by the poet's subversive usage of language in the avant-garde. In what follows, I highlight the phenomenological dimension of Kristeva's conception of the poetic subject, whose philosophical frame of reference prominently features Hegel's phenomenology. I examine the potentials and the limitations of construing revolt in terms of the avant-garde poetic practice, and its bearing on larger social scale linguistic reclamations in the context of the so-called ordinary language usage. I propose that Kristeva's conception of the speaking subject should be given a more robust social sense in agreement with her own broad conception of poetic language as a field of linguistic work, and therefore seek to combine an emphasis on the social dimension of language from Saussure's linguistics with one on the subversive poetic practice from Kristeva's semiotics. My reading thus echoes some of the previously raised concerns about the individualistic and apolitical subject figured by a Kristevean artist (Huffer 1998) and the difficulty of linking this subject to society and of connecting literary practice to actual social and political structures (Moi 1985). My contribution to this scholarship is to show that Kristeva's narrow, subjectivist rendering of revolt runs parallel to a similarly narrow focus on poetic language as an ornament, and that both need to expand to make room for socially significant revolt. My argument is therefore that language matters in social action.

Kristeva's alternative to scientific linguistics is an open semantics that seeks to inhabit an ambiguous juncture between the sign and the subject and to thematize language as being both a structured semiological system and living discourse (*Polylogue*, 321). It maintains the topos of the speaking subject within the process of generating discourse (321) and does not suspend it in favor of a metalinguistic view of language as finished product. Kristeva develops such an open semantics through an engagement with Hegel's logic of negative force, which she interprets as an enabling condition *and* a perennial threat of dissolution within the signifying process (343). She draws on Freud's conception of the unconscious as a nonobjectifiable, bodily drive (*Trieb/pulsion*) that fuels as well as endangers the signifying process, or what "carries, strings together as well as threatens the predicative synthesis" (ibid). In the *Revolution in Poetic Language*, the bodily drive is developed in terms of the semiotic, an ambiguous nonthetic energy that precedes, enables, and exceeds the stability and order of the symbolic, developed largely in relation to the inflexible linguistic and social structures represented by the modern bourgeois world. Finally, she engages the twentieth-century avant-garde poetry wherein the predicative subject-object structures are routinely undone, and the unconscious drives that both energize and destabilize the signifying process are given free rein (*Polylogue* 349–65; see also *Revolution in Poetic Language*, especially part IV).

Kristeva's open semantics takes its clue from her contemporary Emile Benveniste's nonreductive approach to language. Benveniste helps to thematize language more broadly than as a structured system; he distinguishes between the structural level (linguistic coherency), the subjective level (language as discourse, tied to speakers and context), and the historical level (the ideology inherent in language) (*Polylogue*, 324). As a result, Benvensiste does not emphasize solely the structured character of language viewed as a system of signs, but the *predicative process* at work within the linguistic act, which depends on a speaking subject (325). The predicative synthesis involves an assertion (posing a referent) and cohesion (the syntactical form) (326).

While Kristeva adopts the conception of language as discourse from Benveniste, she expands it beyond his emphasis on the assertive and cohesive dimensions of the predicative process to include the experience of the speaking subject and to develop a phenomenological understanding of language as speech. However, she does not adopt Husserl's phenomenology as her basis because the latter conceptualizes language as a phenomenal appearance only, and not as a process (356). To be sure, Husserl's emphasis on the predicative function of language depends on the subject, insofar as the predicate does not only pose the world as a referent of truth-conditional claims (assertions), but simultaneously posits the subject itself as its necessary correlate (see *Revolution in Poetic Language*, part I. 3). However, in agreement with scientific linguistics, Husserl's phenomenology adopts the metalinguistic point of view occupied by the transcendental ego from which language appears as an object only (*Polylogue*, 341). Husserl therefore misses the position of the poetic subject and its involvement within language as a mobile process.

Kristeva turns to Hegel's phenomenology instead, whose dialectical logic approximates the experience of the speaking subject (341).[11] Even though, in Hegel's idealism, signification operates within a speculative optics where everything is always already logical, she argues that the "dialectical logic can be extracted from its idealism" (342) and that one can thematize a pre- and extralogical materiality together with Hegel. Specifically, Hegel's notion of the Concept and its material correlate, the positing and dividing force of "negativity" (*négativité*), provide an alternative logic to the static formalism of subjects and objects. Kristeva writes:

> The Hegelian Concept . . . is a *position* or a determination, but it is also a *process*, at the same time totalizing and diversifying, which encompasses the becoming of objectivity (genesis of the concept) and subjectivity. (341)

Hegel's Concept is therefore a mediating term or, better, a continual conceptual movement between traditionally opposed terms: reflection and being, subject and object, the for- and the in-itself. The dialectical logic implied within this movement contains two distinct yet interlinked moments: the positionality of a logical act, whereby the Subject and Predicate are established as discrete albeit correlated forms (the predicative synthesis, also called the symbolic in *Revolution in Poetic Language*, or what Husserl calls the thetic function), and the possible disruption or dissolution of this synthesis through the unresolvable motoric tension that precedes and inheres in the predicative function (called the semiotic in *Revolution in Poetic Language* and developed as the fourth element of the dialectic in her engagement with Hegel). The dialectical logic of conceptual movement goes beyond the static formalism of subject-object oppositions; it is a dynamism driven by the forces of negativity, which Kristeva, following Hegel, describes thus:

> Neither a term nor a play between terms, negativity is the very possibility of a scission and the position of all terms: the driving force (*moteur*) of the passage between the terms . . . but also of the passage outside of the logical framework. (342)

Negativity is therefore a condition sine qua non of the predicative process ("a scission and the position of all terms"), but its mobile charge perennially threatens to return the same process to a nonsignifiable without. Negativity subtends the predicative process whereby the subject and the object, the speaker and the body, the word and the referent, the addressee and his or her reality, become distinguished (349), *and* it potentially disrupts the whole signifying matrix by an influx of nonassimilable excess of bodily force. Art and madness come closest to the source of this disruptive charge in their signifying practices. Kristeva analyzes especially the nineteenth-century avant-garde literary discourse with an eye to such predicative disruptions, where the traditional distinction between subject and predicate positions gets unraveled in the text. Her magisterial *Revolution in Poetic Language* is an extended homage to this disruptive process as developed especially in the works by Mallarmé and Lautréamont; she observes there, for example, that "modern poetic language . . . attacks not only denotation (the positing of an object) but meaning [*sens*] (the positing of the enunciating subject) as well" (58).

Importantly, such symbolic disruptions constitute a veritable revolution coextensive with revolutions on a larger social scale. She writes:

> Marx believed that capitalism has produced its own gravedigger: the proletariat. Imperialism produces its true gravedigger in the non-subjected man, the man-process who sets ablaze and

> transforms all laws, including—and perhaps especially—those of signifying structures. The productive process of the text thus belongs not to this established society but to the social change that is inseparable from instinctual and linguistic change. (*Revolution in Poetic Language*, 105)

Kristeva argues that, despite the apparent asociality of the signifying process practiced within a poetic text, there "lies the social function of texts: the production of a different kind of subject, one capable of bringing about new social relations, and thus joining in the process of capitalism's subversion" (ibid).

The new poetic subject is a precondition of a revolutionary subject who will engage in social movements on a larger scale. It is a subject of desire who reconnects with the reserve of libidinal energy and deploys it in the production of new literary and/or political works. According to Kristeva, any social movement depends on having secured such a subject as an alternative to an atomistic, unitary, and technocratic one (191); only a desiring and divided subject can forestall the risk faced by any and all large-scale social movements—that of replacing the old dogma with a new, potentially as repressive and stultifying one. This poetic subject intersects the usually opposed realms of subjective experience and objective social practice. As Kristeva argues, poetic text is a practice that subverts the symbolic and social norms by proposing new signifying devices, but it also presupposes an intense experience of *jouissance* through language—that is, its practice is indissociable from the subjective experience of heightened materiality and intense conflict rather than that of clarity and unity (211), privileged within transcendental phenomenology.

How can this poetic subject become an agent in the social world? This is the problem of "introducing the struggle of significance—its process—no longer just into 'individual experience'—where, in any case, it already is, since it is always destroying that experience—but also into the objective process of contemporary science, technology, and social relations" (213). In Bataille's terms, the "minor attitude" of the poet must be translated into the major attitude of a revolutionary (212). The truth of the poetic subject must therefore be "applied to all social practice, including political practice, but also, and increasingly, everyday, scientific, and technical practice. It is as if, after the emphasis that Freud placed on the subject's impossible coincidence with himself in sexuality, a return toward the practice of the text were necessary to recall not only that 'poets' had already discovered this impossibility but also that, as the precondition of their practice, the contradiction inherent in the signifying process is the precondition of all practice" (216). In sum, the poetic subject serves as a condition sine qua non for any revolutionary process that will avoid the risk of social suffocation entailed by any overly restrictive regime—whether it is ideologically conservative or progressive. This subject will maintain a spirit of perennial openness, questioning, and adogmatism that any social movement attentive to the nonconformist singularity of its subjects desperately needs.

Kristeva's conception of the speaking subject provides a powerful alternative to the transcendental egological subject from Husserl's phenomenology to the scientific subject from modern linguistics. It is faithful to the complexity of linguistic experience and leaves room for the internal crises, stalls, and breakdowns within the signifying process. It offers therefore a novel conception of subjectivity and an original contribution to the phenomenology of language. However, even though she defines poetic language broadly, in terms of its incessant signifying work, she uses the language of literature in a narrow sense to demonstrate what an open semantics is about. Thus, although Kristeva overtly resists a narrow, purely "ornamental" conception of poetic language, she never ventures into the realm of the prosaic language of everyday life to analyze the poetic process, and she does not flesh out the experience of the speaking subject in the so-called ordinary context of language use. There is a tension between the declarative and the performative aspects of her analysis: stating that poetic language maps onto language *tout court* but pursuing a specialized study of a range of avant-garde literary texts written by an established lineup of male authors only. Her narrow focus thus belies the broad construal of poetic language as a field of language-at-work.

More importantly, perhaps, Kristeva offers little clue as to what the transition from the minor attitude of the poet to the major attitude of a social actor might look like and whether it must take place at all. Indeed, she leaves little if any theoretical and practical space for resistance and revolt to oppressive linguistic norms by social groups. She states repeatedly in *Revolution* that the poet's subversive textual work has direct ties to social revolt ("The explosions set off by practice-process within the social field and the strictly linguistic field are logically [if not chronologically] contemporaneous, and respond to the same principle of unstoppable breakthrough; they differ only in their field of application" (104), but the validity of this claim is taken for granted and not really borne out by an analysis that remains riveted on literary texts. As Moi forcefully put it,

> it is still not clear *why* it is so important to show that certain literary practices break up the structures of language when they seem to break up little else. [Kristeva] seems essentially to argue that the disruption of the subject, the *sujet en proces* displayed in these texts, prefigures or parallels revolutionary disruption in society. But her only argument in support of this contention is the rather lame one of comparison or homology. Nowhere are we given a specific analysis of the actual social or political structures that would produce such a homologous relationship between the subjective and the social. (*Sexual/Textual Politics*, 170)

To frame this issue in sociolinguistic terms: how is the poet's subversiveness echoed in and reflective of large social struggles for change, including linguistic change, in the case of, for example, homophobic and sexist speech or racial slurs? Isn't linguistic change, such as the successful reclamation and resignification of historically offensive terms like *queer*, necessarily a result of work being carried out by social groups (LGBTQ groups and allies) and their transgressive and transformative speaking practices? Such resignifying practices unfold largely within the so-called ordinary context of language use in the everyday, but they deploy the poetic process whereby language becomes a field of incessant creativity and inventive usage, not unlike within poetic texts in the narrow sense. This daily social practice of linguistic renewal unveils the extraordinary side of ordinary speak in its potential to subvert the received linguistic code and to loosen the weight of conservative norms by unbounded play with words. This social practice therefore fits Kristeva's description of the poetic process as "an activity which liberates the subject from certain psychic and social structures" and "a dynamism which breaks the inertia of linguistic habits" (*Semeiotike*, 117–18, cited above), yet it simultaneously calls into question her seeming equivocation between sociolinguistic conventions and static structures. Sociolinguistic conventions constrain our daily expression, and they can be joyously transgressed in turn. They are stable and organized into abiding systems that get sedimented over time, but they do not fit seamlessly into the models of scientific objectivity from modern linguistics, which Kristeva herself rejected. In agreement with Saussure's writings from the *Nachlass*, language (*la langue*) is a social reality of historically sedimented, contingent, and revisable conventions. Therefore, there is room for resistance and revolt to linguistic (and other forms of) normalization within the evolving practices of language use, manifest not solely within the travails of an individual poet and his or her readership but also in the poetic labor performed by the so-called ordinary people who may deliberately transform the old language of abuse and subjugation into a celebratory chant. Poetic practice need not be first taken out into the streets; it exists (always already) in the social world. Its scope extends beyond that of a mere ornament associated with a narrow and exclusive group within society. Its productive force pervades the life of language broadly construed in its potential to receive, resist, and revolt against normalization, within individual and collective lives. This expanded sense of *poeisis* as linguistic productivity belongs equally to individual speaking subjects and to the social world, and it plays out within refined poetic modes and a more "pedestrian" wordplay. Kristeva's analysis of poetic language thus largely retains its validity in a social context, despite her own myopic focus on European avant-garde writing and inattention to the broader semiotic field of work.

Notes

1. This early work has received limited attention in the scholarship, perhaps because it tends to be regarded as a "structuralist phase" Kristeva went through de rigueur as one of the members of the 1960s Parisian intellectual scene, and which would have been largely surpassed by her adoption of psychoanalytic theory and practice as a primary reference for her thinking about resistance and revolt in her later work from the 1980s. However, when asked directly, Kristeva noted that she does not consider her work in linguistics and poetics as obsolete (personal communication over Skype/Kristeva Circle conference, March 2014); furthermore, this work cannot be easily classified as a "structuralist phase," considering that it investigates language in terms of subjective experience (following Hegel), and not structured systems only.

2. As presented in Simon Bouquet, 1998.

3. See Stawarska (2015) for a critical study of the posthumous *Course* in relation to philosophically relevant themes (the signifier/signified, *la langue/la parole*, and synchrony/diachrony distinctions), and for a positive interpretation of historically authentic materials from Saussure's *Nachlass* as linguistic phenomenology.

4. See Stawarska (2015) for a discussion of the Unconscious in Saussure's general linguistics based on the *Nachlass*, which would complicate Kristeva's critique.

5. As Barbara Johnson notes in her helpful Translator's Introduction to Derrida's *Dissemination*, his reading of the *Phaedrus* in "Plato's Pharmacy" (in *Dissemination*) follows Saussure's principle of anagrammatical dispersal of word-themes by tracing the systematic insistence of the word *pharmakon* and its relatives in Plato's

text. This dispersal illustrates the undecidable polysemy of *pharmakon*, translatable equally well as "remedy" and "poison" (and thus surpassing the boundaries of a single word) and occupying multiple contexts in the dialogue (XXIV–V).

6. See also *Semiotike*, 120, for a discussion of literary text as a response to other texts (*écriture—réplique*), hence a dialogue of texts, both as evocation of other writings (reminiscence) and appeal (*sommation*) to other texts.

7. The Neogrammarians believed that "the factors responsible for linguistic change must also be active in everyday linguistic activity," and an awareness and understanding of the relations between linguistic forms is implied in the two cases (Amsterdamska, 188).

8. For the linguists before him, "everything that departs from the primitive order seems not to be proper" (ibid); there is an assumption that perfection was reached within language's primitive order "without asking if the primitive order was not preceded by another" (ibid).

9. Derrida writes that "one cannot retain the convenience or the "scientific truth" of the Stoic and later medieval oppositions between *signans* and *signatum* without also bringing with it all its metaphysico-theological roots" (ibid.).

10. Judith Butler (1997; 1999), drawing on Bourdieu and J. L. Austin, develops a powerful argument in favor of linguistic reclamation; reclamation is tied to the basic view that language is performative, a way of doing (and redoing, and undoing . . .) things with words.

11. Kristeva's engagement with Hegel in *Polylogue* seems more constructive than the primarily critical reading developed in *Revolution in Poetic Language*, and I therefore focus attention on the former text, with occasional references to the latter.

Works Cited

Amsterdamska, Olga. 1987. "Schools of Thought: The Development of Linguistics from Bopp to Saussure." Dordrecht: D. Reidel.

Barthes, Roland. 1972. *Critical Essays*. Evanston, IL: Northwestern University Press.

Bouquet, Simon. 1998. "Les deux paradigmes éditoriaux de la linguistique générale de Ferdinand de Saussure." *Cahiers Ferdinand de Saussure* 51: 187–202.

Butler, Judith. 1997. *Excitable Speech. A Politics of the Performative*. Routledge.

———. 1999. "Performativity's Social Magic." In *Bourdieu: A Critical Reader*, edited by R. Shusterman, 113–28.

Derrida, Jacques. 1998. *Of Grammatology*. Translated by Gayatri Chakravorty Spivak. Baltimore: Johns Hopkins University Press.

Fehr, J. 2000. *Saussure entre linguistique et sémiologie*. Paris: PUF.

Godel, R. 1960. "Inventaire des manuscrits de F. de Saussure." *Cahiers Ferdinand de Saussure* 17: 5–11.

Kristeva, Julia. 1969. *Semeiotike: recherches pour in semanalyse*. Paris: Seuil.

———. 1977. *Polylogue.* Paris: Seuil.

———. 1980. *Desire in Language. A Semiotic Approach to Literature and Art.* Edited by L. S. Roudiez. New York: Columbia University Press.

———. 1984. *Revolution in Poetic Language.* New York: Columbia University Press.

———. 2006. "The Speaking Subject." In *Structuralism: Critical Concepts in Literary and Cultural Studies,* edited by Jonathan Culler. Vol. 4. London: Routledge.

Saussure, Ferdinand de. 1964. "Lettre de Ferdinand de Saussure a André Meillet." *Cahiers Ferdinand de Saussure* 21.

Saussure, Ferdinand de. 1989 [1967/8]. *Cours De Linguistique Générale. Edition Critique par Rudolf Engler. Tome 1.* Wiesbaden: Harrassowitz.

Saussure, Ferdinand de, and Eisuke Komatsu. 1993. *Troisième Cours De Linguistique Générale (1910–1911): D'après Les Cahiers D'emile Constantin = Saussure's Third Course of Lectures on General Linguistics (1910–1911): From the Notebooks of Emile Constantin.* Oxford: Pergamon Press.

Saussure, Ferdinand de, Eisuke Komatsu, and George Wolf. 1996. *Premier Cours De Linguistique Generale (1907): D'après Les Cahiers D'albert Riedlinger = Saussure's First Course of Lectures on General Linguistics (1907): From the Notebooks of Albert Riedlinger.* Oxford: Pergamon.

———. 1997. *Deuxième Cours De Linguistique Generale (1908–1909): D'après Les Cahiers D'albert Riedlinger Et Charles Patois = = Saussure's Second Course of Lectures on General Linguistics (1908–1909).* Oxford [England]: Pergamon.

Saussure, Ferdinand de, Simon Bouquet, Rudolf Engler, and Antoinette Weil. 2002. *Ecrits de linguistique générale.* Paris: Gallimard.

Saussure, Ferdinand de. 2005 [1967]. *Cours de linguistique générale.* Edition critique préparé par Tullio de Mauro. Paris: Payot.

———. 2006. *Writings in General Linguistics.* Oxford: Oxford University Press.

———. 2013 [1916]. *Course in General Linguistics.* Translated by Roy Harris, with a new introduction by Roy Harris. London: Bloomsbury.

Starobinski, Jean. 1979. *Words upon Words: The Anagrams of Ferdinand De Saussure.* New Haven: Yale University Press.

Stawarska, Beata. 2015. *Saussure's Philosophy of Language as Phenomenology: Undoing the Doctrine of the Course in General Linguistics.* New York: Oxford University Press.

Utaker, Arild. 2002. *La philosophie due langage: Une archéologie saussurienne.* Paris: PUF.

8

Peregrine Genius and Thought-Things

Julia Kristeva and Hannah Arendt on Revolt as Salutary Estrangement

Elaine P. Miller

In her essay on Louise Bourgeois, Julia Kristeva notes the French artist's ability to "re-imagine, re-postulate herself, indefinitely, without foundation," a capacity that forms an integral part of what she calls "intimate revolt" (2008, 249).[1] Playing on the etymology of "revolt" as a return or displacement or change, Kristeva traces this activity of opening psychic life up to infinite re-creation in the art and life of Bourgeois, but also in her own and Hannah Arendt's philosophical work, relating it to their common identity as immigrants living between cultures and between languages. Arendt, like Bourgeois, emigrated from Europe to the United States, where she cultivated a second intellectual and creative identity linked to her adoptive land, just as Kristeva did in moving from Bulgaria to France. Arendt referred to herself, quoting Schiller, as *ein Mädchen aus der Fremde*, "a girl from out of the foreign," which Kristeva interprets to mean that she refuses any absolute intellectual master, style, or identity. In the subtitle to the volume on Arendt of her *Feminine Genius* trilogy, Kristeva links Arendt's concept of natality or second birth to estrangement, another form of revolt. In this chapter I focus on this theme of estrangement as a salutary modification of visual art and of language, whether in poetry, irony, or narration, a theme that is manifest in the concepts of revolt (Kristeva) and natality (Arendt). At the same time, through Arendt, I argue that reimagining oneself infinitely without foundation, which suggests a pure interiority, is incomplete without the exteriority of action and commemoration.

Kristeva develops her conception of revolt in depth in *Intimate Revolt, The Sense and Non-Sense of Revolt*, and recently in "New Forms of Revolt." She opens *The Sense and Non-Sense of Revolt* with the claim that the title is meant to evoke the "current political state and the lack of revolt that characterizes it" (Kristeva 2000c, 1), although she also emphasizes the polyvalence and plasticity of the term "revolt" and announces her desire to wrest the word from its overt and narrow political usage (3). Poetic language and psychoanalysis can be thought of as revolutionary in a fundamental sense because they can access the archaic and overturn conscious meaning (15–16), uncovering something unfamiliar that is nonetheless intimate. It is in this sense that we can think of revolt as estrangement.

Kristeva evinced an early interest in the concept of estrangement in *Desire in Language* and in her 1970 article "The Ruin of a Poetics." The concept of estrangement, or "defamiliarization," was introduced by the Russian Formalist theorist Viktor Shklovsky in order to explain the structure of poetic language. According to Shklovsky and to Roman Jakobson, the function of metaphor in poetic language is the opposite of its function in informative speech. Whereas a metaphor in explanatory discourse aims to make the unfamiliar understandable by translating it into the familiar, the metaphor in poetic language translates the familiar into the unfamiliar, thereby illuminating something new about or exposing a new aspect of the subject under consideration. This theory shares characteristics with surrealist collages, which juxtapose commercial images with those traditionally associated with the domain of art, and with Dadaist collocations of art and everyday items. Defamiliarization also influenced Berthold Brecht's concept of the *Verfremdungseffekt* (translated as "estrangement" or the "distancing effect") aimed for in theater, which would intentionally aim to prevent the audience from identifying emotionally with the play and remind them forcefully of the artifice of the situation on stage by presenting an image, word, trope, or scene outside of its usual context, placing it next to something that it would not ordinarily accompany.[2] This kind of "estrangement" has a salutary implication in contrast to the Hegelian/Marxist conception of *Entfremdung*, or alienation, and may even be considered a corrective to alienation in its task of preventing the easy identification of the audience with the world of the play, allowing for a critical distance on it. Further, defamiliarization prevents easy incorporation into theoretical discourse.

In “The Ruin of a Poetics” Kristeva criticizes Russian formalism for remaining closed to its own philosophical presuppositions, namely, the “presuppositions of discourse concerning meaning as were broken down, in other respects, by philosophers from Husserl to Heidegger, and, in another context, by Marx” (Kristeva 1973, 102–3). These presuppositions include extralinguistic or protolinguistic elements that both surround discourse and make it possible. Mikhail Bakhtin’s research contributed to the formalist insight into language’s structure by questioning literary meaning in relation to both the historical development of systems of signification and the subject’s own coming into being (105). Bakhtin is important, according to Kristeva, because he poses problems or questions to language rather than attempting to solve them (106); this method of using language to question itself eventually became a central focus of her theory of irony, as I discuss later in this chapter. Bakhtin foregrounded ways in which discourse is continually interrupted by representations that are no longer descriptive, shifting the focus of literary analysis from semantics toward the rules of language and of subject formation (117). The attempt to work through these problems motivates much of Kristeva’s early work, in particular the task of opening up a place for consideration within formalist analyses of language of the speaking subject’s psychic drives and the materiality of the body.

In *Revolution in Poetic Language*, Kristeva focuses on the body through the formalist concept of estrangement or distancing by examining poetic language’s mimesis through rhythm, tonality, and other nonsignificative elements of language, which, she argues, arise out of the heterogeneous and contradictory movement of drive activity. This not-yet-signifying language, which in poetry is always co-present with symbolic language, originates in the body of the not-yet constituted subject still fused with the mother. These semiotic elements articulate quantities of energy as a “chora” or nonexpressive and mobile totality; these energy shapes, arranged and rearranged according to familial and social constraints, shift constantly throughout the body (1984, 25). In the non-signifying linguistic modes of rhythm, alliteration, assonance, and timber, these charges reappear in the modified linguistic form of what Kristeva calls a “second-degree thetic.” The semiotic as second-degree thetic appears only indirectly and through the mediation of symbolic language. In this way a plurality of connotations creates a polyvalence of the sign.

In *Strangers to Ourselves*, Kristeva expands on this theme of estrangement as a possible element of language formation and resignification by looking at the foreigner as a character in historical literature, in particular in a specific kind of text that subverts the type of *Bildungsroman*, where the protagonist achieves self-actualization on a journey of discovery. In some Enlightenment texts, the figure of a foreigner plays a significant role in this journey, encouraging an encounter with otherness as a form of self-transformation. Kristeva argues that in texts such as Montesquieu's *Persian Letters* and Voltaire's *Zadig* and *Candide*, the Hegelian process of negation and sublation is displaced; encountering exotic otherness results in a return to self as estranged rather than fulfilled, providing readers with the opportunity and capacity to evaluate and even to laugh at their own culture's limitations or peculiarities (Kristeva 1991, 133). Here the foreigner becomes a mask for the "ironical mind" of a new kind of philosopher, one who has the necessary distance required to effect social or political transformation (133–4).

Kristeva focuses on Diderot's *Rameau's Nephew*, a text that Hegel also uses as an example in the section "Culture: Spirit in Self-Estrangement" of the *Phenomenology of Spirit.* Rather than featuring a foreigner, Diderot's novel is structured around a conversation between "I," a philosopher defending universalist morality and ethical conduct, and "He," a nihilist and libertine whose idiosyncratic behavior is at odds with both social conventions and the rationalist's universalist claims. Hegel argued that *Rameau's Nephew* illuminated the emergence of a specifically modern consciousness that brought about a self-awareness of the culturally embedded nature of many of our deepest convictions and a recognition of the roles we play within society. In the novel, the nephew's persistent and dismantling attack on the philosopher's traditional positions illuminates the fundamental contradiction inherent in Enlightenment consciousness between an adherence to universals (the philosopher) and the simultaneous embrace of individual subjectivity (the nephew). Although for Hegel this contradiction eventually is overcome, Kristeva characterizes the nephew as a kind of intellectual "foreigner" who cannot be simply assimilated.

For Hegel, the ironic attitude of the nephew, while it demonstrates a certain freedom from the substantial universality of the past and attests to the birth of modern subjectivity, is nonetheless dangerous. In his *Aesthetics*, Hegel describes Romantic irony[3] as the anarchistic flip side of political revolution, an overthrow of intellectual authority in favor of limitless creative bravado. Such an attitude exults in the capacity artists have to literally create a world through the imagination. Although it is liberating and exciting, this stance leaves no substantial identity with which ironic subjects could identify, and they become like refugees, persons without a national or linguistic identity. All creation, whether philosophical or aesthetic (or, worse, a combination of the two), begins to have equal value, and this purely inward life, as Hegel sees it, would be as limited and poor as the tradition-bound substantial ethical life rejected through aesthetic revolution.

Kristeva, by contrast, follows Bakhtin and Roland Barthes in conceiving of irony as the task of the critic who utilizes language to put language itself into question (Kristeva 2000c, 213–4). Following Barthes's conception of language as negativity, Kristeva writes that some literature "literally pulverizes the subject as well as its individual representations" (212). Without the critical eye, writing may be conceived of as a kind of eternal truth, and writers as "subjects recording an always-already ancient meaning" (214). The critic situates the writer as a knot in this infinite unfolding, one who has stolen from and recorded fragments of "the old text" of culture, but who also retains the capacity to transform it in unlimited ways (Barthes 1997, 502). The critic seizes and affirms the negativity of writing, and, through irony, "crystallizes" a meaning from it that is ephemeral and subject to change. Through this provisional affirmation, the critic "retains a weakened but persistent effect" of the positive project of the writer, transforming the death drive into the negativity of irony (Kristeva 2000c, 214). Here irony refers to a type of meaning that can be gathered and knotted provisionally, but not conclusively fixed.[4]

Kristeva thus takes the side of the nephew who has no country of origin and whose stance is negative and critical but also transformative alongside and against the seriousness of the philosopher. He exists as a "boundary-subject" who can embody more than one symbolic identity at a time, straddling materiality and thought, personal identity and public expression (Kristeva 1993, 35). Kristeva endorses self-estrangement as a cultural phenomenon that returns all humans, by virtue of the "foreign" unconscious inside us, to our fundamental "otherness or foreign status" (Kristeva 1991, 147). When self-estrangement is historically overcome, as she thinks it is in Hegel's account of culture (146), the richness of this polyvalent subjectivity is lost. What art and poetic language and psychoanalysis can do is to draw attention to the surplus of meaning at the node of estrangement or contradiction, allowing or even forcing the spectator/audience to linger in foreignness for a while.

This process may be achieved not only in language, but also visually and through the other senses, as Kristeva discusses in other works. In *Intimate Revolt*, she considers the medium of film, which combines linguistic and visual elements and can be considered as a condensed, sensuous form of writing. For example, the director Sergei Eisenstein estranges the audience members from their customary way of anticipating the unfolding of a confrontation by distributing the spaces of a scene rhythmically along two opposing diagonal tendencies (Eisenstein 2006; Kristeva 2002, 76–77).

In *The Sense and Non-Sense of Revolt*, Kristeva analyzes two installations from the Venice Biennale in terms of their construction of a symbolic meaning that exceeds both intentionality and symbolic reception, expressing a content that, she argues, the audience can unconsciously sense as much as conceptualize (Kristeva 2000c, 10). The installations, by Hans Haacke and Robert Wilson, had visitors traverse on the one hand a crumbling, shifting, disintegrating terrain, or on the other a ground that sank and caved in under spectators' feet. Both artworks aimed to dislocate the audience from their most familiar stance, both their tacitly assumed bodily positions as they stood or walked, and their unarticulated mental presuppositions. Kristeva defines re-volt in these installations as an effect of temporality, invisibility, refusal, and displacement evoked by audience participation. Here the collapse effected by these works is not only rhythmically or structurally displacing, but also deeply affective. The works literally jolt their audience, giving rise to the instability and disorientation that testify to vitality amid congealed habit (Kristeva 2000c, 10).

Bourgeois, the artist with whom Kristeva seems to sense the deepest affinity, had an artistic style that continually shifted, metamorphosing into what Kristeva calls a series of new beginnings. In her diaries, of which she kept three versions—written, audio recorded, and pictorial—Bourgeois provides a wealth of information on her personal life and the ways in which it directly affected her art. Bourgeois associated her own developing creativity and her capacity to constantly reinvent herself with moving to a new country and culture and existing between symbolic identities. Kristeva zeroes in on Bourgeois's extraordinary ability to sublimate, turning sorrows into ideas and images and transforming herself from a self-described shrunken "little pea" shriveled by loss of love, to a "runaway girl" who uses sculpture to constantly reinvent herself or re-volt (see Kristeva 1984).

In Kristeva's words, Bourgeois and other creators, including herself, live a "peregrine fate," needing to constantly cross frontiers in an attempt to free themselves of themselves. In particular, Bourgeois's sculpture "Topiary IV," which depicts the lower half of a female figure with a bejeweled tree for the top part of her body, fascinates Kristeva. The figure stands on only one leg, with a crutch propped under a tree branch arm, indicating a need for support that belies the beautiful flourishing tree branches of the rest of its body, adorned with jewels. The piece, which Kristeva calls a kind of reverse mermaid, signifies the "psychic plasticity" of a transplanted foreigner who has rebirthed herself into a new medium. Kristeva ends with the enigmatic phrase "the seduction of crystallization" (Kristeva 2008, 251–52). This is a reference to "Cells," another work of Bourgeois's, described as crystals that "pile up, spinning skyward—threatening at every moment to dwindle, thin, deflate, lured earthward, tempted to come crashing down" (Kristeva 2015, 418). Though tempted to "crystallize"—the term, from Stendhal, suggesting an idealization and fixation—she forces herself to continually reanimate herself through the kind of activity Kristeva calls "revolt," and which Arendt referred to as natality.

Kristeva argues that Arendt's concepts of natality, thinking, narration, *inter-esse*, and *sensus communis* all outline a space for a discourse of salutary estrangement, one that has political implications. Kristeva refers to all types of Arendtian thinking as forms of estrangement. First of all, she points out that Arendt wrote *The Life of the Mind* and all her postwar writings in English, which was for her a foreign language, and that this act of thinking in another language not only shaped her ideas but was expressed by her as its own kind of "human condition," one forced upon everyone to a certain extent by virtue of the advent of modernity, but in particular on Jewish refugees after World War II. Not only in terms of this identity, but also in terms of her own thinking, Arendt claimed that she "did not fit" (Kristeva 2001, 185).

There are four senses in which estrangement plays a thematic role in Arendt's work, according to Kristeva, and four parallel senses in which Kristeva takes each of these up for her own work. First, estrangement is the condition of humans' relation to nature, one that is not a perversion of humans' essential nature but rather a fulfillment of it (Kristeva 2001, 141). The history of human action is bound up with what Arendt calls "the fact of natality, through which the human world is constantly invaded by strangers, newcomers whose actions and reactions cannot be foreseen by those who are already there and are going to leave in a short while" (Arendt 1971a, 242). These strangers open us up to newness and enable a birth into further dimensions of the self, a thought that might accompany our consideration of the current refugee crisis.

Second, Kristeva points to Arendt's discussion of thinking, an activity that presupposes a "two-in-oneness." Consciousness itself inserts an otherness into the "one" that each of us is. While for Kristeva this otherness within us refers to the unconscious, for Arendt the two-in-one is a conversation I have with myself in thought (Kristeva 2001, 183). The *bios theoretikos,* she writes, citing Aristotle, is a *bios xenikos,* a strange or foreign life (Arendt 1971b, 53, 198; Kristeva 2001, 106, 190). Thinking is further estranged from its logical sequence in a linear and chronological temporality—our thoughts can shoot toward past or future, back and forth, at will—as well as from any particular place. Asking "Where are we when we think?," Arendt answers with Plato in the *Sophist,* "no where" (Arendt 1971b, 11; Kristeva 2001, 193). For Arendt, "difference and otherness," the phenomenon of estrangement, "are the very conditions for the existence of [the human being's] mental ego," which "exists only in duality" (Arendt 1971a, 187).

Likewise, when thinking takes possession of a thing, it "loses its reality and acquires a curious kind of eeriness" (Arendt 1971b, 183). Because thinking requires the mind to go beyond mere appearances, there are entities that can be called "thought things," in contradistinction to the material world around us. In this category Arendt includes memories, fantasies, as well as philosophical concepts like Kantian ideas or Platonic forms. However, she identifies certain types of artworks as the potentially most estranged and estranging products of the activity of thinking, resulting in objects that create a gap in the flow of time from past to future. In such a gap, peculiar to human temporality, a beginning not fully determined by the past might open up. Her primary example of such a phenomenon is Kafka's early prose pieces, which present objects transformed by thought by being taken out of one context and abruptly transferred into another (184). Art is the result of human beings' overreaching themselves, producing useless things that are unrelated to material or even intellectual needs.

Third, estrangement refers to narration, which takes the thought thing and integrates it into a new story. Here, we can begin to conceive more clearly the political implications Kristeva sees in Arendt's concept of estrangement. There is an inherent connection between thought, action, and language in that they all presuppose a plurality of people and a politically organized whole that always encompasses difference (Kristeva 2001, 85–86; Arendt 1971b, 184). Narration, which Kristeva defines in Arendt as "the concept of human life as a political action revealed in the language of story and *history*" (Kristeva 2001b, 13), brings together language and politics, even that of strangers. In narration, the dialogue of the two-in-one of thought, the actualization of consciousness in the thinking dialogue between me and myself—another form of estrangement—is presupposed and externalized, and translated into discourse that can be received publicly.

Estrangement opens up a gap in the world when life becomes more than a simply a struggle to survive, and thought and action begin to be commemorated. Poetry in particular changes an existence oriented around self-preservation and the temporality of biological life into a historical, political, or public one by transforming remembrance into a tangible memory (Arendt 1971a, 169). This transformation is important because what gives art its meaning is not its mere relation to itself, but its context among other things.

Like Kafka's stories, narration takes events out of "reality" and turns them into "thought-things." There is a second, complementary activity of narration in which the spectators "complete the story in question through *thought,* a thought that follows upon the *act*" (ibid.). This completion can be thought of as a commemoration. According to Kristeva, history has two parts in Arendt, namely, the history of action, and that of "evoked memory," where the spectators of the action narrate and fix it in the mind of others, turning the *polis* into "an organization that is creative of memory and/or history/histories" (Kristeva 2001b, 16).

Finally, and most explicitly politically, Kristeva analyzes Arendt's reading of Kant's *Critique of Judgment*, which is organized around the argument that Kantian aesthetic judgment is eminently political. Arendt was inspired to teach a course, the sessions of which have been recorded in *Lectures on Kant's Political Philosophy,* by the Kantian idea that both aesthetics and politics presuppose a community on the basis of the communicability of judgments (Arendt 1989). Arendt reads Kant's "common sense" as a natural "sense of community," implying that human beings are not politically autonomous, that they need each other's company for the purpose of deliberation and reflective judgment. As Kristeva writes, judgment is "an activity that is central to the political space because it is through judgment that thought leaves behind its solipsism in order to participate in 'extended mentality' and 'common meaning' " (Kristeva 2001b, 67).

Kristeva refers to Arendt's critique of identity politics as a "radical estrangement that pokes holes in the various sanctuaries of identities or groups"; Arendt, she writes, was "loyal to the essence of the life of the mind that consists of combining the abrasive force of solitary questioning . . . and the greater community of judgment" (Kristeva 2001a, 105). The "who" of Arendtian political theory, thought through Kant's critique of judgment, always aims to speak in such a way that her words are universally communicable. Kant writes that in making a judgment that a particular thing is beautiful, the logical quantity of that judgment is singular, but nonetheless its scope is universal. When I judge something to be beautiful, rather than just claiming that it is to my liking, I make an implicit appeal to the judgments of all other humans, who, after all, have the identical cognitive structure to my own. Even if, empirically, all other people may not agree with my judgment, to say something is beautiful is to appeal to others in a public manner in a way that judgments of agreeableness, which are purely private, do not.

Arendt expands on Kant's brief remarks on the *sensus communis*, linking it to his claim that aesthetic judgments, in order to be universal, must be disinterested. By this Kant means that in making a judgment of taste we separate ourselves not only from our biases, but even more importantly from any desire, which would be bound to the object's real existence. Arendt interprets disinterestedness in a related but different manner. To be disinterested is to remove oneself from being among things. Paradoxically, in order to achieve a political consciousness, to create a new network of interrelationships, one must first estrange oneself from the web of relationships one has to the world, relationships that may blind one to the needs and rights of others. This severance is necessary in order for those needs and struggles to become visible for the first time.

Depriving human beings of the possibility of communicating their thoughts publicly would be tantamount to depriving them of the freedom of thought altogether. Impartiality can only be achieved through the process of taking others' viewpoints into consideration. Arendt writes that for Kant the faculty that makes this publicity possible is imagination, which allows us to bring to mind that which is absent or merely possible, namely, the viewpoints of others to which we attempt to compare our own views, taking a critical distance upon our biases. This critical distancing is a form of estrangement in Brecht's sense, which operates by isolating or removing something from its usual context. This capacity for distancing thought or estrangement is definitively lacking in someone like Adolph Eichmann, whom Arendt discusses in her articles on his trial for *The New Yorker* and in "Thinking and Moral Considerations" (1971c). As a result, he could seamlessly move from one context to another without feeling any contradiction, from the contextual determination of a Nazi official to that of an ideal prisoner and defendant.

Imagination removes the object of contemplation from direct sensation, subjecting it rather to reflection, and thereby allowing us to attain an "enlarged mentality" (Arendt 1989, 67). This process parallels Kant's judgment of taste ("this is beautiful") because in such a judgment one attempts to the best of one's ability to separate oneself from biases or interests brought about through mere liking or contingent past experiences, and to speak in a "universal voice" (Kant 1987, 59, Ak. 216). Arendt writes that the reason "love of beauty" can be encompassed within "political judgment" is that both types of judgment require publicity and presuppose a common world: "The common element connecting art and politics is that they both are phenomena of the public world" (Arendt 1989, 103). At the same time, it is important to underscore that the common world can only be attained by estranging oneself from one's particular context and biases and striving to inhabit the position of the world citizen.

For Kristeva, intimate revolt relates psychic life to the external world; as such it is necessarily dialogical and interactive.[5] In her latest work on revolt, Kristeva relates intimate revolt to maternal reliance, the process by which the maternal body/psyche prepares for its role in harboring and nurturing another being that will eventually have a subjectivity separate from it. As such, it opens up realms "where the One (identity) does not achieve being, or is not content with simply being one" (Kristeva 2014a, 81). In her lecture accepting the Hannah Arendt Prize for Political Thought in 2006, Kristeva describes the foreignness of Arendt's "who" as appearing only through mutual reliance. In addition, we can note the etymology of Arendt's natality, linking the political to the figure of birth into the world, and into relations with the other. In her Toronto lectures on Arendt, Kristeva writes that a "*total experience of the fact of birth* necessarily 'includes': being born, giving life, acquiescing to the uniqueness of each birth, being reborn continually into the life of the mind, a mind that *is* because it begins anew in the plurality of others and in that condition alone can act as a living through that surpasses all other activity" (Kristeva 2001b, 88). This polyvalent sense of birth implicitly links intimate revolt to a more political concept of revolt. Reliance implies a relation to the mother that is the necessary condition for rebirth into the world, but also one that must be cut off in this latter process, just as being a member of a universal community involves detachment from biases that bind us to our own particular needs and desires.

The "new forms" of revolt Kristeva discusses in the essay by that name are more explicitly political, and address struggles occurring in various parts of the world, particularly where religious fundamentalism has become oppressive or even violent. These forms of revolt can be described, in her words, as the "visible side of a reassessment of the religious domain" (Kristeva 2014b, 1), tracing a current that goes beneath the surface of the flow of images, exchanges of words, and tensions of identity politics and struggles, resisting fear of failure in order to open up the possibility of political rebirth. They are primarily concerned with inner life or the interiority of the subject, rather than either naming a revolution within language (as in *Revolution in Poetic Language*) or one that topples a government. Nonetheless, they necessarily involve an openness to and engagement with the other, a "broadened mentality" in Kant's language of the *sensus communis.*

Among several examples of this new form of revolt, the case of Rafah Nashed, a Syrian psychoanalyst, the social aspect of whose work Kristeva emphasizes, takes priority. Nashed's consulting practice progressively became a safe place where people suffering from the prohibition on free speech could simply come to talk and be listened to (Kristeva 2011). In this kind of analytic situation, Kristeva argues, psychoanalysis inscribes the being of the desiring subject into the events related, thereby integrating action and memory into a narrative; she thus argues that the relation of "amorous transference and counter-transference" is a form of *inter-esse* or between-beings (ibid.), a term she takes from Arendt.

The concept of the *inter-esse* is one that reappears in many places in Arendt's work. What distinguishes Arendt's discussion in the lectures on Kant's political philosophy from the other places where she uses this term is that politics is linked not to the *inter-esse* itself, but to a judgment that is without interest. We can better understand what she is doing here, in her last work, by comparing it to the way in which Kristeva appropriates the *inter-esse* into her own notion of transference-countertransference as political.

Kristeva compares the relationship between poetic genius and commemoration to that between the subject's memory and consciousness in the analytical situation. Unconscious, repressed memories can only come to the surface and be transformed into language and memory with the help of the dialogical situation that opens up between patient and psychoanalyst. The analysand is always more hidden to herself than to the analyst, just as the aesthetic exemplar will be proven not in the interiority of a merely subjective judgment but in its openness to the broader political and historical community.

Kristeva posits likewise that the success of a psychoanalytical cure would rest upon the movement, via the process of transference and countertransference through which the "who" of the patient is revealed or "born" to the analyst, toward the end of the cure. This new birth is followed by the opening up of new ties and new, plural worlds that come into being just as a new self is born in the process of natality. Insofar as Arendt calls the revelation of the speaking being that occurs with the appearance of her discourse political, Kristeva writes that "thus understood, the analytical experience is eminently political in the Arendtian sense" (Kristeva 2011).

For Kristeva, Arendt's "who," always attuned toward others in the *sensus communis*, is, like the unconscious of the analysand, open more to the temporality of others' memory than to the poet herself (ibid.). However, through commemoration it may be revealed (Arendt 1971a, 169). The "who" is an identity that only makes sense in a life that is not merely singular or self-oriented, and it manifests itself in action and speech, as well as in art. Poets and artists enact a story that repeats the events of life in imaginative form, transforming them into memories or thought experiences that would not survive were it not for this activity (173). Kristeva thus refers to Arendt's "who" as the "*inter-esse* of creative singularities" (2006).

The listening of the speaking being opens up possibilities for new bonds to form, as well as a revolution and revaluation of values and norms, "bonds which constitute the very essence of the political" (Kristeva, 2006). She calls transference and countertransference, as well as Arendt's *inter-esse*, "original worlds of appearance, which do not preexist narration itself, but are progressively constructed as the ego puts itself in question or 'in anamnesis,' so that a subject emerges with new, open and endless bonds" (ibid).

The message of Nashed's work, Kristeva suggests, can be summed up as "Be not afraid." In addition to her work giving individuals a safe place in which to speak and be listened to, Nashed and her colleagues undertook an interrogation of Sufism, a mystical division of Islam, investigating the "maternal" relationship between God ("thee") and the mystic ("me") that Kristeva sees as another dimension of the intimate relationality of reliance that follows according to an "acceleration of liberating transformations" (Kristeva 2002, 13).

Although Kristeva calls Arendt's "two-in-one" a "radical split between me and myself," she does not think it radical enough because it does not take the unconscious into account. Over and over again Kristeva remarks on Arendt's proximity to or compatibility with the Freudian psychoanalytic doctrine (Kristeva 2001a, 194f), in particular the act (of transference) whereby the interior of a subject becomes known to herself only through her openness to another. Of course, Kristeva writes that Arendt herself did not value psychoanalysis, but that nonetheless her work opens up a way of thinking how psychoanalysis might contribute to the political process, and in particular to the "restructuring of the political bond" (Kristeva, 2006).

A counter-claim might be made against Kristeva that even the most successful psychoanalytic cure, one that would result in the reopening of ties to the world, can only contribute to politics if it results in either action or commemoration, not just self-knowledge. Thus Kristeva's and Arendt's work is complementary. Today, in a time of hyperbolic narration, where even the lowliest of experiences can be recorded and repeated and broadcast to multiple ears and eyes almost instantly through new media, it is not narration, which always holds the danger of leading to least common denominator thinking, that artists must preoccupy themselves with. Arendt foresaw the increasing superficiality, with modernization, of the representation of human action, and Kristeva's critique intensifies the focus on this problem. Kristeva implies that art's role today is to re-estrange the overly familiar, just as Bourgeois's works did, and Arendt might have agreed even more strongly if she had lived to this point in history. This re-estrangement reflects the split nature of the subject herself, a split that will never be overcome, but whose contours can be explored and engaged in the work of art.

Notes

1. See also Kristeva 2002 and 2001c.

2. According to Jacques Rancière, this blurring of boundaries between art and non-art, in particular between high art and commercial art, is "as old as modernity itself": "The time when great art was constituted . . . is the same time when it began to become commonplace in magazine productions and corrupted in bookstore trade" (Rancière 2009, 49).

3. Hegel primarily has the German Romantic writers Friedrich and August Wilhelm Schlegel, who explicitly embraced irony, in mind here.

4. As Kristeva writes, following Jacques Lacan: "language, constituted as symbolic through narcissistic, specular, imaginary investment, protects the body from the attack of drives by making it a place—the place of the signifier—in which the body can signify itself through positions; and if, therefore, language, in the service of the death drive, is a pocket of narcissism toward which this drive may be directed, then fantasies remind us, if we had ever forgotten, of the insistent presence of drive heterogeneity" (Kristeva 1984, 49).

5. For more on this topic, see Oliver 2014.

Works Cited

Arendt, Hannah. 1954. *Between Past and Future: Eight Exercises in Political Thought.* New York: Viking Press.

———. 1971a. *The Human Condition.* Chicago: University of Chicago Press.

———. 1971b. *The Life of the Mind.* Chicago: University of Chicago Press.

———. 1971c. "Thinking and Moral Considerations." *Social Research* 38 (3).

———. 1989. *Lectures on Kant's Political Philosophy.* Chicago: University of Chicago Press.

———. 2007a. "Franz Kafka, Appreciated Anew." In *Reflections on Literature and Culture,* edited by Susannah Young-Ah Gottlieb. Stanford: Stanford University Press.

———. 2007b. "The Jew as Pariah." In *The Jewish Writings,* edited by Jerome Kohn and Ron H. Feldman. New York: Schocken Books.

Barthes, Roland. Preface to *Sade, Fourier, Loyola.* Translated by Richard Miller. Baltimore: Johns Hopkins University Press.

Birmingham, Peg. 2006. *Hannah Arendt and Human Rights: The Predicament of Common Responsibility.* Bloomington: Indiana University Press.

Eisenstein, Sergei. 1996. *Selected Works: Vol 4.* British Film Institute.

Hegel, G. W. F. 1975. *Lectures on Aesthetics.* Vol. 1. Translated by T. M. Knox. Oxford: Oxford University Press.

Kant, Immanuel. 1987. *Critique of Judgment.* Translated by Werner Pluhar. Indianapolis: Hackett.

Kristeva, Julia. 1973. "The Ruin of a Poetics." In *Russian Formalism,* edited by Stephen Bann and John E. Bowlt. New York: Harper & Row.

———. 1984. *Revolution in Poetic Language.* Translated by Margaret Waller. New York: Columbia University Press.

———. 1991. *Strangers to Ourselves.* Translated by Leon S. Roudiez. New York: Columbia University Press.

———. 1993. *Nations Without Nationalism.* Translated by Leon S. Roudiez. New York: Columbia University Press.

———. 2001a. *Hannah Arendt.* Vol. 1 of *Female Genius: Life, Madness, Words.* Translated by Ross Guberman. New York: Columbia University Press.

———. 2001b. *Hannah Arendt: Life Is a Narrative.* Translated by Frank Collins. Toronto: University of Toronto Press.

———. 2001c. *The Sense and Non-Sense of Revolt.* Translated by Jeanine Herman. New York: Columbia University Press.

———. 2002. *Intimate Revolt.* Translated by Jeanine Herman. New York: Columbia University Press.

———. 2006. Speech accepting the Hannah Arendt Prize for Political Thought. http://www.kristeva.fr/Arendt_en.html.

———. 2008. "Louise Bourgeois: From Little Pea to Runaway Girl." In *Louise Bourgeois,* edited by Frances Morris and Marie-Laure Bernadac. New York: Rizzoli.

———. 2011. Conference on Rafah Nashed. October 9, 2011. Accessed January 7, 2015. http://www.apadivisions.org/division39/publications/review/2012/04/rafah-nashed.aspx.

———. 2014a. "Reliance, or Maternal Eroticism." Translated by Perry Zurn. *Journal of the American Psychoanalytic Association* 62 (1).

———. 2014b. "New Forms of Revolt." *Journal of French and Francophone Philosophy* XXIII (2).

———. 2015. *Teresa, My Love: An Imagined Life of the Saint of Avila.* New York: Columbia University Press.

Oliver, Kelly. 2014. "Kristeva's Reformation." *Journal of French and Francophone Philosophy* XXIII (2): 20–25.

Rancière, Jacques. 2009. *Aesthetics and its Discontents.* Translated by Steven Corcoran. Cambridge: Polity Press.

9

Eurydicean Revolt and Metam-Orphic Writing in Arendt and Kristeva

Sarah Kathryn Marshall

In the tenth book of the *Metamorphoses*, Ovid (2010) recounts the well-known tale of Orpheus and Eurydice. Hymen, the god of marriage, is said to have presided over the couple's wedding ceremony in vain, as he did not afford his customary blessings. His torch smoldered with lachrymose fumes, fueling no benedictory fires, only a pervading sense of trepidation. These foreboding omens of a failed union were soon consummated in Eurydice's fated death and Orpheus's backward glance, returning her to grips of the underworld. In the *Georgics*, Virgil (2004) details her descending lament as she demands: "what wretched luck has ruined me—and you, oh Orpheus, what burning need?" His wife wrested from him twice, Orpheus endured a "disconsolate" existence, renouncing any "thought of love, or marriage" and disavowing the world of the living henceforth bereft of Eurydice's presence (Virgil 2004, 92). The doleful widower thus took to the lyre, inspired by his mourning to write songs of youths "dazed by unnatural desire" and penalized "for their lust" (Ovid 2010, 271). But Orpheus, too, paid the ultimate price when the Maenads, who "thought themselves to be scorned by such devotion," vengefully "tore him apart" (Virgil 2004, 93). Even death would not bring consolation to the unfortunate Orpheus, whose elegiac compositions survived the dismemberment of his limbs and lyre and their dissemination on the tides of the Hebrus. Only Apollo's pitying intervention would save Orpheus's head and reunite the lovers in the underworld.

Hannah Arendt and Julia Kristeva, each in her own way, give this myth a novel significance within the context of their own works. For Arendt, the story cautions against losing oneself to a solipsism divorced from a political life shared with others. Orpheus comes to represent the abstract thinking of the philosophical tradition, which, in its "burning need" for truth, does violence to a Eurydicean world of common sense where meaning is possible. Arendt seeks to reconceive both realms and maintain their relation in order to secure a truly human life in the wake of a totalizing modern political trend. In the first volume of her *Female Genius* trilogy, Kristeva attends to Hannah Arendt's use of the Orpheus myth to reconsider Arendt herself as a challenge to the authority of the Western tradition. At the same time, however, she investigates a "burning need" within this tradition that perpetually sacrifices femininity and the body to a phantasmatic phallic order of univocal signification. Despite the prejudices Arendt shares with this order, Kristeva deciphers another translinguistic order at work in Arendt's writing, one that allows Arendt to subtly revolutionize philosophical thinking. Following Kristeva's call to recount the desensing that makes Arendt's thought possible, this essay attempts to resurrect the myth of Orpheus and Eurydice through a reading of two thinkers who champion differential negotiation as the only salvation for a fractured human condition.

The Human Condition and the "Backward Glance" of the Storyteller

In *The Human Condition*, Arendt identifies a prevailing trend in the history of philosophy that privileges theoretical contemplation over political involvement as constitutive of human existence. Suspicious of the tendency, she proposes "a reconsideration of the human condition" in light of a pervasive modern scientific worldview she finds to be increasingly technologizing, normalizing, and automatizing. Arendt acknowledges that such a reconsideration is "a matter of thought," and she characterizes her project as "nothing more than to *think* what we are doing" (Arendt 1958, 5). But rather than thematizing *thinking* itself, which would place her square within the philosophical perspective she intends to reevaluate, Arendt focuses her attention on what it is human beings are *doing*.[1] On her view, the life of contemplation, translated from the Greek *bios theōrētikos* into the Latin *vita contemplativa*, has been extolled by the history of philosophy as "the only truly free way of life," devaluing the public-political life in the "realm of human affairs," which was problematically translated from *bios politikos* into *vita activa* (14). According to Arendt, "the enormous weight of contemplation in the traditional hierarchy has blurred the distinctions and articulations within the *vita activa*." And although she accepts "the validity of the experience underlying the distinction" between the *vita activa* and the *vita contemplativa*, Arendt argues that the distinctions within each of these domains of human experience have been effaced (17).[2]

Of the three activities comprising the *vita activa*—labor, work, and action—Arendt considers action to be the only one that is essentially political, because it "goes on directly between men" under the condition of plurality (Arendt 1958, 7). While all three activities attest "directly or indirectly" to a shared human world, Arendt contends that "it is only action that cannot even be imagined outside the society of men" (22). It is true that labor and work deal with the lives and world of human beings living together by sustaining the life of the species and crafting things that house humans and form the human world, yet they can and sometimes must be done in private, without direct contact or communication with others.[3] By contrast, Arendt characterizes action as that which must be performed in a public space. The actor acts for and with others, through words and deeds; indeed, for Arendt, actions have no existence except insofar as they appear before others in a shared world. Arendt departs from the tradition by aligning being or reality not with abstract truths like the Platonic forms, but with the world human beings share in common. "The only character of the world by which to gauge its reality is its being common to us all," Arendt notes, observing that "[i]t is by virtue of common sense that the other sense perceptions are known to disclose reality and are not merely felt as irritations of our nerves or resistance sensations of our bodies" (208). On her view, "appearance—something that is being seen and heard by others as well as by ourselves—constitutes reality" (50).[4]

Arendt's emphasis on political action in a common world situates her unique account of subjective experience. Perceptions, thoughts, feelings, pain—none of these is, strictly speaking, *real*, at least in an unaltered state. Rather, each must undergo a process of transformation that renders it capable of being shared with others. Because common sense is the only guarantor of reality in a fundamentally plural world, Arendt maintains that "even the greatest forces of intimate life," including "the passions of the heart, the thoughts of the mind," and "the delights of the senses," are characterized by "an uncertain, shadowy kind of existence unless they are transformed, deprivatized and deindividualized, as it were, into a shape to fit them for public appearance." "While the intimacy of a fully developed private life" will, Arendt thinks, "always greatly intensify and enrich the whole scale of subjective emotions and private feelings, these intensifications will always come to pass at the expense of the assurance of the reality of the world and men" (Arendt 1958, 50). A radical heterogeneity thus separates subjective experience from reality. And even though private, subjective experiences provide actors with a certain "depth" of appearance in public life, they must nevertheless be brought to light in the world of common sense in order for them to have any bearing on reality (71).

Rather than disparaging the private realm in order to exalt the public sphere (which would, in a certain sense, merely reverse the traditional hierarchy), Arendt stresses the importance of each as part of a robust political existence. It is the private realm that allows individuals to take refuge, rest, or reflect before reemerging in the public sphere through word and deed. These comings and goings constitute the locus of what Arendt considers to be a uniquely human life, one where action transforms anonymous existence into a singular "who" (Arendt 1958, 178).[5] Arendt describes "the disclosure of who somebody is" as a rebirth into a "web of human relationships" preexisting the individual entering the scene (183). Because action "always establishes relationships and therefore has an inherent tendency to force open all limitations and cut across all boundaries," the emergence of the "who" inaugurates a new beginning that changes any preceding constellation of human affairs (190). Arendt sees in this tendency the potential for rebirth in the public sphere humans share in common. Such reconfigurations, she thinks, demand to be recounted:

> The disclosure of the "who" through speech, and the setting of a new beginning through actions, always fall into an already existing web where their immediate consequences can be felt. Together they start a new process which eventually emerges as the unique life story of the newcomer, affecting uniquely the life stories of all those with whom he comes into contact. It is because of this already existing web of human relationships, with its innumerable, conflicting wills and intentions, that action almost never achieves its purpose; but it is also because of this medium, in which action alone is real, that it "produces" stories with or without intention as naturally as fabrication produces tangible things. (Arendt 1958, 184)

The fact that individuals initiate changes in the web of human relationships through action inspires storytelling as a means of recounting those events. While Arendt stresses that "nobody is the author or producer of his own life story," she maintains the story as that which "reveal[s] an agent" (Arendt 1958, 184). On Arendt's view, only someone other than the actor can tell the story of her words and deeds. A story can only begin once "the fleeting moment of the deed is past," at which time "the light that illuminates processes of action" in their "full meaning" becomes available to the other who narrates the events after the fact. Because the actor seeks meaning in the undertaking of deeds as they unfold, the story that will have been a result of these deeds is not immediately significant to the actor. "Action," on Arendt's analysis, "reveals itself fully only to the storyteller, that is, to the backward glance of the historian, who indeed always knows better what it was all about than the participants" (192). The historian-narrator's stories compose the "fabric of human relationships and affairs," but they are remarkably fragile. "Their reality depends entirely upon human plurality," Arendt explains, "upon the constant presence of others who can see and hear and therefore testify to their existence." If these narratives are to take on a worldly existence as "deeds and facts and events and patterns or thoughts or ideas," Arendt observes that "they must first be seen, heard, and remembered and then transformed, reified as it were, into things—into sayings of poetry, the written page or the printed book, into paintings or sculpture, into all sorts of records, documents, and monuments" (95). In other words, for the storyteller's tales to become a permanent fixture in the real world, they must be memorialized in works of art.

And yet, according to Arendt, "[t]he immediate source of the art work is" nothing other than "the human capacity for thought." It is not merely fortuitous that one of the few passages in *The Human Condition* where Arendt treats the activity of thinking can be found in the section on the work of art; the work of art is an important place of articulation between the public sphere and the private domain. "Thought," Arendt contends, "is related to feeling and transforms its mute and inarticulate despondency" until it is "fit to enter the world and to be transformed into things, to become reified." She deems this a case in which "a human capacity which by its very nature is world-open and communicative transcends and releases into the world a passionate intensity from its imprisonment within the self." Thinking, Arendt claims, is always already *potentially* public. Moreover, this capacity to transcend one's private experiences in thinking is the very same capacity that allows for the transformation and communication of the passions.

In the reification specific to artworks, however, Arendt identifies a "transfiguration" beyond "mere transformation"; for her, the art work is "a veritable metamorphosis" (Arendt 1958, 168). Arendt's account of the artwork relates the private realm of feeling to the public world of common-sense, through the intermediary of thought. This implies the presence of an inspired storyteller, one who is touched by the events to which she bears witness. This passion allows the storyteller, along with the web of human relations of which she is a part, to accomplish a transcendent metamorphosis in her recounting of the event she narrates by transforming feeling into thought and thought into art.

Still, there is a cost associated with this metamorphosis, and as Arendt explains, "the price is life itself: it is always the 'dead letter' in which the 'living spirit' must survive, a deadness from which it can be rescued only when the dead letter comes again into contact with a life willing to resurrect it, although this resurrection of the dead shares with all living things that it, too, will die again" (Arendt 1958, 169). Orpheus transforms his mourning into an artwork; he composes lyrical verses that persuade Hades and Persephone to resurrect his dead wife. Rather than safeguarding Eurydice's existence, however, Orpheus's backward glance annihilates her once more. Because "the living activities of action, speech, and thought" are, like Eurydice, "of an entirely unworldly nature," Arendt maintains that their "reality and materialization" depend on "the help of an altogether different nature," the Orphic "workmanship that builds all the other things in the human artifice" (95). In *The Human Condition*, Arendt does not develop a complete account of the trafficking between the "living spirit" and the "dead letter" that preserves action; for this her reader must turn to *The Life of the Mind*, where she explores the role of thinking and its relationship to the human world of common sense.

The Invisible Life of the Mind

In the introduction to the *Thinking* volume of *The Life of the Mind*, Arendt discloses a motivating interest in pursuing her study of mental activities; the question "What is thinking?" has been "plaguing" her since undertaking the project that culminated in *The Human Condition* (Arendt 1981, 6). Taking inspiration from "Wittgenstein's famous aphorism 'what we cannot speak of we must be silent about' " and Hegel's observation in the "Sense-Certainty" chapter of *The Phenomenology of Spirit* "that 'the This of sense . . . cannot be reached by language,' " Arendt locates the source of philosophy and metaphysics in "the discovery of a discrepancy between words, the medium in which we think, and the world of appearances, the medium in which we live" (8). This discrepancy leads her to affirm the alterity of thinking with respect to sensation and vice versa, as well as the incommensurability of words and things. Unlike Kant's "professional thinkers," however, who have historically privileged one of these domains as the only means of accessing truth, Arendt seeks to follow Kant's attempt to put the two in dialogue (3). The reason that this task has failed historically, on Arendt's view, is because no one has properly attended to Kant's distinction between "reason [*Vernunft*]" and "intellect [*Verstand*]," not even Kant himself (15). On Arendt's reading of the *Critique of Pure Reason*, the activity of reason is thinking, which is concerned with finding existential meaning, whereas the activity of intellect is knowing, which is concerned with cognition of the truth. The problem with traditional investigations into the activity of thinking is that philosophers "were demanding the kind of criteria for certainty and evidence that are the results and the criteria of cognition"; yet Arendt emphasizes that "*[t]he need of reason is not inspired by the quest for truth but by the quest for meaning. And truth and meaning are not the same*" (14). With this distinction, Arendt initiates her exploration into the life of the mind and the activity of thinking.

She begins by affirming the autonomy of mental activities in relation to the life and world from whence they arise. Human beings have the capacity to transcend worldly conditions in thinking, willing, and judging, that is, in mental life, though never in reality. With a manifestly Kantian flavor, Arendt stresses the importance of this unconditioned mental life for engendering worldly actions capable of impacting reality. And yet she characterizes inner life by an invisibility with respect to the world of commonsense appearances shared with others in speech and action. Inner life is, for Arendt, divided between the activities of the mind and the sufferings of the soul. Both are nonvisible, yet the activities constitutive of the mind, on the one hand, are "self-made," within one's control, and can be stopped or started at will; on the other hand, the sufferings constitutive of the soul are by contrast the result of the world's impositions and comprise a "more or less chaotic welter of happenings" from whence "passions, feelings and emotions arise," showing themselves in the world through and despite the individual (Arendt 1981, 72). Arendt associates the soul's *pathēmata* with the silent inner workings of the bodily organs in their specific uniformity, asserting that both are unfit to appear in the plural world of common sense. Unlike the mind's operations, which can be expressed in "metaphorical speech," the workings of the soul "are much more adequately expressed in a glance, a sound," or "a gesture." Beyond these "physical signs," Arendt maintains that feelings must undergo reflection before they can be manifested in the world; this gives them a "highly individualized form" appropriate to and meaningful for shared experience (31). "Soul-experiences" in their "unadulterated state" are, therefore, "body-bound" unless they are transformed into speech and action (32). A mental act, by contrast, does not rest content with what is given; rather, by its very nature, "it always transcends" sensation and passion through the transformation of the object into "an experiment of the self with itself" (73–74).

In the reflexivity of mental activity, Arendt finds an inherent duality in the nature of consciousness. Passive self-awareness, which accompanies all mental activities, actualizes an original "split between me and myself" (Arendt 1981, 75). Yet she does not identify the active component of consciousness, what she calls the "thinking ego," with the self (43). "[A]geless, sexless, without qualities, and without a life story," the thinking ego is "unconsciously conscious" of and through its activity, but it immediately "disappears as though it were a mere mirage when the real world asserts itself again." The thinking ego transcends what is given, transforming its objects—be they sensory or affective—and becoming conscious of itself through its willful activity of self-experimentation. The world, however, ceaselessly impinges upon this invisible realm, requiring that consciousness abandon its transformative musings to contend with reality. According to Arendt, there is an even more fundamental abandonment that makes this mental activity possible: a "deliberate *withdrawal* from appearances" inaugurates mental activities (75). "*Every mental act*," she stresses, "*rests on the mind's faculty of having present to itself what is absent from the senses*" (76). For Arendt, a "special concern for the general" motivates a renunciation of the world that is always presented in multitudinous particularity. It is the work of thinking, in an imaginative act of "re-presentation," which transforms an actually absent visual image into a present invisible image. Thinking, Arendt explains, "must prepare the particulars given to the senses in such a way that the mind is able to handle them in their absence; it must, in brief, *de-sense* them" (76–77). Thus, not only do worldly demands dissolve the conscious self-experimentings of the thinking ego, but thinking itself presupposes a renunciation of the world's sensible particularity as a condition for its imaginary activity.

At the same time, what is done in response to the "urgencies of everyday life" ultimately depends, for Arendt, on mental activities—that is, on "the principles by which we act and the criteria by which we judge and conduct our lives" (Arendt 1981, 71). The visible things we must do in the world of appearances are founded upon a withdrawal into an invisible mental life, which is, in turn, made possible through a disavowal of manifest reality. The radical alterity of these two realms leads to a vacillation between thinking and doing, presence and absence, visibility and invisibility, activity and passivity, but also between life and death. As in *The Human Condition*, Arendt maintains that the plurality of a world shared with one's "fellow men" is "one of the basic existential conditions of human life on earth"; she thus follows a Roman idiom that depicts being alive as *inter homines esse*, "to be among men," and death as *inter homines esse desinere*, "to cease to be among men."[6] Because the "outstanding characteristic" of mental activity is being by oneself and having intercourse with oneself as opposed to being aware of the "realness of world and self," Arendt aligns the visible-shared world of doing with life and the invisible-solitary activity of the mind with death (74). Still, she holds that "there is nothing in this ordinary life that cannot become food for thought, that is, be subjected to the twofold process of transformation that readies a sense-object to become a suitable thought-object" (77–78). Withdrawal from the world of "common-sense experience" arises out of "the quest for meaning," manifest in "men's need to tell a story of some happening they witnessed or to write poems about it." This nonetheless requires an abandonment of the commonsense world of everyday speech that is shared with others. Accordingly, thinking not only introduces death to a self who is aware of its reality, but it also destroys the other who is "removed from our presence" in order to be brought back as a remembered object of thought (78). Arendt thus reveals that the human desire to find meaning in life requires the annihilation of the self and the other to create a life of the mind; mental life, on the other hand, is constantly threatened with extinction from the demands of a world that requires one to do something to maintain her existence.

Ultimately, the original split in consciousness sets off a perpetual "intramural" war between thought (which is, in its supreme expression, philosophy) and common sense (which is crystalized in the figure of the Greek hero) (Arendt 1981, 80). Sensory experience, Arendt confesses, is in itself incoherent and devoid of meaning, but thinking's dominion results in the "inversion of all ordinary relationships," including a "reversal" of life and death, near and far, past and future (83–85). Through this inversion, the everyday world of common sense is associated with death, while the imaginary world of *desensed* recollection is exalted as the true life. What is actually close at hand is removed from presence in favor of a distant past now absent. The future is sacrificed to memories made present in an eternal *nunc stans* that paralyzes action and the possibility of change (84–85). The perspective of the thinking ego occludes awareness of this inversion and its basis in the disavowal of common sense. "[I]t is rather as though the invisible had come forward," Arendt explains, "as though the innumerable entities making up the world of appearances, which through their very presence distract the mind and prevent its activity, had been positively concealing an always invisible Being that reveals itself only to the mind" (87–88). Thus, the thinking ego perceives the intrusion of the world as a "withdrawal" or "oblivion" of Being and a collapse into meaninglessness (88).

For Arendt, the thinker's way of life is therefore always that of the stranger; it is a "*bios xenikos*" (Arendt 1981, 53). To illustrate just how strange this inverted world is for the one experiencing it, Arendt invokes the myth of Orpheus and Eurydice. "Just now," she elucidates,

> I chose to speak first of de-sensed sense-objects, that is, of invisibles belonging to the world of appearances that have temporarily disappeared from or have not yet reached our field of perception and are drawn into our presence by remembering or anticipation. What actually occurs is told for all time in the story of Orpheus and Eurydice. Orpheus went down to Hades to recover his dead wife and was told he could have her back on the condition that he would not turn to look at her as she followed him. But when they approached the world of the living, Orpheus did look back and Eurydice immediately vanished. More precisely than could any terminological language, the old myth tells what happens the moment the thinking process comes to an end in the world of ordinary living: all the invisibles vanish again. (Arendt 1981, 86)

Here Orpheus can be understood as a depiction of the thinking ego, which has withdrawn from real life in favor of the life of the mind. For him whose solitary descent into an eternal nostalgic hell, living—Being and significance—consists in a disavowal of an actual shared world where meaning is present and transformative. What matters is instead an absent but imaginatively re-created Eurydice. The demands of reality threaten this dead-realm of non-sense, annihilating the invisible life that the remembering widower has resurrected in thought. Reality, which is normally so full of presence, life, and immediacy, is bereft of all these qualities for the mourning Orpheus. Yet, in his attempt to reject an existence devoid of meaning, he is confronted with a severe, and no doubt painful, reality check—the vanishing of the invisible Eurydice. Unlike Ovid, however, Arendt does not abandon Orpheus to the bacchantes. For her, these two realms can be put in relation through the human linguistic capacity.

It is "only through speech," Arendt explains, that "[m]ental activities, invisible themselves and occupied with the invisible," can "become manifest" in the plurality of a world shared with others (Arendt 1981, 98). Speech, as Arendt conceives it, must be metaphorical insofar as it "bridges the abyss between inward and invisible mental activities and the world of appearances" (105). "The greatest gift language could bestow on thinking," the metaphor, is "poetic rather than philosophical in origin" (102). Quoting Shelley, Arendt describes metaphorical language as that which "marks the before unapprehended *relations* of things and perpetuates their apprehension" (102–03). She follows Aristotle, who says in the *Poetics* that "[e]very metaphor discovers 'an intuitive perception of similarity in dissimilars' " (103). The metaphor thus brings the two worlds together in their very alterity by finding a common ground. It does this by "turning the mind back to the sensory world in order to illuminate the mind's non-sensory experiences for which there are no words in any language" (106). "The metaphor," Arendt explains, "achieves the 'carrying over'—*metapherein*—of a genuine and seemingly impossible *metabasis eis allo genos*, the transition from one existential state, that of thinking, to another, that of being an appearance among appearances" (103). By way of a relationship of differential resemblance between words and thoughts, Arendt identifies thinking as "the mental activity that actualizes those products of the mind that are inherent in speech and for which language, prior to any special effort, has already formed an appropriate though provisional home in the audible world." Taking metaphorical language as a "token" that human beings have been "naturally endowed with an instrument capable of transforming the invisible into an appearance," she affirms that "the mind's language by means of metaphor returns to the world of visibilities to illuminate and elaborate further what cannot be seen but can be said." For Arendt, "[a]nalogies, metaphors, and emblems are the threads by which the mind holds on to the world even when, absentmindedly, it has lost direct contact with it." "The simple fact that our mind is able to find such analogies, that the world of appearances reminds us of things non-apparent," she goes on, "may be seen as a kind of 'proof' that mind and body, thinking and sense experience, the invisible and the visible, belong together, are 'made' for each other" (109). "There are not two worlds" for Hannah Arendt, "because metaphor unites them" (110).

Femininity and the Possibility of Eurydicean Revolt

Kristeva's response calls for "a desensing" of Arendt's analysis. "The creative imagination manipulates the elements of the visible world," she notes, "but only after those elements have been desensed, evaporated, killed—in a word, disappeared, like Eurydice's body, from the perceptions of sense and sight." For Kristeva, Eurydice comes to represent a sacrificing of femininity as well as bodily and psychic suffering to an Orphic imagination responsible for the life of the mind. Nevertheless, she understands Arendt's work to allow for the preservation of these traditionally sacrificed elements by making "Eurydice into an Orpheus who is capable of recounting the story of desensing" (Kristeva 2001, 98). She thus hints at a novel interpretation of the myth through a consideration of Arendt herself as example. Following an analysis of *The Human Condition*, in which Arendt exalts narrated action in the public sphere as constitutive of the *bios politikos*, Kristeva wonders about the "the woman" in Arendt's work.

> Does Arendt-Orpheus demolish Hannah-Eurydice? This commentary does not give the reader the impression that our author identifies with a sacrificed Eurydice, nor that she regrets Orpheus's productive imagination. Perhaps it is because the only way to save the elements of the sensory realm, and to start with, femininity, is to make Eurydice into an Orpheus who is capable of recounting the story of desensing. Only in this way, through a narration of this sort, can the story of desensing somehow become sensitive to each of the participants in action. To accomplish this eminently political act, we must operate from two sides at the same time, and we must possess, of course, a healthy dose of reflective wisdom, but especially of political *phronēsis*.

> In that sense, Eurydice, the sensory realm, and femininity do not evaporate under the pen of our politically minded narrator. (Kristeva 2001, 97–98)

Kristeva proposes a recounting of the myth, in which a Eurydice turned Orpheus saves the sensory realm and femininity by means of another perspective on suffering loss. This tale condenses several important themes Kristeva draws on throughout the Arendt volume. To seriously consider her proposition and create a new beginning for Orpheus and Eurydice, it will be necessary to explore Kristeva's account of female psychosexual development and its relationship to writing as a sublimatory activity.

Her analysis in *The Sense and Nonsense of Revolt* is particularly pertinent to the Arendt biography, because it is here that Kristeva situates the subject of feminine sexuality in relation to the political. Through an analysis of the female subject's relationship to the phallic order, she brings the private and the public together by emphasizing the contamination of sensuality and language in thought, the attestation of which, on her view, women are particularly well positioned to articulate. Although Kristeva's perspective is that of "private life, psychological life, art, and literature," it is not, she claims, "socially irrelevant" (Kristeva 2000, 7). According to Kristeva, revolt—from the Latin *volvere*, to turn or return—is the condition for not only the life and happiness of the psyche but also that of the social sphere. The revolt that she identifies, however, is not merely transgressive; it is also reparative, returning to "the archaic" to "overturn conscious meaning." Were it not for a revolt of this sort, she maintains, "life would become a life of death, that is, a life of physical and moral violence, barbarity" (15). Kristeva's task, as she defines it in this text, then, is "to illuminate the experiences of formal and philosophical revolt that might keep our inner lives alive, this psychological space we call a soul and that is no doubt the invisible source of what is Beautiful" (8). To accomplish this task, she therefore finds it necessary to allot a significant portion of the text to reworking the Freudian theory of female sexuality in order to account for an archaic mother-child bond that subtends and disrupts the paternal symbolic order. For Kristeva, it is this pre-oedipal experience that lays the groundwork for revolt as a human capacity for sublimatory thinking.

Kristeva reframes Freud's psychosexual theory in order to exalt, rather than disparage, the specificities involved in the development of the subject sexed female. The depreciation of the female body, derived from infantile fantasy and historically reinforced through cultural norms, renders women well suited to challenge a patriarchal symbolic order, provided they are able to work through the psychic and somatic suffering that such an order imposes on them. Kristeva remains quite close to Freudian theory, subtly reworking Freud's ideas by drawing out the implications of underdeveloped aspects of his thought. Like Freud, she maintains the primacy of the penis in the early psychic development of all sexes. On the one hand, Kristeva claims, the penis is "narcissistically invested" because "it is visible" and "eroticized" (Kristeva 2000, 72). On the other hand, however, its tumescence and detumescence in the boy, along with its absence in the girl, make the penis a threatened organ, allowing it to take on a representative capacity through castration anxiety and the acquisition of language and the law in the Oedipus complex. "Starting with this latent absence," Kristeva follows Lacan in maintaining that "the penis can become the representative of other ordeals of separation and lack experienced earlier by the subject" (72–73). Because it subsumes other lacks in the experience of the developing subject, starting with "birth, oral deprivation, and anal separation," "[t]he penis ceases to be a physiological organ to become a phallus [. . .], the symbol of the signifier and the symbolic capacity" (73). Kristeva nonetheless stresses the specificity of the phallic reference for *infantile* sexuality; it is repressed in the latency period and subsequently operative only in the adult unconscious. Because the castration complex is repressed as part of the infantile oedipal fantasy, Kristeva extends traditional psychoanalytic theory in asserting that the phallus and the symbolic order it makes possible are fundamentally "illusory" (98).

Clearly, Kristeva also follows her predecessors in maintaining the universality of the oedipal triangle. Although she admits that the "child-mother-father" relationship may have variations involving members of the extended family or same-sexed parental partners, Kristeva nonetheless situates her discussion of this developmental ordeal in the context of a traditional, opposite-sexed family structure. Thus, she argues that "[f]or all individuals, men or women, 'incest' implies the return to the female parent, the mother" (Kristeva 2000, 75). The prohibited mother is "an object forever lost and sought" for Kristeva, a loss for which the investment in signifying practices never adequately compensates. Thus, the impossible desire for the mother sets up impossibility "at the heart of the psyche," making it possible for the individual to become the subject of a language that can never fully capture objects with words (76). Kristeva extends the Freudian-Lacanian account, however, contending that "the little girl" undergoes a "two-sided" oedipal (99). Like the child sexed male, the child sexed female simultaneously discovers and invests both the sexual organ and thought in the phallic stage, allowing for her separation from the maternal container in order to become a unique and differentiated being (97). This "copresence" of desire and meaning inaugurates the Oedipus complex; however, the imaginary basis for the phallus, the penis, is perceived by the female "as extraneous, radically other" (99, 97). The experience of extraneousness in the oedipal alters the course of psychosexual development for the female subject, for whom "a dissociation is structurally inscribed between the sensory and the signifying" (99).

Although the experience of extraneousness renders subsequent symbolic investments disappointing for the female subject, Kristeva affirms that the female does become a subject of pleasure and the signifier; what is more, she often excels in symbolic endeavors and may "cultivate a secret sensoriality" that is not bound to the phallic signifying order (Kristeva 2000, 101). This is because, unlike the child sexed male, the child sexed female changes objects in what Kristeva calls "Oedipus^2." The experience of phallic extraneousness "reactivates" a more archaic sensorial experience of "sameness" with the maternal container, to which the female subject turns and returns throughout her life (100). As Kristeva puts it in "Fatigue in the Feminine," a conference talk she gave two years after the publication of the Arendt volume, "[d]eprived of a penis, and depreciated by the fact in all known cultures, [the female] adheres to the phallic order by bearing the unconscious trace of *oedipal prime*, of her polymorphous sensoriality, devoted to the desire of the mother and for the mother" (Kristeva 2010, 119). It is from this earlier, more fluid, and sensual identification with the mother that the child sexed female takes on the mother's desire: "the love of the father" and the phallic-symbolic order. (Kristeva 2000, 103). According to Kristeva, Oedipus^2 "assures her erotic individuation as a woman who loves men," while Oedipus^1 "assures her structural place as subject" (80). Because of this two-sided oedipal structure, however, female subjectivity is attuned to the fundamental illusoriness of the phallus.

Kristeva understands "illusory" in its Lain etymology, from *illudere*, "to make light of" (Kristeva 2000, 100 n11). Taking on the first person, she explains that "this law, this pleasure, this phallic power, and simultaneously, their lack, to which I acceded through the phallus—that of the stranger—is a game. [. . .] The phallus that 'I' invest is what makes me a subject of language and the law; there 'I' am. There is something else, however, a *je ne sais quoi*" (100). For Kristeva, this "something else" is "an endemic and ineluctable female homosexuality" based on the semiotic link to the archaic maternal experience, one that is ultimately "subordinated to female heterosexuality" (80). "In my interpretation," Kristeva claims, "the *feminine oedipal* does not 'undergo catastrophe,'" as Freud would have it, "but completes eternal returns due to the pregnancy of oedipal prime under and in oedipal two and leads the female subject to an eternal psychosexual incompletion" (Kristeva 2010, 120). On the one hand, the a-teleological nature of this process puts her at risk for exhaustion and melancholic symptomology, but on the other hand, it gives her the chance to acquire a specifically feminine plasticity and endurance, along with endless possibilities of rebirth. While "[t]he Freudian tradition has the advantage of having underscored the structuring role of Oedipus and the phallus," Kristeva laments that "it perhaps has the disadvantage of having done so without indicating forms of modification, transgression, and revolt vis-à-vis this order" (Kristeva 2000, 87). Her reworking of Freud's theoretical framework, however, provides some insight into the forms such revolt could take. "I see in the psychical bisexuality of the woman," Kristeva ventures, "a maintenance and an estrangement of illusion as illusion." And while "pointing out the incommensurable psychical effort required in acceding to this psychically bisexual being that is women," she suggests that such a being "never adheres to the illusion of being, any more than to the being of this illusion itself" (106). By including her own discourse within this phallic illusion of permanence, Kristeva suggests that the differentiating role of the symbolic order, while indispensable for alterity, signification, and sociality, is nonetheless sociohistorically conditioned, phantasmatic, and subject to metamorphic disruption.

In both aforementioned texts, Kristeva promotes writing as a vehicle through which the phallic order can be traversed. The subject invests in language as compensation for the loss of the maternal, which is thereafter sought endlessly because the symbolic order can never fully signify the desire for the lost object. Nevertheless, Kristeva holds that the "two sides" of sensuality and significance "will try to connect" through the "bridge of language." "You cannot say this traumatic excitability," she explains, "but, more exactly, you say it without knowing it, unconsciously. This other scene of the unconscious will take shape in language, which will become the space of another translinguistic representation" (Kristeva 2000, 82). In her reading of Roland Barthes's critical project, Kristeva theorizes writing as a phenomenon distinct from "the linguistic substance of language" characteristic of the phallic-symbolic order (194). She conceives it instead as a "formulation" of the negative (212), "a sort of diagonal line that, through language, inserts the intimate into the historical." Writing achieves another representation by inscribing "a translinguistic meaning that is never verbalized in the categories of language" (194). For her, writing denotes "the inexhaustible aspect of meaning, accessible only through infinite interpretation" alongside but irreducible to "the appearance of signs" (203). As a "movement that questions all 'identity' (whether linguistic, corporeal, or historical)" (193–94), writing allows for the emergence of a "subject-in-process" via "an endless refraction and reformulation of the system of language, the unity of the speaking subject, and the transparency of the social link itself" (214). Writing thus puts the phallic illusion into play as such, reconstructing the configurations of its terms and the invisible relations between them. In so doing, it remodels language, changing the significance of the signifying matrix by imbuing the positive and univocal symbolic with the negative and polymorphous workings of the semiotic. For Kristeva, the writer-semiotician avoids the despair of meaninglessness at the same time that she resists merely reinscribing her desire extraneously into the phallic-symbolic order by putting on display the equivocal, phantasmatic, and nonsensical aspects of the signifier. She thus "gives meaning to non-meaning [*donne sens au non-sens*]" by investing language, the communicative link to the other, with the sensual, nonrepresentative, and intimate depths that make each being not merely an instantiation of Being, but a unique and singular becoming (214 [*445*]). Kristeva's Orpheus, then, is no longer alone in the realm of the visible; instead, Eurydice inscribes herself within a metam-Orphic creation and, by infusing the symbolic with the sensual, disrupts and transforms the structure of the communicable. Eurydicean revolt, thus, revolves and involves these two realms, maintaining and repairing the bond between the archaic-semiotic and the phallic-symbolic, perpetually reconfiguring their links and sharing this experience with others in a common world.

Kristeva's Desensing

It is with this sense of the myth in mind that Kristeva desenses the Arendtian corpus. Using Arendt's very texts, Kristeva reconfigures their meaning by attending to Arendt's investments, the philosophical and personal commitments that make it possible for Arendt to reconfigure traditional concepts and hierarchies, despite the biases to which she remains beholden. Thus, Kristeva's critique of Arendt is indissociable from a clear admiration and gratitude toward Arendt's thought, and taking Arendt's life and works seriously means, for Kristeva, engaging Arendt's corpus in a transformative writing process. It is no surprise, then, that Kristeva challenges Arendt's apparently limited account of narration in texts such as *Men in Dark Times* and *Essays in Understanding*, where she disparages poetry and contemporary narrative structures for their failure to "seek the public's approval" (Kristeva 2001, 92). Kristeva affirms modern literature as a revolutionary *praxis* that recollects the bonds between binary poles, exposes and puts into question psychic conflicts, and creates space for renewal. "Life as revolt is actualized in the nonthought of writing," she asserts. No doubt gesturing to her own work on the subject, Kristeva asks, "Are we capable of envisioning other strains of discourse and action that would be the modern figures of this mutability, of this perpetual outburst of *meaning and the senses* that Arendt sought?" (44, italics added). In a direct reference to *Thinking*, Kristeva suggests

> [w]e might fault Arendt for failing to grasp that the poetic language of a narrator . . . is a way to join the "thinking ego" and the "self as it appears and moves in the world." More effectively than could any philosophical concept or mystical vision, poetic language of this sort can translate the *nunc stans* of the senses and breathe life into a recovered past. (Kristeva 2001, 92)

Here Kristeva champions the language of poetry as a means to overcome the dualism between the withdrawn and solitary "thinking ego" and the present and involved self of sensory awareness in the world with others. Binding this original split would involve, first, a "translation" of the *nunc stans* or "stop-and-think" that brackets the sensory imposition of the world, and, second, it would bring together the self involved in the world of appearances and the transcendent ego lost in thought. Such a translation would make it possible to resurrect memories within the present world of sense.

Yet Kristeva clearly understands Arendt's account of narration to indicate that meaning can be created within the world of appearances and not merely within an individual thinking ego. She cautions against deeming "Arendt's adherence to narrative" as "a denial of poetry." While Arendt's emphasis on narrative in *The Human Condition* is "inextricably linked with action, which in the end is always political," Kristeva points out that "poetry was intrinsic to the narrated word" for Arendt (Kristeva 2001, 95). She affirms that Arendt "rightly proposed the possibility of transforming hubris and morbid obsession into the *phronēsis* of narrated action: an action constantly renewed and strange, and for those very reasons resurrecting." It is this transformative narrated action, which Kristeva identifies with "the

Arendtian experience itself," that, on Kristeva's view, "is able to maintain the tension between *bios theōrētikos* and *bios politikos* without retreating into arid speculation, without taking delight in the banality of the vital process, and without destroying one with the other" (96). Kristeva thus shows that, for Arendt, it is the poetic nature of narrated action that bridges the abyss between the private mental activities and the public world of common sense.

Kristeva nevertheless admits that the narrated action that discloses a "who" in the world of appearances still occurs within the logical framework of the thinking ego: it is only "achieved through a constant attack on biological life" (Kristeva 2001, 174). She quotes Arendt from *The Human Condition*: "the essence of who somebody is—can only come into being when life departs, leaving behind nothing but a story" (175). Arendt associates the private, inner workings of the body with labor and women, placing them in opposition to the narrated disclosure of a "who" in the shared political sphere. The body is "generic," a site of "objectless, exclusively corporeal, and incommunicable pain" (178). The psyche is similarly "not 'appealing' "; its "pervasive ugliness" is "hidden" from the world, and it is the "same" for everyone, except in cases of "disorder or abnormality" (178–79). Like the sufferings of the soul, women and the body must be surrendered to the creation of a hero who is recollected in thought. Thus, even as a commonsense figure, the disclosure of a "who" appears to preserve a dichotomous and sacrificial logic. Kristeva identifies these tendencies as "Arendt's defenses" (180). Arendt sublimates these aspects of the human condition into her account of a narration that secures and glorifies the hero in the political sphere. In her attempt to "avoid subjecting [the hero] to an unchecked unconscious," Kristeva objects, Arendt "runs the risk of depriving the 'who of someone' of its body, making it cumbersome, perhaps, but also incredibly flexible" (181). It is this possibility of returning to archaic and sensorial experience that makes Kristevean revolt possible; if Arendt deprives "the who" of its body, she then severely limits the potential for political transformation.

While acknowledging these biases, however, Kristeva contends that "Arendt's reasoning is more complicated" (Kristeva 2001, 182). Through a comparison of passages from *The Jew as Pariah* and *The Human Condition* in which Arendt acknowledges sexual difference (her own as well as that found in Genesis) with a passage from *The Life of the Mind* where she aligns the body with the "given" of the "individual" experiencing self, Kristeva illuminates an implicit assumption within Arendt's thought. On her view, "the text suggests that human diversity is an essential precursor for action, with the original difference between man and woman at the very beginning of plurality. [. . .] Accordingly, femininity would not be merely an original given, but an intrinsic difference that is indispensable to the action that Arendt considered" (183). Kristeva goes on to examine Arendt's use of English in her later writings. Disavowing but nonetheless retaining her German mother tongue, Kristeva notes Arendt's feminine tendency to "preserve" rather than "dissolve" bonds even in challenging them (187). This acknowledgement, on Kristeva's reading, saves Arendt's thought from a "neutral," "asexual universalist logic" or a "poetic dissemination," allowing her work to inhabit the "realm of incarnation," which is characterized by an original difference that creates the possibility for action and meaning (187–88). Despite the absence of thematic considerations of femininity and the body in Arendt's corpus, Kristeva reveals their structural presence as indispensable to her unique perspective. Arendt's works are symbolic interventions that revolve around archaic and personal investments whose presence in her writing transforms the discourse to which she contributes.

It is Arendt's distinctly feminine vantage point, Kristeva goes on to show, that allows her to challenge philosophy while maintaining thought's necessity for life. She points to *The Life of the Mind* and Arendt's impatient elaboration of the dichotomies to which thought gives rise. Kristeva takes care to note the "non-sense and meaninglessness" generated in thinking's withdrawal from the world of phenomena (Kristeva 2001, 189). She attends to the opposition between the imaginary realm of the thinking ego and the sensation of reality provided by the world of "common sense" (189–90). She considers Arendt's notion of "desensing" as constitutive of the split between thought and the real (190–91). And she confirms an awareness of death as the only reality for the thinking ego withdrawn from the sensory realm (200). But Kristeva elaborates on the dissolution of reality that necessarily accompanies thinking. Referring to *The Life of the Mind*, Kristeva quips, "*bios thēorētikos is a bios xenikos*" (190), and she asserts that the thinker's "fundamental estrangement [. . .] demands to be taken seriously" (192). This loss of world, the strange experience of a morbid reality, is no doubt isolating, painful, destructive, and dangerous, but it is also creative. Kristeva explains that the "initial loss stimulates questioning concern, discursive thinking, and philosophy itself" (193). Accordingly, she rebukes those inclined to read Arendt as having dismissed the realm of thinking for its negativity in favor of a public world of appearances. Rather, Kristeva interprets her as "highlighting the conflicts inherent in the experience of thinking" while at the same time hailing thought as that which makes one "fully alive" (191, 200). For Kristeva, Arendt's work illuminates "a viable antidote to alienation":

> Thinking is what reveals and uncovers the "split" or the duality of the thinking ego, but it also provides the most effective therapy for the thinking ego when it sustains the dialogue between the parties that constitute the split and when it can question their differences while avoiding getting stuck in any one part of the dichotomies that gave rise to this experience. (Kristeva 2001, 195)

Kristeva thus presents Arendt's project as an instance of metam-Orphic writing, a structurally feminine endeavor, insofar as Arendt constantly renegotiates the links between commonsense and philosophy, passion and thought, the political and the private, Eurydice and Orpheus. It is Arendt's life, the singular semiotic experience to which she returns and expresses, that allows her to challenge oppositions without merely reversing traditional hierarchies. Here is "the woman" in Arendt's corpus (97).[7]

For Arendt and Kristeva, division is a fundamental condition of the human experience. Kristeva reveals Arendt's genius in her championing of the bond between a thinking ego withdrawing in search of meaning and a soul suffering the force of reality in worldly interactions. This emphasis on the bond, which is created in a narrative dialogue between opposing factions, allows for a novel interpretation of the myth of Orpheus and Eurydice to which Kristeva only hints. Telling the story anew requires a desensing—indeed, all thought does—but also a recounting of that desensing, of being lost in a foreign realm, of suffering the void of meaninglessness. All of this must be brought to bear on the shared world of appearances. These authors challenge the authority of the thinking Orpheus to a partnership with the suffering Eurydice, for they share a joint fate. Saving subjective experience, the world of appearances, the semiotic, and Eurydice also means saving imagination, thinking, the symbolic, and Orpheus. Salvation of this sort could never amount to a sublation, conflation, totalization, or reduction of Orpheus and Eurydice into an undifferentiated homogeneity. It instead calls for a negotiating tension that appreciates difference, a Eurydicean-Orpheus or an Orphic-Eurydice who is sensitive and articulate, thoughtful but passionate, vulnerable yet capable, solitary while involved. For Kristeva, this requires a certain encounter with femininity, which returns to an archaic, pre-oedipal experience of the maternal, investing the signifying process with its other. This semiotic rupturing, which restructures the symbolic register, allows for a rethinking at the social level and hence the possibility for another revolutionary politics. Kristeva's conception of the political is therefore one that is indissociable from Eurydicean revolt. Metam-Orphic writing is one way in which such revolt can be shared in a fundamentally plural world. By creating alternative narratives, Arendt and Kristeva each recuperate the role of Hymen in uniting Orpheus and Eurydice in thinking otherwise than the sacrificial logic that has dominated the Western tradition.

Notes

1. Arendt makes regular use of the third-person male pronoun to indicate human beings in general, and I retain her usage when quoting her directly, because Kristeva takes issue with this in her uptake of Arendt.

2. She will have left her investigation into the various distinctions within the *vita contemplativa* largely to her final and incomplete work, *The Life of the Mind.* Her main contention in *The Human Condition* is instead that human beings live meaningfully only insofar as they participate in the *vita activa.* In her later work, she will broaden the term *vita contemplativa* and instead refer to "mental activities" as constitutive of the life of the mind. Even in *The Human Condition,* however, Arendt distinguishes between cognition, logical reasoning or intelligence, thought, and contemplation as fundamentally different phenomena. See Arendt, *The Human Condition,* 170–72, 291–92.

3. A more complete account of labor and work is not within the scope of this chapter. For more on these activities, see *The Human Condition* (Arendt 1958). Briefly, labor encompasses "the biological process of the human body, whose spontaneous growth, metabolism, and eventual decay are bound to the vital necessities produced and fed into the life process" (7). The activities of labor "feed" life, and they are Sisyphean insofar as they must be repeated to ensure the continued survival of the organism. Work, by contrast, is teleological; it fabricates durable artifacts to create a specifically human world that aims at bestowing permanence "upon the futility of mortal life" (8).

4. This is a formulation she will retain throughout her work. See *The Life of the Mind* (Arendt 1981): "In this world which we enter, appearing from nowhere, and from which we disappear into a nowhere, Being and Appearing coincide. [. . .] The worldliness of living things means that there is no subject that is not also an object and appears as such to somebody else, who guarantees its 'objective' reality" (19).

5. For Arendt's account of the "who," see 175–83.

6. This idiom also appears in *The Human Condition* (Arendt 1958, 7, 51).

7. It may be true that Kristeva's own project demands a desensing. Despite gestures to the contrary, her Western, white, and heterosexual biases are evident. To desense Kristeva's work (an undertaking in which she is no doubt already engaged;

see, for example, the conclusion to her Female Genius tryptic [Kristeva 2004, 403–27]) would demand the kind of attention to the translinguistic in her writing that Kristeva attends to in the writings of Hannah Arendt. If white supremacy, colonialism, and heteronormativity are indeed part and parcel of the symbolic order Kristeva describes, then it could be possible to traverse this phantasm with inscriptions that attest to other experiences. Such a task is quite clearly beyond the scope of this chapter; nevertheless, Arendt and Kristeva inspire a certain ethics in their readers, one that calls for revolt at the sites where alterity is effaced. It would, therefore, be an infidelity to both authors were one to disavow this issue.

Pleshette DeArmitt (2014) had begun to address this in her book *The Right to Narcissism: The Case for an Impossible Self-Love.* Attending closely to Kristeva's logic and the structural implications of her analyses, Pleshette insists that the third party, which allows for individuation from the semiotic maternal container, cannot be strictly identified with the father. What is imperative for Pleshette is that the mother have some other desire mediated through the symbolic register in which the child can begin to differentiate itself and an other.

Works Cited

Arendt, Hannah. 1958. *The Human Condition.* Chicago: University of Chicago Press.

———. 1981. *The Life of the Mind.* San Diego: Harcourt Inc.

DeArmitt, Pleshette. 2014. "Derrida: The Mourning of Narcissus." In *The Right to Narcissism: A Case for an Im-Possible Self-Love,* edited by Pleshette DeArmitt, 91–138. New York: Fordham University Press.

Kristeva, Julia. 2000. *The Sense and Nonsense of Revolt.* Translated by Jeanine Herman. New York: Columbia University Press. (1996. *Sens et non-sens de la révolte.* Paris: Fayard)

———. 2001. *Hannah Arendt.* Translated by Ross Guberman. New York: Columbia University Press.

———. 2004. *Colette.* Translated by Ross Guberman. New York: Columbia University Press.

———. 2010. "Fatigue in the Feminine." In *Hatred and Forgiveness,* translated by Jeanine Herman, 144–25. New York: Columbia University Press.

Ovid. 2010. *Metamorphoses.* Translated by Stanley Lombardo. Indianapolis: Hackett Publishing Company.

Virgil. 2009. *Georgics.* Translated by Peter Fallon. Oxford: Oxford University Press.

10

At the Risk of Thinking

On Writing an Intellectual Biography of Julia Kristeva

Alice Jardine

Part 1

Kristeva. I have to assume that everyone reading this shares a semiotic sense of who we are referring to, around whom we are circling at so many events and in so many publications. We circle her, follow her, read her, listen to her, teach her, value her. There is comfort in the stability of her image, even across time.

Yet even this remarkable woman whom we presume to know is the first one to admit she is quite at a loss to know who is Julia Kristeva. It was the very first thing she said during the first of my many interviews with her via teleconference and in person over the past couple of years. Here's how she began our "biography tapes":

> It's very difficult. Sometimes I do not recognize myself in the demands people make of me to talk about Julia Kristeva. Because I'm not entirely sure who this woman is. There is an image, there is a received idea, there is even sometimes a cult . . .[1]

She asks: who is this woman Julia Kristeva? She travels around the world, accepting honors and speaking to huge audiences wherever she goes—

often to her genuine astonishment. She knows, as a practicing psychoanalyst, that autobiography is a "false genre." And on top of that, she has been psychoanalyzed, leading to what she sees as a complete "transvaluation of the self."

But what about biography? What about someone else taking on the role of biographer? Why should someone else care "who Kristeva is"? Why should I care? Who am I to care?

In her book *Risking Who One Is*, my friend and colleague Susan Suleiman raises the question of how to operate critically as an intellectual when the work one is interpreting has been produced by a contemporary, by a living artist, philosopher-critic, or writer with whom one feels deep affinity (1994). She unpacks, through multiple examples, how complex this question is in terms of identity, and I would add, especially in the twenty-first-century context of seriously competing identity models: for example, the model celebrating postidentity global, cosmopolitan citizenship versus models of authoritarian, often nationalistic when not proto-fascistic reactions worldwide today against all new forms of what Kristeva calls "happy cosmopolitanism." For those of us politically and epistemologically engaged by many of the same urgent questions as the still-living subject-object of our biographical, artistic, and/or critical fascinations, in the context of world politics today and the relative silence of intellectuals confronted by those politics, the question of how to proceed with integrity can be paralyzing. And what about when one knows one's subject-object personally? Maybe even likes the person? Perhaps even considers the person a friend?

On top of, or alongside the question of, writing about one's contemporaries in the current global political climate, I have lately been asking myself many of the same questions Suleiman asks about "strong autobiographical reading"—reading autobiographically even when one doesn't intend to. In the post-postepistemological, political, and artistic situation today, what does it mean to engage in strong autobiographical reading practices to sort through the chaos of how to live, think, and work? Does that kind of reading as a search for the sense of one's own life and work amount to intellectual narcissism at a moment when intellectuals need to adopt perhaps a more historically familiar "committed" model of intellectual labor? Does the practice of "strong autobiographical reading" apply in the same way to critical and philosophical narrative that it does to fictional, poetic, or imagistic story telling? Must it most often work through identification or through rejection—or can it somehow involve both? What about writing biography through strong autobiographical reading? Would it be possible to do strong autobiographical reading through writing biography without resorting to analogy, or allowing oneself to get in the way of the biographical project, without occupying all the space?

I am asking many of these questions because I am currently writing an intellectual biography of Julia Kristeva, asking what constitutes her originality and authority for the twenty-first century, with emphasis on her call for the urgent revival of the humanities. There is no doubt that Kristeva is one of the most important intellectuals of the twentieth and twenty-first centuries, yet her work is often marginalized, critiqued, even maligned on the Right and also on the Left. I have never fully understood why—although sometimes I think I do. What I know for sure is that since I first started reading Kristeva in the mid-1970s, I have mostly remained fascinated by her loyal defense of the creative, psychic process at the heart of the literary and artistic humanities and her ability to maintain that defense across mind-numbing historical change. Do I still read Kristeva today because of that defense? Or is it because of my fascination with her status as a "migrant female intellectual"? Or is it her identity as an intellectual and writer who is also a mother? Or is it her advocacy for those who are marginalized in scary new ways in an increasingly technologically flattened-out world? Or is it my attraction to risk: to the risk of thinking, to the idea of putting at risk my sense of who I am while embracing Julia Kristeva's call for all of us to take the risk of thinking? *Period.*

Sometimes I wonder whether the strong resistance to Kristeva's thought, particularly on the Anglo-American Left, is an allergy to thinking—*period.* Whatever the reason, the critiques are serious, loud, and often difficult to answer:

> —There is the familiar accusation of elitism, most often accompanied by an allusion to the famous difficulty of her prose, a stylistic approach associated with postwar High French poststructuralism and its emphasis on the power of language to shape reality.
>
> —There are the accusations of Eurocentrism, the argument that her emphasis on "caring for Europe" (*soigner l'Europe*), her emphasis on and celebration of the singularities at the heart of European intellectual history, have led her to naive ethnocentric tourism (for example, in China) and, more importantly, to false theoretical generalizations about the "others" she so values. This leads to accusations that she isn't Marxist enough, or postcolonial enough, or feminist enough.

—And then, to add fuel to the fire, there is the often virulent critique of her persistent interest in religion, especially the history of mysticism at the heart of Judeo-Christianity. She has, after all, been called one of the most important theologians of the twentieth century as she has laid out the benefits of spirituality for a secularized world.

—Or there is the often hysterical complaint about her association with and intellectual camaraderie with a small gang of—to put it mildly—controversial French postwar male writers and thinkers, particularly those not critiquing forcefully enough the hegemonic power of advanced neoliberal capitalism.

—And then there's her allegiance to psychoanalysis, with all of its nineteenth-century echoes of the heteronormative bourgeoisie. Most recently, I couldn't believe the angry hullabaloo about her psychoanalytic focus on male adolescence, and the adolescent's need to believe in ideals, and how when those ideals are shattered it can lead to nihilism, indeed to crisis, with Kristeva making reference not only to Western male adolescents, but also to young men in Middle Eastern cultures being pulled into nihilistic extremism. You would have thought she was saying there are no other reasons for terrorism than teenage angst . . .

—But by far the longest, loudest, most frequent—and snarky—complaint about Kristeva, particularly on the part of feminists, is her long, loyal, passionate, very public love affair with Philippe Sollers—from their earliest days to now:

—In Philippe Sollers's words . . .

> What is a *coup de foudre*? A *coup de foudre*, it's a very common expression. It seems it actually happens from time to time . . . [Kristeva: ". . . with clouds full of electricity . . ."] There are attractions . . . But what is a *coup de foudre* that endures? That, well, that's something else. It's complex. It must have to do with very complex individuals who can eventually reignite each other from time to time . . .[2] (Damisch, 2011)

What is a *coup de foudre* that endures over time?

I must ask *myself* this question, of course, because I had one of those for Julia Kristeva in my youth. Of the intellectual kind at least. . . . And it has endured. I remain fascinated by Kristeva's work—in an unresolved kind of way. I made peace, for example, a long time ago with Colette, Simone de Beauvoir, Virginia Wolf, Margaret Atwood. I made peace with those texts on which I had operated an obsessively "strong autobiographical reading" for decades. My fascination for Kristeva's work is different. I am writing an intellectual biography of her by engaging in a strong autobiographical reading of her, putting myself at risk in part, I must confess, in order to be able to fully engage with the abovementioned critiques of a body of work I admire and find vitally important. But I am also searching for an etiology that is not an origin, but a start to figuring out what it means to be an *intellectual* in the twenty-first century. Not an aesthete. Not an expert. But what Kristeva calls a contestatory intellectual. That's what I try to be. But it's hard. And I haven't succeeded yet.

I first met Julia Kristeva when I was twenty-four years old, a young, naive woman in my first year of graduate work at Columbia. I was work-study, and the then chair of French, Michael Riffaterre, asked me if I wanted to be Julia Kristeva's research assistant. The Kristeva I met then—only ten years my senior—was mesmerizing to me in every way. I was particularly struck by the fact that, even as a relatively young intellectual, she could be viciously attacked by Marxist graduate students and by right-wing faculty—without batting an eye! She didn't really care. She was too busy devouring Mallarmé.

But what I remember most acutely about her was her simultaneous intellectual brilliance and her devotion to her baby son, David, born in 1975. I have a vivid memory of Kristeva holding David in one arm and talking on the phone at her shoulder while sorting through the books I had just brought her from the library. In the beginning, it was the way Kristeva looked at David that fascinated me the most.

Over the years, I have stayed very attached to David, first babysitting him when he was very small, singing "Twinkle, Twinkle Little Star" with him over and over and over again. Over the years, it has never entered my head to ask Kristeva about David's developmental and cognitive delays and disabilities. He was—and is—gorgeous. Always just himself. Just David. And adored by both of his parents, who have done everything humanly possible to make space for his exquisite singularity.

Most recently, I spent some time on the Ile de Re with David, listening to his thirty-nine-year-old self recite LaRochefoucauld by heart. It was also there where I conducted a series of intensive interviews with Kristeva about her life. Yes, I decided to take the risk . . . the risk of figuring out who Julia Kristeva is for me through strong autobiographical reading and the writing of her biography. I decided to take seriously one of the strongest things I have learned from Kristeva—the importance of the intimate. I am following my desire to understand better how she connects her "vie intime" with the thought processes she makes public through constant writing. That is something I want to learn to do better myself.

But I also want to engage those pesky critiques I mentioned. Recently Kristeva said in an interview with the *Huffington Post* that she is an "energetic pessimist"—which, yes, describes me exactly. And this world we are living in right now feeds my energetic pessimism so acutely that I have come to be very sure that

> —This world we're living in needs Kristeva's strong ethical drive as a cosmopolitan and contestatory intellectual;
>
> —It needs her insistence on thinking not about identity, but about how to achieve and value singularity;
>
> —It needs her strong insistence on secularism and a new, renewed form of humanism, a transvaluation of classical religion, with the infinite Chain of Being coming to us through books rather than through God and religion;
>
> —It needs her valuing of the arts and literature as unique forms of thought, as when she emphasized recently in China, agreeing with a colleague, that the only way to face up to totalitarian thought is to learn about and teach to new generations [the value of] the plurality of languages, literatures, and mentalities of the world and how to problematize and analyze them (Kristeva 2010);
>
> —It needs her ability to embrace, indeed embody, marginalization and vulnerability. It needs her insistence on all the edges of subjectivity: mental illness, delinquency, mysticism, maternity—for example, through her recent work on disability as an opportunity, not as a lack to be fixed through charity, not as a deprivation, but as irreducible singularity. She reminds us that

> Jesus was the disabled God, carrying our mortality for us, carrying our fear of our own mortality;
>
> —The world really needs Kristeva's resistance to mediatization, to mechanization, her pushing back against an increasingly digitalized, commodified technocracy. This is especially so at a time when the complex dance between what she calls "the need to believe" and "the desire to know" is being replaced by a trudging obsession with how one might fit into the marketplace, where everything and everyone can be bought and sold—preferably in English.

Kristeva has sutured my attention to her insistence on the importance of revolt, even small, localized, "intimate revolt" in the West, a continuous revolt against allowing our inner life—whether one calls it *soul* or *psyche*—to be colonized by media spectacle, capitalist consumption, and information overload.

I want to emphasize all of those things in this intellectual biography, against her critics, and for the sake of my own intellectual narrative.

But, first, I want to insist on the fact that at the heart of Kristeva's own strong thinking over forty years, there is an intimately experiential shape that I especially want to highlight in my text. Kristeva arrived in Paris in 1965 very much the young woman educated in the Eastern bloc, an immigrant. During the 1960s and 1970s, she was at her most theoretical, developing her abstract vocabularies with breathless rapidity. While focused on gendered subjectivity, she was careful to distance herself from feminism; when she focused on nationality, she looked to the United States or to China, not to Eastern Europe; her own status as a mother was mostly hidden from public view. Any conceivable autobiographical voice there might have been at that point was buried under some very heavy prose.

Kristeva's work published in the 1980s and 1990s shifted radically, and very quickly, toward a more forthright consideration of what she saw as a serious crisis at the heart of Western civilization, a crisis brought on in large part by the assault of technology and the media on human subjectivity. Since 2000, Kristeva has continued her call begun in the 1990s for new, complex, flexible, hybrid subjectivities and for the socio-political acceptance of otherness in Europe and around the world. But she has left behind the scientifically abstract, theoretical prose of the first two decades of her work as well as the predictive prose of the following twenty years, and returned to her own experiential beginnings. She writes more personally of foreignness, migration, and immigration; she explores more openly femininity, women, and motherhood; she questions world religions, atheism, and current relationships to the sacred; she worries about the ends and echoes of the Cold War and its effects on the formerly Communist world, particularly Eastern Europe. She also acts publically on behalf of the vulnerable.

It is the return of Kristeva's work in the early twenty-first century to her own, earlier life experiences that I want to explore most deeply in the work ahead of me, while exploring for myself the shape of that experiential/intellectual trajectory.

Part 2

Julia Kristeva would be first in line to say that one is not, cannot be determined by one's childhood:

> Many things from my childhood resonate with what I am doing today. But if I am a Freudian, it is because I believe, like Freud, that we are not determined by our childhood—contrary to what many think about Freudianism. Our childhood provides us with the seeds of our personality, but what one rediscovers in analysis is that one has reconstructed one's childhood. Something was given to us, but we have rebuilt it. Therefore one never finds the exact, current situation in the past. Lots of people who think they will are actually disappointed by analysis. They complain: "But I can't find The Memory that can explain who I am now . . . I can't find the Delicate Flower . . . The Love . . . The Enigma . . ." That's why I say that memories are not deterministic, they are invitations to travel . . .[3] (Damisch, 2011)

And yet . . .

Kristeva was born in Sliven, Bulgaria, on June 24, 1941—two days after World War II became a daily reality in that part of the world with the German invasion of the Soviet Union. Sliven is at the foot of the Balkan Mountains and not far from the Black Sea. She would live there until the family relocated to Sofia after the war.

Her parents could not have but felt like she was a glimpse of bright joy in the midst of the darkness of war. Kristeva was born into the chaos of war:

> There was a song that we sang during my childhood—a Russian song—that goes like this [JK sings the song with clear delight] . . . So it was the 22nd of June 1941, at 8 o'clock in the evening I think . . . Kiev was bombed and we were at war . . . And so me, I was born two days after. Sometimes when I hear this song, I imagine how dramatic it must have all been for my parents. Bulgaria was entering the war and, very quickly, it was the German presence that made itself felt since Bulgaria and Germany were allies. To give birth to a child in those circumstances was no doubt a great joy, but also at the same time a huge uncertainty. What was going to happen?

Bulgaria entered World War II in 1941 as a member of the Axis powers but declined to participate in Operation Barbarossa and actually saved its Jewish population from deportation to concentration camps. It was the only Nazi-infiltrated country in Europe not to do the Nazis' bidding when it came to Jews. As the war turned against Germany, Bulgaria did not fully comply with Soviet demands to expel German forces from its territory, resulting in a declaration of war and an invasion by the Soviet Union in September 1944. The Communist-dominated Fatherland Front took power, and Bulgaria then joined the Allies until the war ended. The left-wing uprising of September 1944 led to the abolition of the monarchy, but it was not until 1946 that a single-party people's republic was established. It became a part of the Soviet sphere of influence under the leadership of Georgi Dimitrov (1946–1949), who laid the foundations for a Stalinist state that was highly repressive, executing thousands of dissidents.[4]

That is, from birth to the age of five, Kristeva's earliest childhood memories, earliest stories and photos, and earliest psychic echoes are infused with what she calls the great "Bulgarian Ambiguity." In this land where Greek myth, Christianity, Judaism, and Islam meet; where first there were Nazi boots on the ground, then Soviet boots; where the monarchical government aligned itself with the Nazis but adamantly refused to deport the Jews; where Russians took over but only became fully Stalinist late in the game, taking their time—this was the historical cauldron in which Julia Kristeva was formed.

One of Kristeva's earliest memories is of sneaking down to the basement with her parents to listen to Radio London. She first saw Nazi boots, then Stalinist boots marching past the windows at the top surface of the basement walls. Safety was down below, in the basement: with Europe, with family.

> I only remember a few things. In this house where I was born, there was a basement. And the house was rented by teachers, who were probably Communists—resisters . . . So my parents and I went down to the basement to listen to Radio London . . . so that no one could hear . . . because there were Germans who lived there too . . . and who passed by . . . I vaguely remember seeing the soldiers in German uniform pass by . . . And I can still hear the sound . . . dun dun dun da . . . the signal of Radio London . . .

Kristeva recently reflected: "Politics, it's not for me. I prefer the micropolitical, the microcosms of the Macropolitical world . . ."

When Kristeva evokes the Bulgaria of her childhood, however, as with most us, it is the intimacy of family she remembers best. She was surrounded by affection.

> When I speak of and think about Bulgaria, about Sofia—both of which abound with memories—these memories, everytime I evoke them, are never fixed, determinant. What matters in my experience of memories is the voyage towards and through them . . . it's about a perpetual questioning . . .[5] (Damisch, 2011)

Kristeva's father lost his parents as a child—Kristeva's paternal grandfather died in the war of 1912, her paternal grandmother dying shortly thereafter. Her father was raised by a country peasant woman who also took care of Kristeva as a very young girl, passing away when Kristeva was about three years old. Kristeva called her "grandmother."

Because her father was an orphan, he had only two choices in life—à la Julien Sorel: he could join the military or he could become a priest. He decided to join the seminary, later studying at the Theology Faculty of Sofia. He was a practicing Orthodox Christian, but he had a sharp, critical, restless mind. What he was really enthusiastic about was literature—especially Russian literature: Dostoevsky and Tolstoy. He spoke many different languages—Russian was obligatory—and this was what he wanted for Kristeva too. He introduced Kristeva to literature and poetry from a very young age. The other thing he loved was music, and Kristeva remembers well his beautiful voice booming through the church—although Kristeva is quick to point out that he passed on his musical talent not to her but to her sister, born in 1945. During the early part of the war, under Nazi occupation, her father was part of the resistance to the deportation of Jews, belonging to a brave group of intellectuals who went straight to the czar with their demands that the deportations not take place. At the end of the war, with the Russians in charge and the passage to Communism, Kristeva's father left the Seminary and Kristeva took her last communion at the age of five. Her father then studied to be a doctor. That was until he found out—as would take place later in Maoist China—that he was going to have to go out into the countryside as a "barefoot doctor" to supposedly "treat" the poor (with no supplies and no help). So he quit his medical studies and worked in Sofia at the Soviet Style Ministry of Religion, interpreting Christian Orthodoxy for the young Soviet state. Kristeva describes herself as having been a true "fille a papa"—her father adored her: he was a father in love. The feeling was mutual: Kristeva adored him as well.

Kristeva's mother came from more of a bourgeois background, with Kristeva's maternal grandparents working in small business. What is especially interesting about them goes back two generations, into what Kristeva calls the "religious polyphony" of the Balkans. There, on her mother's side, one finds dissident Jews who became Muslims and, eventually, Christians. But in spite of this hybridized spiritual history, Kristeva's mother was not at all religious; she was completely secular. She was a scientist, had studied biology, and was a follower of Darwin.

The young Julia Kristeva was, in fact, caught—almost every night—in the middle of good-humored but passionate debates at dinner, where her religious father was "the dinosaur" and her scientific, Darwinian mother the "progenitor of monkeys":

> Life was pretty restrained. But there were certain freedoms for a time. For example, my father took us to communion in the orthodox faith until I was about 5 or 6. After that, he didn't want us to be seen taking communion because people who were religious were repressed. As for me, I very quickly adapted because of school and mama was also very secular. She never

> disputed papa's ideas although one could sense that she went to church only to please him, that she herself did not believe. She had studied biology and so her ideas were the opposite of my father's. At the dinner table, once I was in school, we would tease my father. We called him a dinosaur and we would say that, as Darwin had argued, we descended from monkeys. My mother was a strong Darwinian. And papa would get furious! He would yell: "yes, of course you are both descendants of monkeys (because my sister would follow me in my teasing of him). Yes, yes, it's very easy to see! One just has to take a look at you to see that you descend from the monkeys!"

Kristeva has been recently reflecting a great deal on the struggles in the twenty-first century between science and religion, suggesting that we may have more to learn right now from the dinosaurs than from the monkeys.

Kristeva was a very independent young girl in the young Soviet state. She remembers it as a time of having everything she needed, but not what she wanted. She tells the story of seeing, when she was about five, the little girl next door being fed water one spoonful at a time. This felt like the libidinal economy of those Communist times—spoonful by spoonful, drop by drop, one got what one needed, but only that. She rebelled against that economy, preferring instead to run wild in her grandmother's garden among the flowers, or among the beautiful old Byzantine churches by the sea. These are very physical memories she has. But, of course, she was also a very good student in school.

Because Kristeva's father was not a member of the Communist Party, Kristeva couldn't go to the public school. She was disappointed not to be able to carry the flag, but she didn't cry about it. She almost never cried. Her parents enrolled her in the "French Maternal" school, where she was taught by French Catholic nuns—Dominican nuns, to be more precise. There she absorbed languages, especially French, like a sponge and was taught to memorize songs, especially French literary texts. The nuns taught her poems by La Rochefoucauld and Hugo, and, of course, she read lots of stories by Colette. Kristeva loved her Dominican nun teachers and was devastated when, in the early 1950s, they were arrested, condemned as spies, and chased out of the country.

Kristeva has obviously reflected a great deal in her writing on the beautiful fragility of the poetic imagination and in particular on the importance of the French literary imagination. This emphasis becomes less mysterious when we realize that whatever else she was up to as a child, French literature was at the center of her young life.

Like most excellent students, Kristeva longed for symbolic recognition. And in this regard, there are two stories she really wants everyone to know about her Bulgarian childhood—and she has in fact written about both. First, as far as we know, Bulgaria is the only country in the world that celebrates the alphabet every spring, and she was an avid participant in those celebrations, receiving a "Prix D'Excellence."

And she also wants everyone to know that Georgi Dimitrov, the leader of the Communist government in Bulgaria, who had once been accused by the Nazis of setting the Reichstag on fire, was instrumental in stopping the Jews from being deported from Bulgaria during the Nazi occupation. In fact, it was he who helped make it possible for Jews to actually immigrate to Israel after the war (his wife was Jewish).

She wants us to know that it isn't her in the official picture presenting the flowers to Dimitrov. It should have been her—she was first in her class—presenting flowers to Dimitrov. But she was so nervous that she got sick and couldn't go. She still gets sick when she is really nervous—like before meeting the pope!

Then there are two stories from Kristeva's Bulgarian childhood that *I* really want you to know. One has to do with Kristeva's love of books and her impatience with anything that smacked of girlish destiny. She especially didn't like any kind of dolls, although they were continually thrust upon her. She remembers her intense disappointment at once receiving the gift of a dollhouse:

> I remember that I once received the gift of a dollhouse—the representation of a house . . . where there's a doll, a bathroom, a kitchen, a dining room, etc and then there's the little girl who's supposed to take care of all that! Me? I was really disappointed because I didn't want to take care of all that! I never played with it much. It's still pretty much all in one piece. It stayed in a cupboard. I thought it was ridiculous for little girls to push strollers. Me? I had my books. They might have been kept in a drawer, but I really used them and they ended up completely torn apart through use. So this gift of a dollhouse disappointed me a little. On the other hand, in that package of things that little girls were supposed to have—the bathroom, the kitchen, etc—there was that little dollhouse doll which could sit up in

> order to be bathed because there was a hole in its buttocks . . . a hole in order to be able to sit her up on a little peg . . . I found it all so absolutely stupid. In all of that, the only thing that interested me was to see what was inside of the hole! My mother said I would be a doctor and it's true that for a long time, I wanted to be a doctor.

The other story I want to share with you about Kristeva's Bulgarian childhood is that she almost never cried. She was often disappointed—disappointed she couldn't wear the flag to parades because of her father not joining the Communist Party, disappointed that her long-awaited gift was a dollhouse, and so forth—but she didn't cry when she was disappointed. Or even when she was sick or hurt. In fact, this "stay calm and carry on" posture became integral to her character. This became clear to me during what I call the "running story": Kristeva as a child didn't walk, she ran! She ran and ran as fast as she could until she fell down! And then when her mother—tearful and worried—caught up with her, Kristeva touched her mother's cheek and said: "Don't cry, Maman, I will take care of you."

> It's something that's just part of my character: not to cry. My mother used to tell me about it. As soon as I could walk, I wouldn't walk but would, rather, run. And I ran very, very fast! So I started running . . . and there's a park in Sofia called Le Parc des Rosiers where I would run and run until I would fall . . . and Maman would yell "But stop! Stop!" And I would fall and she would catch up with me. I would stand up, with my knees all bloody and my mother would plead with me, "please stop! your knees are all bloody!" And I would reply: "listen mama, don't be upset. Let me comfort you." And then I would take off running . . .

Very recently, Kristeva has reflected on the fact that she "takes care of herself by taking care of others" . . . "Je me soigne en soignant les autres." She has admitted that family for her is about complex caring, not about comfort.

For high school, Kristeva attended the Alliance Française, where she continued her linguistic and literary studies. She soon took up journalism and wrote stories constantly for the high school newspaper, getting paid enough that she was able to become even more independent. She was able to finish her studies through a correspondence course, and she became a successful, full-time, well-paid journalist just before she left for Paris on a scholarship.

And that was the turning point—for her and, it turns out, for us and for the rest of Kristeva's readers worldwide. It was the time of Sputnik. It was time to make big decisions about her future. She was excellent at math and science and decided she would become an astrophysicist and go off to Siberia in the Soviet Union to study (and probably to work on new Cold War weapons for the Soviet state). She applied for a fellowship she clearly should have won. But, of course, her father was not a member of the Communist Party, so she wasn't be chosen. The envelope finally arrived:

> So one day I saw an envelope addressed to my father in the mailbox and I understood immediately what it was (the response to my application). So I opened it, thinking to myself that maybe I had been accepted . . . but . . . no. They told my father that his daughter perhaps had all the necessary qualities for acceptance, but that they only accepted the children of those who were members of the Communist Party and that since that wasn't the case with him . . . And with that, my father completely broke down in tears. But not me. I didn't cry. I pursued my studies of the humanities [les sciences humaines].

She didn't know it yet, but the French government was about to offer a scholarship to a top Bulgarian student to go study "les sciences humaines" in Paris. And so, for us, "the rest is literature."

Kristeva has reflected at some length on the fact that she has never planned her life. She has never had a program, or strategy. She had never thought about leaving Bulgaria before she actually left. She never thought: I will go to France. She says she swims through life, traveling through herself. "Je me voyage." She swims through experiences; she doesn't add them to an itinerary. What is important to her is to move along in life and writing, pulled by pure curiosity, just seeing where it all leads . . .

> Even though I think of myself as very Cartesian, rational, etc., I do not follow a program. I don't say: I will do this and I will do that, and then that. I do not follow a trajectory fixed in advance. I do things a bit as they come to me, as if I were swimming. I let myself be carried by the waves. I swim, but

> there is also the movement of the waves. I never thought that I would leave Bulgaria—never! But it is true that in a way all of my studies have been escapes, a way of taking distance from my parents while staying close, distancing myself but at the same time transcending them where they were.

Yes, Kristeva has talked to me a lot about how she has always just tried to construct herself as she swims through the waves of the world and history.

And my attention to "reading for strong autobiography" really perks up here! For that is the way I have lived as well, with far less illustrious results, I'm afraid. But it's the same lack of Plan. So what can I—at sixty-four years old—learn from my contemporary, my friend, at seventy-four years old, right now, about how to live, how to work, how to be, how to contest? One thing I already know is that, over the past few years, Kristeva and I have both come to share a deep concern about the world of our children and students, where everyone is becoming so programmed they are never present to themselves. They are becoming so rapidly commodified and mechanized—with vulnerability absolutely not allowed:

> Humanity is so caught up in the rat race for a so-called "happiness"—a "well-being" made up of enjoyment, performance, brilliance—that all vulnerability is considered to be an intolerable menace, unthinkable. This is a vision of humanity that is commercialized and mechanical. (Damisch, 2011)

This kind of programming runs totally countercurrent to self-making through reliance on curiosity and ethical passion . . .

> I try to construct myself through the waves of the world and history . . . and there's a lot of chance involved, a lot of necessity too, but I do not think I have a destiny. And I've had a lot of deaths and resurrections in my life. When one leaves one's language, one's country, childhood, one loses a lot of things . . . and a lot of things are erased just as one erases writing in the sand . . . But there are always re-beginnings and it has been living through these tests, these deaths and resurrections, that I have achieved satisfactions in life that would have been unimaginable to me beforehand. . . . (Damisch, 2011)

Whomever history ultimately determines Kristeva to have been, can we embrace the fact that someone so accomplished, such a cosmopolitan and contestatory intellectual, could be living life so in the moment, so caught in the waves of curiosity? And how can her utter lack of strategy help me—her autobiographically inclined biographer—find my way forward—with integrity?

Kristeva often quotes the words on Colette's tombstone: "To be reborn has never been too much for me." Having done some strong autobiographical reading of Julia Kristeva, perhaps it's time for me—for us?—to contemplate some rebirth, or at least some re–self-invention.

Taking on the challenge of strong thinking, traveling through oneself, constructing oneself, walking the tightrope between intellect and revolt, between the intimate and the public, between work and play, with no plan, no program, no strategy or directive—that is the kind of contestatory intellectual I want to be henceforth—for whatever time I have left on this earth! And you? It's worth the risk, don't you think?

Notes

I presented a slightly different version of this work as the Keynote Address at the March 28, 2014, Kristeva Circle at Vanderbilt University. Warm thanks to Kelly Oliver and Rebecca Tuvel for their conference-organizing genius and also for their warm reception in Nashville. I also want to thank Anna Jardine for her patient, loving help with the PowerPoint I used for my address at Vanderbilt. Special thanks to Loren Wolfe—co-interviewer and co-producer of the "biography tapes." A different version of this article will appear in the volume *Being Contemporary: French Literature, Culture, and Politics Today*, edited by Lia Brozgal and Sara Kippur. Liverpool: Liverpool University Press, 2016.

1. All quotations unless otherwise attributed are from my private taped interviews with Kristeva, conversations expressly focused on my biographical project.

2. Sollers made these remarks while sitting with Kristeva outside their home on the Île de Ré.

3. Kristeva makes these remarks while looking at photos of herself as a child.

4. This short paragraph of historical context is constructed from multiple sources, including Wikipedia.

5. Kristeva makes these remarks as images from her childhood and from historical Sofia scroll in the background.

Works Cited

Damisch, Teri. 2011. *Histoires d'amour et de passerelles*. Documentary. The complete documentary is available on Kristeva's public Web site, www.kristeva.fr.

Kristeva, Julia. 2010. "Un Institut des Humanités à Paris-Diderot," http://www.kristeva.fr/un-institut.html.

Suleiman, Susan Rubin. 1994. *Risking Who One Is: Encounters with Contemporary Art and Literature*. Cambridge: Harvard University Press.

Contributors

Sara Beardsworth is associate professor of philosophy at Southern Illinois University. Her book *Julia Kristeva: Psychoanalysis and Modernity* (State University of New York Press, 2004) is the first systematic overview of Julia Kristeva's work in relation to philosophical modernity. She has published numerous essays on Kristeva, Adorno, Irigaray, Freud, psychoanalysis, feminist philosophy, and continental philosophy. She is editor of The Library of Living Philosophers.

Melinda C. Hall is assistant professor of philosophy at Stetson University. She specializes in bioethics and continental philosophy, and her research interests include the intersection of contemporary bioethics and disability studies, the ethics of human enhancement, and the social and cultural construction of disability. Hall is the author of *The Bioethics of Enhancement: Transhumanism, Disability, and Biopolitics*, published by Lexington Books in 2016. Her work is also published in the *International Journal of Feminist Approaches to Bioethics*, the *Disability Studies Quarterly*, and *Philosophy Compass*, among other venues. She received her PhD in philosophy from Vanderbilt University.

Sarah K. Hansen is assistant professor of philosophy at California State University Northridge. Their writings have appeared in *Philosophy Today*, *philoSOPHIA: A Journal of Continental Feminism*, the *Journal of French and Francophone Philosophy*, and the *International Journal of Feminist Approaches to Bioethics*. Sarah is also co-founder and co-director of The Kristeva Circle, an academic organization dedicated to promoting research on the work of Julia Kristeva.

Alice Jardine is professor of Romance languages and literatures and of studies of women, gender, and sexuality at Harvard University. Her research focuses on twentieth and twenty-first-century French and Francophone literature, critical theory, and gender and sexuality studies. She is best known for her *Gynesis: Configurations of Woman and Modernity* and for her coedited volumes such as *The Future of Difference; Men in Feminism; Shifting Scenes: Women, Writing, and Politics in Post-68 France*; and *Living Attention: The Life and Work of Teresa Brennan*. She is currently writing a biography of Julia Kristeva, *At The Risk of Thinking: An Intellectual Biography of Julia Kristeva*, as well as her own memoir, *Alice's Adventures in Paris: A Literary Memoir*.

Julia Kristeva is professor of linguistics at the University of Paris VII and the author of numerous books, including *The Sense and Nonsense of Revolt* (Columbia University Press, 2000), *Intimate Revolt* (Columbia University, 2002), *Hatred and Forgiveness* (Columbia University Press, 2010), and *The Severed Head: Capital Visions* (Columbia University Press, 2012). She is the recipient of the Hannah Arendt Prize for Political Thought and the Holberg International Memorial Prize.

Sarah Kathryn Marshall is a PhD candidate at the University of Memphis. She specializes in continental philosophy, feminist theories, psychoanalysis, and the history of social and political thought. Her writings have appeared in *Evental Aesthetics* and *The Journal of French and Francophone Philosophy*.

Elaine P. Miller is professor of philosophy at Miami University of Ohio. She is the author of *Head Cases: Julia Kristeva on Philosophy and Art in Depressed Times* (Columbia University Press, 2014) and *The Vegetative Soul: From Philosophy of Nature to Subjectivity in the Feminine* (State University of New York Press, 2002) and has published articles on themes in feminist theory, contemporary continental philosophy, and eighteenth- and nineteenth-century philosophy of nature and art (particularly in Kant, German idealism, and Nietzsche).

Elena Ruiz is assistant professor of philosophy and global studies at Michigan State University. She specializes in nineteenth-century philosophy, Latin American philosophy, and feminist theory. Her essays have been published in *Hypatia*, the *APA Newsletter on Feminism and Philosophy*, and *Human Studies: A Journal of Hispanic/Latino Issues in Philosophy*.

Surti Singh is assistant professor of philosophy at American University of Cairo. She received her PhD from DePaul University in 2012. She specializes in Frankfurt School critical theory, aesthetics, social and political philosophy, and feminism. Her current book project is titled *Adorno's Concept of Experience: Rethinking the Postmetaphysical Turn in Critical Theory.*

Beata Stawarska is professor of philosophy at the University of Oregon. She has published widely on contemporary European philosophy (especially phenomenology and poststructuralism), philosophy of psychology, and feminist philosophy. Her first book, *Between You and I: Dialogical Phenomenology,* appeared with Ohio University Press in 2009. Her second book is titled *Saussure's Philosophy of Language as Phenomenology: Undoing the Doctrine of the Course of General Linguistics* (Oxford University Press, 2015).

Amy Ray Stewart is a PhD candidate in philosophy at Southern Illinois University Carbondale, where she teaches Women, Gender, and Sexuality Studies. She specializes in psychoanalysis, feminist continental philosophy, and LGBTQ studies. Amy is currently working on a dissertation that explores the intimate and imaginative revolt of transgender embodiment. Her writings have appeared in *Psychoanalysis, Culture & Society* and *philoSOPHIA: A Journal of Continental Feminism.*

Rebecca Tuvel is assistant professor of philosophy at Rhodes College in Memphis, Tennessee. She specializes in social-political philosophy, feminist philosophy, and animal ethics. Her essays and reviews have appeared in *Hypatia: A Journal of Feminist Philosophy, Societies: An Open Access Sociology Journal, Journal of Critical Animal Studies, Environmental Philosophy,* and *philoSOPHIA: A Journal of Continental Feminism.*

Index